THE
GUNPOWDER
PLOT DECEIT

THE GUNPOWDER PLOT DECEIT

MARTYN BEARDSLEY

PEN & SWORD
HISTORY

AN IMPRINT OF PEN & SWORD BOOKS LTD.
YORKSHIRE - PHILADELPHIA

First published in Great Britain in 2018 by
PEN AND SWORD HISTORY
an imprint of
Pen & Sword Books Ltd
Yorkshire - Philadelphia

Copyright © Martyn Beardsley, 2018

HB ISBN 978 1 52672 568 4
PB ISBN 978 1 52675 142 3

Printed and bound in the UK TJ International Ltd,
Padstow, Cornwall

Typeset in Times New Roman 11/13.5 by
Aura Technology and Software Services, India

Pen & Sword Books Ltd incorporates the imprints of Pen & Sword
Archaeology, Atlas, Aviation, Battleground, Discovery,
Family History, History, Maritime, Military, Naval, Politics, Railways,
Select, Social History, Transport, True Crime, Claymore Press,
Frontline Books, Leo Cooper, Praetorian Press, Remember When,
Seaforth Publishing and Wharncliffe.

For a complete list of Pen and Sword titles please contact
PEN & SWORD BOOKS LIMITED
47 Church Street, Barnsley, South Yorkshire, S70 2AS, England
E-mail: enquiries@pen-and-sword.co.uk
Website: www.pen-and-sword.co.uk

942   or

PEN AND SWORD BOOKS
1950 Lawrence Rd, Havertown, PA 19083, USA
E-mail: uspen-and-sword@casematepublishers.com
Website: www.penandswordbooks.com

Contents

Introduction...vii

Author's Note ix

Chapter 1   The Background.. 1

Chapter 2   The Plotters 7

Chapter 3   The Jesuits and Supporters.. 17

Chapter 4   The Official Story..24

Chapter 5   The Scene of the Crime..32

Chapter 6   Spymasters, Subterfuge & Set-Ups....................................39

Chapter 7   The Monteagle Letter...46

Chapter 8   The Arrest of Guy Fawkes..59

Chapter 9   The Published Confessions: Guy Fawkes 66

Chapter 10   The Published Confessions: The Declaration of Thomas
              Wintour, 23 November 1605 79

Chapter 11   The Subsequent Arrests..91

Chapter 12   Trial 97

Chapter 13   Consequences.. 104

Chapter 14   Verdict 107

Appendix A King James' Speech To Parliament Regarding the Plot 126

Appendix B Extracts from the King's Book... 136

Bibliography.. 183

Notes 186

Index 189

Introduction

When I was a boy, the biggest highlight of the year after Christmas and birthdays was November the Fifth and everything that went with it. Bonfire Night itself was obviously the pinnacle. The impact of the event has in recent years become diffused by being spread over any number of days, but back then the celebrations were always on the fifth unless it was a Sunday, and the smell of the smoke of a thousand bonfires and the gunpowder from ten thousand fireworks hung in the air and could even be detected into the following morning. But just as enjoyable was the traditional making of the 'guy' – rummaging through wardrobes for old clothes to be stuffed, making or buying the mask – followed by the trip out onto the streets in search of a 'penny for the guy' from passers-by. Then, around 4 November, came the trip to the local shop and the depositing of a huge pile of low-denomination coins on the counter in return for the biggest box of fireworks the money would stretch to.

Although we still have fireworks at that general time of the year, the penny-for-the-guy tradition has, as far as I can see, completely died. My feeling is that for most children, the dubious American import of Trick or Treat has overtaken Bonfire Night as the main such event of the year.

When the money had all been collected and the big night arrived, the guy was hauled to the top of the bonfire and secured, and we all stood round to experience the great thrill as the match was applied and the whole lot whooshed up in flames. We knew something of the story behind it – particularly what Guy Fawkes had planned to do – but it never occurred to us, certainly not me, that we were ritually celebrating the horrific execution of a real man. We didn't appreciate that a man as real as any of our fathers had been horribly tortured and then dragged in front of a crowd one cold January morning; that he had been hanged, and that his body had then been horribly mutilated. Neither did we wonder what had driven him to attempt to perpetrate such a terrible, desperate act as blowing up Parliament. All we knew was that by good fortune he had been caught at the last minute with the lighted match in his hand.

Or had he?

I was researching a children's novel involving priest holes and timeslips, featuring a modern boy who finds himself in the time of Guy Fawkes, when I came across a curious old book which questioned many of my assumptions about the Gunpowder Plot story. That book was *What Was the Gunpowder Plot?* and it was written in 1897 by a Jesuit Priest, Father John Gerard. I became fascinated. The plotters were Catholics who had received spiritual guidance from Jesuit priests who themselves came under suspicion, so it wasn't surprising that one should try to pick holes in the government of the day's version of events. What impressed me was the astute and painstaking case Gerard made, delivered with all the forensic attention to detail and marshalling of evidence of a barrister in a murder case. I was struck by the sheer weight of the evidence indicating that there was far more to the story than is generally supposed.

Most books about the Gunpowder Plot raise some of the issues, but usually briefly, as asides, as minor diversions from the main story. The story promulgated by the authorities at the time is pretty much the one which has been passed down from generation to generation; it is the one which even today most people will be familiar with and assume to be true and uncontroversial. In fact, there is plenty of evidence to suggest that at least some important elements of the popular story are built upon shaky foundations, and that we have been fooled for centuries by a cleverly engineered campaign of subterfuge and propaganda. I felt that Gerard's case deserved to be brought before a modern audience.

Author's Note

One of the key figures in this story is Robert Cecil, the Lord Privy Seal at the time of the Plot who also acted as the king's spymaster. He became the First Earl of Salisbury six months before the arrest of Guy Fawkes, thus some writers refer to him as 'Salisbury' and others 'Cecil', while some switch from Cecil to Salisbury from the point in the story when he was ennobled. This makes sense, but I have opted to prefer to go with 'Cecil' throughout.

Still on names, spelling was a fluid art in the times we are looking at (the way Shakespeare spelt his name in different ways being often held up as an example). Two of our plotters, brothers, are known as Winter in some sources and as Wintour in others. As the latter version seems to have been the one they preferred, that is how they will be known in this book – but the way this particular plotter's name should be spelt perhaps goes deeper than mere pedantry, as we shall see when we look at his signed declaration later in the book.

Just to complicate matters further, two Father John Gerards make an appearance in this story. The earlier one was a contemporary of Guy Fawkes, who ministered to certain of the plotters. His thrilling escape from the Tower of London is worthy of a volume in itself but since it happened before the events we are discussing it is outside the scope of this book. In an attempt to avoid confusion, I refer to him at all times as 'Father Gerard', and to the Victorian author of *What Was the Gunpowder Plot* just as Gerard.

Gerard himself deserves further mention. As well as being a Jesuit priest, he was the author of several historical and religious books, a regular contributor to *The Month* (the magazine of the Society of Jesus), and a Fellow of the Linnaean Society. He was born in Edinburgh in 1840 and educated at Stonyhurst College in Lancashire, where he later became a Prefect of Studies, or senior master. He founded the Stonyhurst magazine and became the college's historian. When Gerard died in London in 1912 an obituary in *The Catholic Press* said that 'his pen was always forcible and candid' and testified to 'his fairness in controversy'.

Finally, I would like to thank Bob Bradley, contributor to the healeyhero. co.uk mining history website and former surveyor, and Dr Geraint Thomas of Aberystwyth Univesity, both of whom kindly took the time to provide me with their very helpful expert opinions.

Chapter 1

The Background

In the autumn of 1605, a group of men attempted to commit what in modern terminology could only be called a terrorist attack in the heart of London. It could have been much worse and its effects much more far-reaching than any of those carried out by the IRA in the twentieth century or Islamic groups in Britain in the early twenty-first century. As well as the blast devastating a densely populated area with a radius calculated at nearly 500 metres,[1] it would have wiped out the monarch and much of the government, and, if all had gone to plan, would have marked the launch of a revolution and the restoration of Catholicism as the state religion.

Like the activities of most terrorists, the devastating act would also have killed randomly: those of the same religion; those who supported their cause if not their methods; those who had no strong feelings one way or the other and who were just getting on with their lives.

To help put the overall situation at the time into some sort of perspective, it is worth bearing in mind that from the time that Christianity first arrived on these shores during the Roman occupation until the sixteenth century, the plotters' faith had been of the strain that we would now call Roman Catholic. Thus, Britain had been a Catholic country for far, far longer than it had been a nominally Protestant or Anglican one, and that remains true even to this day. We will have to wait for roughly another 800 years before Protestantism is no longer the new kid on the block.

We will never know what emotional effect it had on the ordinary English person to be told by their 'betters' that they had been worshipping in the wrong way for generations and would now have to do things – and believe things – differently. Some no doubt agreed with the changes. The new way probably struck many as being more egalitarian, freed from the shackles of a Rome that the average peasant might have seen as an impossibly distant and almost mythical place, yet one which had grown corrupt and too big for its boots. They may have seen the new way as being more in keeping with what Jesus intended. They were, after all, still Christians after the Reformation. They weren't being asked to kick out God, Jesus and the Bible.

But to what must surely have been the majority for a good number of years, this was not just a religious change but a fundamental cultural one. Religious belief, tradition and practice was much more intimately entwined in people's lives then than now, and it is difficult for us to appreciate just how profound, how devastating this change must have been. But we can at least see why the 'old way' lingered – sometimes openly, often in secret and at the risk of fines or worse. If you are the latest in a line of many generations raised in the same faith and its stories and celebrations and rituals and believe that your soul's very salvation depends on preserving those ways, you are not going to abandon that just because some official – or even a king – tells you to. In his 1897 book, *What Was the Gunpowder Plot,* Gerard makes a convincing case that at least half the population of England if not more was Catholic when James came to the throne.

So, just as the previous old ways – the pagan religions – no doubt continued to be quietly practised for a long time after Christianity had officially supplanted them, so too did the old Christian ways long after Protestantism (or at least Anglicanism) became the state religion. This was especially true of the North and the West Midlands of England, where Catholicism clung on much more doggedly than in places like London. The overwhelming majority of the players in our story were from Yorkshire and the Midlands, with not one known to have been born in London.

It is in a sense understandable that in an Elizabethan era beset by real or imagined Catholic plots (particularly involving Mary Stuart and others wishing to depose Elizabeth in her favour), worrying reports of the slaughter of thousands of Huguenot Protestants by French Catholics – the 'Saint Bartholomew's Day Massacre' – in 1572, and the seemingly ever-present threat of invasion, things had grown worse for adherents of the old religion. Though no worse – and perhaps less so – than for Protestants under Bloody Mary. Elizabeth had, at least initially, endeavoured to allow Catholics a fair amount of leeway. Christopher Lee has pointed out in his book *1603,* that these matters were actually more political than religious, even though the two were often inextricably linked. It wasn't so much a question of Mary, Queen of Scots and Philip of Spain wanting to add England to the Catholic fold, even though that was part of it, but more a question of personal and national ambition. Whatever one's view of these things, during Elizabeth's reign it became riskier and costlier – sometimes financially, occasionally mortally – to be a practising Catholic.

Things were worse if you were a priest, and worse still if you belonged to the Jesuit order – seen at that time as far as England was concerned (with some justification), as the Catholic Church's own 'special forces'. It was illegal to attend Mass, the primary requirement for any Catholic, either publicly or even privately. There were fines for doing so, for not attending the Protestant parish church (although this affected Puritans too), and there was the threat of capital punishment for harbouring a priest. Catholics couldn't legally follow the rituals of their own faith when it came to the fundamental landmark occasions of human life – births, marriages and deaths. And all this even though ancestors of the Elizabethans had for centuries partaken in those holy celebrations in the very same ancient churches where Anglican services were now held.

Contrary to popular belief many, probably most, Catholics were loyal to their monarch, then embodied by Elizabeth; but when she finally died after a long reign they may have been forgiven for breathing a sigh of relief and allowing themselves to dare to harbour hopes of better future. The rumours that things would change under James were not unrealistic or without foundation. He had been, after all, baptised a Catholic and had married one. A Jesuit priest of the time wrote of the prevailing optimism, pointing out that the new king's mother, Mary, Queen of Scots was a Catholic whose faith had in a sense cost her her life, and that people of the time would never have believed that the mother's merits would fail to win from God the grace of His true knowledge for her son or that 'the king would take up so intimately and confidently with those, indeede and only those, who betrayed his mother, and in the end killed her...'[2] The writer was Father Tesimond, often referred to by his alias of Father Greenway. He knew the plotters (and in fact went to school with Guy Fawkes) and his name will crop up often in our story.

James did indeed make conciliatory noises at first. He had been in touch with Rome via the papal nuncio in Brussels and had been informed by Pope Paul V that the Vatican had no intention of backing plans or schemes by English Catholics aimed at overthrowing the monarchy. Initially, things seemed promising for Catholics and they enjoyed more religious freedom than they had known for a generation or more. One of the most obvious and notable signs of this was that fines for recusancy were all but ignored for the first two years of the new king's reign. Jardine, writing in 1857, in *A Narrative of the Gunpowder Plot,* says that over £10,000 was collected in fines and forfeitures during the last year of Elizabeth's reign, whereas in the following two years the sums were just over £300 and £200 respectively.

To what extent James was being disingenuous with his promises and hints in those early days regarding his attitude towards Catholics, and to what extent he started out with genuinely good intentions, is debatable. His ordering the release, within days of arriving in London, of the Jesuit priest William Weston following spells of imprisonment amounting to around seventeen years for performing exorcisms, must have been taken as a sign of things to come. Known Catholics and crypto-Catholics were appointed to office by James, most notably Henry Percy, ninth Earl of Northumberland, who had inveigled his way into James' confidence while Elizabeth was still alive and who was soon made a Captain of the Gentleman Pensioners. This might sound like a rather quaint society, but they were in fact the monarch's bodyguard. Northumberland wasn't openly Catholic, but he came from a staunchly Catholic family and few doubted where his religious allegiances lay. Of greater interest to us is that he was related to Thomas Percy, one of the plotters.

But it was not only the new king, central though his part was, whose attitude towards Catholics would play a part in the developments of the next few years.

Robert Cecil, who was to become the first Earl of Salisbury during the year of the plot, was following in the footsteps of his own father William, Lord Burghley, but especially of Walsingham, Elizabeth's famous spymaster. Both men had been close to Elizabeth and deeply involved in her government's intelligence service activities. Robert Cecil succeeded his father as the queen's chief adviser, and his attitude towards Catholics were similarly ambivalent to that of James. Initially, he had no particular axe to grind against those who kept their heads down and remained loyal to their monarch, but as time progressed he became increasingly anti-Catholic, and virulently anti-Jesuit. And to be fair to him, it was his job to be able to distinguish between those who simply refused to conform to the state religion and those who represented a threat to his employer and to the state. However, once the Gunpowder Plot was uncovered (if not before) he seemed to become obsessed with proving that the Jesuits were behind it, regardless of the lack of evidence and the fact that it almost certainly wasn't true. Father Gerard wrote in his *Narrative of the Gunpowder Plot* that 'they kept it so wholly secret from all men, that until their flight and apprehension it was not known to any that such a matter was in hand', which could have been a lie of course, but it was written when he was safely out of the country, never to return, and is backed up by conspirators themselves. Confessions by both Guy Fawkes and Thomas Wintour say that the plotters heard Mass and received communion from Father Gerard in London. They also took an oath in relation to the Plot but, as Fawkes' confession of 9 November reveals, 'he saithe that Gerrard [sic] was not acquainted with their purpose'. However, this sentence is underlined, and was deleted from the version of the document that was used as evidence at trial. Not only that, but Sir Edward Coke, the Attorney General, explicitly stated as a matter of fact that the Gerard oversaw the oath concerning the Plot. This kind of cherry-picking and manipulating of evidence when it came to the plotters' supposed own words was, as we shall see, typical of the way the case against not only the plotters but the Jesuit priests associated with them was conducted.

The Jesuit mission was a personal, spiritual one, rather than representing the stealthy vanguard of an invasion or overthrow of the king. It is hard to believe that Cecil – a shrewd man with an efficient network of agents and informers – wasn't fully aware of this himself.

The way the amount collected in recusancy and similar fines dropped dramatically in the early years of James' reign has already been highlighted. A sign of the way things quickly changed is that in February 1605 – the year of the plot – the recusancy fines were re-introduced and the figure leapt dramatically to over £6,000. But even before this, the French ambassador, de Beaumont, reported a conversation soon after James arrived in London in which he referred to the appointment of the Catholic Lord Howard to the privy council as being a 'tame duck' who might help him to catch 'many wild ones' – a point we shall return to later. He also 'maintained openly at table that the Pope was the true Antichrist, with other like blasphemies'. This, coming so early in James' reign, could reasonably be taken as an indication that his initial protestations at tolerance were little more than soothing noises designed to humour the Catholics and so pave the way for a smooth accession. Alan Haynes in *Gunpowder Plot* (1994), describes James' attitude towards Catholics as being the same as that towards the Puritans; 'a hostility that was much more political than religious'. But he also adds that 'He hated toleration, and this matched the view of the man who emerged as his chief minister – Sir Robert Cecil'.

In February 1604, possibly as a result of the 'Bye Plot' (which we will come back to later) James issued a proclamation giving all Catholic clergy a month to leave the country; in April, James prompted parliament to introduce a bill which would categorise Catholics as excommunicates. In addition to any spiritual considerations, there were practical and financial effects to this, as Tesimond explained:

'In consequence, they were no longer able to make their wills
or dispose of their goods. The effect of this law was to make

them outlaws and exiles; and like such they were treated. There was no longer any obligation to pay them their debts or rents for land held from them. They could not now go to law or have the law's protection. They could seek no remedy for ills and injuries received. In a word, they were considered and treated as professed enemies of the state.'

In the same year, Spain signed a peace treaty with Britain and King Philip decided against insisting on a clause protecting the rights of English Catholics, so no help would be coming from that direction. Just weeks after the excommunication move, Robert Catesby arranged a meeting with Tom Wintour and Jack Wright. In the words of Haynes, 'Rational men, hitherto of discretion, began to fume at James for shifting policy'. The time had come to strike back.

Chapter 2

The Plotters

The Plot Before the Plot

On Sunday, 8 February 1601, between two and three hundred armed men set out to march the short distance from a mansion on the Strand into the City of London, where they planned to confront Queen Elizabeth to demand a change of government, removing the influential Cecil in particular, though they made it clear that they were 'for the queen' herself. Making their way up Ludgate Hill, they were confronted by a party under the command of Sir John Leveson. This attempted coup was to become known to history as the Essex Rebellion.

Robert Devereux, the second Earl of Essex, had been a rising star at the court of Elizabeth. Some even felt that he was Elizabeth's lover – perhaps we would say 'toyboy' today since she was old enough to be his mother, but that is another story. But then his star waned. Badly. He was accused of letting the queen's preferential treatment of him go to his head, causing him to take liberties that ordinary mortals would have trembled to even dream of. Eventually, a lacklustre military campaign in Ireland further tarnished his reputation, lost him his place at court and a great part of his income. He became a bitter and angry man. Gathering men about him at his house, which he had taken the precaution of fortifying, he concocted a plan to march on the City and get rid of what he saw as the rotten apples. It was doomed to failure, and with support haemorrhaging even before the band reached its destination, a demoralised Essex turned back to his house after a little more than a scuffle had taken place and awaited the inevitable arrest. He was executed for treason in February 1601, just over four years before the events of the Gunpowder Plot.

Essex's dislike of Cecil, his influence and his machinations, may have had some justification; but the former possessed neither the cunning nor the subtlety of the latter. It served as an illustration of what happened to men who crossed the secretary of state and those whom he perceived as a threat, and was a foreshadowing of what was in store for the plotters.

Of the thirteen primary Gunpowder Plot conspirators, six had been involved in the Essex Rebellion, but all were let off with fines rather than being consigned to the same fate as Devereux. During the rebellion, Francis Tresham was one of the men left to guard the queen's messengers who had come to his house to dissuade him from his venture, only to be held hostage. Legend had it that Thomas Wintour was also involved, but according to one of the confessions he made after the plot was uncovered, he was in Rome at the time.

Another who took part in Essex's fiasco was William Parker, Lord Monteagle – the man to whom the letter that supposedly exposed the Plot was sent. Once again, we will come back to his role later.

The Essex Rebellion might have been a miserable failure, but it was no small matter. The authorities knew the men involved. Cecil, in particular, knew them: what type of people they were; where their religious allegiances lay; who they consorted with (even when travelling abroad) and so on. Yet these are the men whom we are asked to believe spent months planning and preparing to kill the king and overthrow the government, stockpiling enough gunpowder to blow up half London, meeting at various inns in the city and elsewhere to discuss strategy, recruiting new members, and renting 'safe houses', all without the government having any idea until undone by a mystery letter at the eleventh hour. This is the basis of the story we are going to examine, but first we need to look more closely at the cast of characters. Other than the Essex Rebellion connection, one thing readers will notice is how many of the plotters either knew each other, sometimes from childhood, or were even related, and how many were Catholic converts rather than lifelong adherents to that faith. For the most part, this was not a disparate group hand-picked for different skills and abilities. In many ways it is a case of 'the usual suspects', with several men being roped in for the money they could add to the pot, or simply when an extra pair of hands was needed for physical labour.

Robert Catesby

Catesby was the acknowledged leader and instigator of the plot. He was from Warwickshire and aged about thirty-five at the time these events took place. His father, Sir William, had spent a number of years in prison for recusancy[1] (to the great detriment to his health) during Elizabeth's reign, and also suffered severe financial penalties. Despite this, he remained a wealthy man and Robert inherited a substantial amount as well as several large estates when William died. However, the fine imposed on Robert for his part in the Essex rebellion obliged him to sell one of the estates passed down to him by his father, and it is said that he was low on funds at the time of the plot.

Physically, he is described as around six feet tall, and Father Tesimond tells us that he was 'More than ordinarily well proportioned...of good carriage and handsome countenance'. As regards character and temperament, he was 'grave in manner, but attractively so. He was considered one of the most dashing and courageous horsemen in the country. Generous and affable... much devoted to his religion...' But Tesimond was sympathetic towards the plotters themselves if not their ultimate aim, and another source has said of Catesby that he 'was very wild; and as he kept company with the best noblemen of the land, so he spent much above his rate, and so wasted also good part of his living'. At least one commentator has suggested Catesby himself as being an agent provocateur, and it is interesting to note that he married a Protestant wife and that their son was baptised in the local parish church.

Augustus Jessopp, in his article on Catesby for a Victorian edition of the *Dictionary of National Biography*, says that the anti-Catholic strictures to which his father and then he were subjected:

> 'made him more and more desperate and embittered and that he seems after this to have brooded fiercely on his wrongs and to have surrendered himself to thoughts of the wildest vengeance. Casting aside all caution he consorted habitually with the most reckless malcontents'.

He also believes that Catesby was probably in prison when James came to the throne, one of those rounded up to prevent trouble before or during the accession.

John (Jack) Wright

He may have been the first person to hear of Catesby's scheme. Tom Wintour was also involved in the conversation, but Wright was already at Catesby's house in Lambeth when Wintour arrived and one suspects that Catesby would have at least given him a hint as to what it was all about while they awaited Wintour's arrival. He was a similar age to Catesby, having been born in 1658, but was from further north. Wright was one of several Yorkshiremen, and went to school with Guy Fawkes (and possibly Father Tesimond[2]).

He was reasonably tall and athletic and had a reputation as a swordsman – but he was perhaps a little too handy with that weapon because he was also inclined to get into fights and arguments. Tesimond tells us he was 'somewhat taciturn' and had few friends; but within that small circle were, in addition to Catesby, presumably Guy Fawkes and also Tom Wintour – whose sister he married.

Like some of the others in the group, he was not originally a Catholic but converted at around the time of the Essex rising, in which he took part. Tesimond says his conversion had a calming, beneficial effect on his previously truculent character.

Thomas Wintour

The third man in on the plot at the start, this Worcestershire man was a thinker and a warrior. He was short but 'well-built' and had fought in Flanders; he was also a linguist who, Father Tesimond believed, had studied philosophy. He was often in Europe, where he seems to have had numerous contacts, and before the Gunpowder Plot came into existence he was involved in sounding out whether Spain would support a Catholic uprising in Britain. Frustration at the lack of enthusiasm by Philip III on that score was one of the factors that contributed towards the creation of the Plot. He was also not originally a Catholic. Wintour's continental travels and experience also led to him being chosen to make contact with someone with explosives expertise.

Guy Fawkes

Wintour informed Fawkes that plans were afoot to strike a blow for the Catholic cause and accompanied him back to England in early 1604. Fawkes had been abroad for ten years or more, mostly engaged in fighting for Spanish Catholic forces against the Dutch and the French. This was when he eventually adopted the Latinised version of his Christian name: Guido. It is usually said that he chose the name himself, but I suspect it was given to him by his comrades. His reputation as a soldier had grown during this period. At the time he was recruited to the Plot, he had reached the rank of *alferez*, literally translated as 'ensign' but roughly equivalent to a second lieutenant, and was in line for promotion to captain.

He was originally from York, the son of a church lawyer, and was thirty-five at the time of the Plot. York was a Catholic stronghold, but Fawkes was baptised in the Anglican church of St Michael-le-Belfrey and is said to have converted to Catholicism some time after the death of his father, and his mother's subsequent remarriage to a Catholic.

He was tall and strongly built, with auburn hair and beard. Despite his soldierly background and the generally rough and gruff image of him which is often promulgated, he was, Tesimond tells us, 'pleasant of approach and cheerful of manner, opposed to quarrels and strife…he was a man liked by everyone and loyal to his friends'.

Thomas Percy

The fifth person to join the conspiracy was an acquaintance of Catesby and also the brothers Kit and Jack Wright (whose sister he married in 1591). At around forty-six, he was the oldest of the group, and it is said that by this point his hair had turned grey or white, which made him look even older. He was another Yorkshireman, and also another of the plotters described as being tall; he had, according to the arrest warrant issued after Fawkes' arrest, a florid complexion.

Percy was related to the Earl of Northumberland, and as such had been made constable of the earl's estates in the north, including Alnwick Castle, as well as being a Captain of the Pensioners-in-Ordinary. This latter post required his attendance at court – something which will obviously have a bearing on this story as it develops. Despite all his social status, Percy, like Jack Wright, had also been something of a rogue in his youth; but, also like Wright, he was a Protestant convert who calmed down (in a 'remarkable fashion' according to Tesimond) after his conversion, if the stories about him are to be believed. He is one of several men who visited James even before Elizabeth's death in an attempt to assure the king-to-be of the loyalty of his future Catholic subjects, and thus hopefully pave the way for a more tolerant royal attitude.

There have always been question marks over his character. There are accusations of ruthlessness and even corruption concerning his dealings with Northumberland's tenants, and he was once imprisoned on a murder charge, though subsequently released.

Robert Keyes

Some months after the assembling of the original five plotters, who might be said to constitute the core members, a man was taken on initially to look after a house Catesby rented across the river in Lambeth where the gunpowder was to be stored. Like Fawkes, Keyes might be viewed as more of a hired hand, and no matter how much the conspirators trusted and respected each other, one suspects there was something of an 'officers and men' divide within the group as a whole.

Less is known about Keyes than some of the others. Gerard refers to him as 'an obscure man of no substance' and says that 'his circumstances had always been desperate, as well as his character'.

From a Derbyshire family, he was another of the older men, being around forty in 1605. The details we have of his appearance have a familiar ring: tall, with reddish beard, a Catholic convert who had been born into a Protestant family (his father was a rector, though his mother was a Catholic) and related to other plotters – in this case, his cousin had married Ambrose Rookwood.

Thomas Bates

In December 1604, Catesby's retainer was added to the mix. He is sometimes referred to as Catesby's 'servant', and it is perhaps an intentional detail in the famous picture of the plotters that Bates is the only one depicted as being bare-headed. The 'servant' appellation is perhaps technically true but also somewhat misleading, since his position seems to have been closer to that of a kind of estate manager like Percy, and in fact Keyes had a servant of his own. It was because of his closeness to Catesby that Bates was inducted into the group – the former realised that the latter was growing suspicious about all the mysterious comings and goings, the clandestine meetings, the appearance on the scene of shadowy figures like Fawkes. In the presence of Tom Wintour, Catesby asked Bates outright about his suspicions, and it emerged that although he hadn't quite figured out everything, he was aware of enough to make it expedient to draw him into the circle:

> 'Catesby noting that his man observed him extraordinarily, as suspecting somewhat of that which he the said Catesby went about, called him to him at his Lodging in Puddle-Wharf, and

in the presence of Thomas Winter, asked him what he thought the business was they went about, for that he of late had so suspiciously and strangely mark'd them. Bates answered, that he thought they went about some dangerous matter, whatsoever the particular were: whereupon they asked him again, what he thought the business might be? and he answered, that he thought they intended some dangerous matter about the Parliament-House, because he had been sent to get a Lodging near unto that place. Then did they make the said Bates take an Oath to be secret in the Action, which being taken by him, they then told him that it was true, that they were to execute a great matter; namely, to lay Powder under the Parliament-House to blow it up.'[3]

But the way things panned out, it seems likely that Catesby would have recruited him eventually anyway, regardless of whether he had noticed what was going on.

Bates was born in Warwickshire and was around thirty-eight years old in the year of the Plot.

Robert Wintour

When the plot unravelled and a description was circulated to aid in his capture, he was described as being 'rather lower than otherwise' and 'stooping', and Father Gerard said he was 'of mean stature, but strong and comely and very valiant'. He was though, another member of the gang sporting a reddish-brown beard. Robert was born in 1568 but the location is uncertain. One source has it as Yorkshire, but he is most closely associated with the Worcestershire area where his family's estates lay. He was from a quite well-to-do family, and Wintour's money is purportedly one reason, if not the main one, why he was asked to join the conspiracy. He was aged around thirty-eight at the time of the Plot. His family ties illustrate the almost nepotistic nature of the group, in that his brother Tom was involved, as was brother-in-law, John Grant; he was cousin to Catesby, and half-brother to John Wintour, a peripheral figure who seems to have played little part other than getting drawn in probably without knowing what he was letting himself in for the day before Guy Fawkes was arrested.

Robert wasn't initially as keen as his brother had been to become involved, but finally gave in when he met Catesby, along with the next plotter on our list, at the Catherine Wheel Inn, Oxford, early in 1605.

John Grant

Another member of the conspiracy whose place of birth is unknown for certain, but he lived in Warwickshire where he became Lord of the Manor of Norbrook, not far from Stratford-Upon-Avon. He married into the Wintour family, and in fact called his son Wintour. Described by Father Tesimond as taciturn and melancholy, he had a reputation for giving pursuivants[4] a hard time when they came looking for priests (whom he did harbour) at his moated mansion. He took part in the Essex rebellion.

Christopher (Kit) Wright

The younger brother of John but drawn into the plot at a later date, supposedly when they needed more manpower to help with their tunnelling activities. He is said to have been tall and strongly built, and was about the same age as John Grant, with whom he had participated in the Essex rebellion. Like other plotters, he and Grant had been imprisoned towards the end of Elizabeth's life as a precautionary measure. He was another convert to Catholicism and had taken part with his schoolfriend Guy Fawkes in the 'embassy' to Philip III of Spain in the vain hope of eliciting backing for an English Catholic uprising.

Kit married the sister of Thomas Ward, the man whom we shall later come across as being in the employ of Lord Monteagle, and who alerted the plotters to his master's receipt of the mysterious letter of 26 October.

Ambrose Rookwood

In his late twenties, Rookwood came from a wealthy family of Suffolk Catholics and received a Jesuit education in Flanders. His parents and other family members had suffered fines and imprisonment for their recusancy. Rookwood himself was charged with the same crime even after he had been drawn into the plot. Jardine says he was an 'intimate' friend of Digby; he also seems to have been close to Catesby and is said to have been related by marriage to no less than three of the families of his fellow conspirators: the Wrights, the Wintours and the Keyes.

One writer[5] quotes a contemporary as saying 'I knew him well and loved him tenderly. He was beloved by all who knew him', and according to Jardine he was 'the descendant, and at this time the head, of one of the most ancient and opulent families in the kingdom'.

It appears that he was taken aback when the full details of what Catesby and the others intended to do were revealed to him, having qualms about the potentially enormous loss of life and fearing that there would be a terrible backlash against all Catholics: '…the said Rookwood being greatly amazed thereat, answered, That it was a matter of Conscience to take away so much blood.'[6]

The persuasive Catesby managed to reassure him that their cause was a just and necessary one: '…he was resolved, and that by good Authority, (as coming from the Superiour of the Jesuits) that in Conscience it might be done, yea, though it were with the destruction of many Innocents, rather than the Action should quail.'

Physically, he was short but handsome, according to Father Tesimond, and a rather flashy dresser.

Sir Everard Digby

Like several of the other plotters, Digby came from what was, ostensibly at least, a Protestant background and converted, although there are hints that he was secretly a Catholic all along but that it suited him to keep it under his hat at least until he came of age. Gerard in *During the Persecution* (1886) claims that 'not one' of his family were Catholics and that his mother was 'a thorough heretic'. Jardine says Digby 'dwelt much in the Queen's court in his youth', having been made a ward of court following the death of his father, and like Percy he was appointed a Gentleman Pensioner. Opinions are divided as to his character. Tesimond was full of praise for his wisdom and the brilliance of his mind, while Jardine describes him as weak and bigoted. Needless to say, his wealth was a blessing to the plotters. Father Gerard, who ministered to Digby when he was seriously ill and not expected to recover, found him to be a kind, brave and devout man.

At twenty-four, he was the youngest of the plotters.

Francis Tresham

Born in about 1567, making him another of the group in his late thirties, Tresham was the final piece of the jigsaw, the last of the main group of conspirators to be brought in – and the most controversial.

His place of birth is not known for certain but his father, Sir Thomas Tresham, who had been converted to Catholicism by the first Jesuit mission to England, lived in Northamptonshire. Like many others of his kind, Thomas endured fines and years of imprisonment for his beliefs. Francis was his eldest son, and a cousin to Catesby as well as apparently also being related to the Wintours and friend to the Wrights. Tresham's father died only shortly before the Plot was due to come to fruition, and the fact that he inherited the estate and suddenly became very wealthy might at least partly explain his late inclusion. He was another of those incarcerated when Elizabeth was ailing, and he had been a prominent Essex rebel. In fact, his disrespectful attitude towards the important prisoners he was guarding at the height of that uprising almost led to his execution. Only the intervention of powerful sympathisers behind the scenes saved his skin.

He had a reputation for hot-headedness and was imprisoned more than once, including on one occasion for assaulting a pregnant woman and her husband. Even Father Tesimond, whose character assessments of the plotters was generally sympathetic, said he was a man 'who knew how to look after himself, but was not to be trusted'.

He and Catesby – and their families – seem to have been close when they were growing up, but as we shall see later, Catesby was to come to regret bringing him into the Plot and is said to have harboured dark suspicions about his cousin's part in its downfall.

Certain patterns begin to emerge in these brief biographies. Most of the conspirators were from the Midlands or Yorkshire; at least eight of the thirteen were originally Protestants; five took part in the Essex Uprising; at least four were imprisoned when the elderly Elizabeth fell ill. Additionally, the network of those plotters who were either friends with or related to others forms a complicated spider's web of connections, with Catesby at its centre. This last point is neither particularly surprising nor something to arouse suspicion, since it was safer to recruit men from within a circle of known and trusted people. But one or two of the other points will be worth coming back to later.

Chapter 3

The Jesuits and Supporters

There is no doubt that the plotters received spiritual support of the English Jesuits, but there is much less evidence that any of the priests were given the whole story regarding what the Plot really entailed, and virtually none that they agreed with or encouraged what Catesby and his band intended to do. Nevertheless, three Jesuit priests died because of their connections with the plotters, and two others only survived by fleeing into exile.

We have seen earlier that Cecil was determined to catch the Jesuits with the same net in which he had the plotters, and the *King's Book* leaves its readers in no doubt as to their guilt, referring to 'the traiterous advice and procurement of the said Henry Garnet, Oswald Tesmond, John Gerrard, and other Jesuits', and that the plotters:

> 'should receive several corporal Oathes upon the holy Evangelists, and the Sacrament of the Eucharist, That they the Treasons aforesaid would traiterously conceal and keep secret, and would not reveal them directly nor indirectly, by words nor circumstances; nor ever would desist from the execution and final accomplishment of the said Treasons... And that thereupon, as well the said Thomas Winter, Guy Fawkes, Robert Keyes, and Thomas Bates, as the said Robert Catesby, Thomas Piercy, John Wright, Christopher Wright, and Francis Tresham, did traiterously take the said several corporal Oathes severally, and did receive the Sacrament of the Eucharist aforesaid by the hands of the said Henry Garnet, John Gerrard, Oswald Tesmond, and other Jesuits.'

The priests were even dragged into the supposed tunnelling scheme:

> 'by the like traiterous advise and counsel of the said Henry Garnet, John Gerrard, Oswald Tesmond, and other Jesuits, for the more effectual compassing and final execution of the

said Treasons, did traiterously amongst them selves conclude and agree, to dig a certain Mine under the said House of Parliament.'

The official account repeatedly links the Jesuits' providing of Mass and giving of the sacrament to Catesby and the other with specific knowledge, support and encouragement of the plot. Whenever the plotters and their dastardly plans are outlined in this publication, the names of Garnet, Tesimond and Gerard are always included as if they were as much a part of the group as Fawkes.

Father Henry Garnet

He was in his early fifties at the time of the Plot, born in Derbyshire but spending his early years in Nottingham. He is thought to have been a Protestant in his youth but travelled to Rome while in his twenties and joined the Jesuit order in 1575. Just over ten years later, he was called to England by Father Weston, who was not only the Jesuit superior, but at that time the only Jesuit who had not been incarcerated by the authorities. Within months, Weston himself was caught, and Garnet found himself head of the English Jesuit mission. He oversaw the expansion of the clandestine Jesuit presence, thus allowing members of the faith around the country to hear Mass and receive communion.

We will see later how Garnet almost inevitably become embroiled in the Plot, and his bitterness at having been, in his opinion, duped by Catesby into giving tacit approval for what he had in mind and the loss of life that would have ensued.

We have a physical description of Garnet which was promulgated to aid his capture:

> '… of a middling stature, full faced, fat of body, of complexion fair, his forehead high on each side, with a little thin hair coming down upon the middest of the fore part of this head; his hair and beard griseled… His beard on his cheeks close cut, and his chin very thin and somewhat short. His gait upright, and comely for a feeble man.'

He was with the group of plotters, together with the prominent Jesuit supporter Anne Vaux and others, who made a pilgrimage to St Winifrede's

Well in Wales. They were in search of a miraculous cure for the priest who had acompanied Garnet to Britain, Edward Oldcorne, who had throat cancer. (It did indeed clear up.) It was during this trip that Anne became concerned at what Catesby might be planning, but Garnet passed on the reassurances he had received from Catesby that his only aim was to go and fight in Flanders.

When news of Guy Fawkes' arrest and what had really been planned came to light, it was of no comfort or use to Garnet that he was dismayed that the conspirators should have thought of going to such extremes. He, too, was a marked man and he knew it. He was caught emerging with Father Oldcorne from a priest hole at Hindlip Hall and taken to London for questioning. Even while he was on his way to the capital, Fawkes and the other arrested conspirators were being executed there.

Although Garnet was interrogated extensively (on twenty-three separate occasions) he wasn't tortured, and in fact was treated relatively well. His protestations of innocence, however, were never going to save him and after a fifteen-minute deliberation he was sentenced to be hanged, drawn and quartered. The execution took place at St Paul's Cathedral in May 1606. Mercifully, before he could be removed partially strangled from the noose so that the more gruesome work could begin, sympathetic onlookers grabbed his legs and put him out of his misery. Cecil had got his wish, and Garnet was officially one of the plotters: the thirteen had become fourteen. Not only that, but he had posthumously supplanted Catesby as the ringleader. Gerard tells us that from the time of the gentle priest's execution, in any government writings about the plot the gunpowder conspirators were described as 'Garnet, a Jesuit, and his confederates'.

Father John Gerard

Like Garnet he was from Derbyshire, having been born in Etwall in 1564. He was the son of a Catholic Lancashire landowner who had been involved in a plot to spring Mary Stuart from Tutbury Castle and had served time in the Tower for treason. John associated with Anthony Babington, who also plotted to rescue Mary and who was eventually executed for the same crime.

As a boy, he was educated at the Catholic college in Douai, then a Jesuit college in Paris and later Oxford University. He eventually travelled to Rome, where he ordained as a Jesuit in 1588, and while there met Edward Oldcorne. Gerard was sent to England to join the small Jesuit mission there.

He travelled about the country in the disguise of a 'gentleman of moderate means', ministering to the Catholic gentry. His luck ran out in 1594, when he was arrested and sent to the Clink prison in Southwark, where he continued to carry out his priestly duties to other Catholic prisoners, before being transferred to the Tower.

Like Guy Fawkes, he was subjected to the manacles, in his case in an attempt to extract information on other Catholic priests – especially Father Garnet, the Jesuit superior in England at that time. Gerard seems to have given nothing away, and in 1597, in an exploit worthy of any thriller, he staged an audacious escape from the Tower with a fellow prisoner which involved shinning along a rope across the moat to a boat waiting on the Thames. Nicholas Owen, operating on the outside, almost certainly had a big hand in this daring escapade.

He continued his work in England, but after the Gunpowder Plot fell apart he became even more of a marked man, especially after he was specifically implicated in the Plot by Thomas Bates, a charge he vehemently refuted and which Bates himself later retracted. It didn't help matters that Guy Fawkes' testimony that Gerard although tending to the plotters' spiritual needs, was not let in on the reason for their meetings. After narrowly avoiding capture while hiding in a priest hole when the house he was staying in was raided, he finally slipped out of the country to live out the rest of his days in Europe. During this time, he wrote *The Autobiography of a Hunted Priest*. He died in Rome in 1637 aged 73.

Father Edward Oldcorne

Like Guy Fawkes, Oldcorne was born in York, but almost ten years earlier, in 1561. He trained for the Catholic priesthood in Europe, the only avenue open to any Englishman, and after joining the Society of Jesus he accompanied Father Gerard to England in 1588. After travelling to London to rendezvous with the senior Jesuit priest Father Garnet, he eventually headed to the West Midlands, establishing himself at Hindlip Hall, home of Thomas Habington, who had been involved in the Babington Plot. From this base he became a well-respected and much sought-after preacher whose ministry led to numerous converts.

Once the Plot was exposed, Oldcorne, in common with his Jesuit companions, became a priority target of a government determined to link them to the conspiracy and consign them to the same fate as Fawkes and co.

Nicholas Owen (see below) had been working his magic at Hindlip and there were several well-concealed priest holes. In January 1606, Hindlip was raided after a tip-off by Humphrey Littleton, in an attempt to save his own skin[1], at a time when others were also in hiding there. These included Garnet and Nicholas Owen himself, who had almost certainly built the priest hole upon which his life depended.

Although the initial search found nothing, the pursuivants were sure they were on to something and persisted for days. Although Owen's priest holes defied the best efforts of the searchers, time itself did for those on hiding. After eight days, Oldcorne and Garnet could endure the cramped, dark confines no longer and surrendered themselves. Although Oldcorne was taken to the Tower for interrogation, where unlike Garnet he was subjected to torture, he was returned to the West Midlands for execution, where he met with the inevitable fate of hanging and mutilation.

Father Oswald Tesimond

Often referred to by one of his aliases, Greenway, the *King's Book* refers to him as 'Greenwell' throughout. Although he may have been born in York like so many others connected with the Plot, and certainly went to the same school as Guy Fawkes, it is also possible that he was originally from Northumberland. He was a couple of years younger than Oldcorne but travelled to Rome and became a Jesuit about four years before him and also arrived in England slightly earlier. Catesby is thought to have told him in full about the Plot during confession. Like Gerard, he managed to remain in the shadows and avoid capture, finally sailing to France in the guise of a merchant. Moving on to Rome, he had a successful career in the Church and lived to the age of seventy-three, leaving behind a written account of his escapades in England and valuable information on the plotters themselves.

Nicholas Owen

He was servant to Father Garnet, and like the Jesuit priests operating in England he went under a variety of aliases, 'Little John' being the best-known. The nickname was on account of his very small stature. Born in Oxford, he was a skilled carpenter and joiner who found his niche in life as a priest hole builder of great skill and imagination. A deformed leg, the result of being crushed by a horse, didn't prevent him from constructing some of the most ingenious concealed hiding places in Catholic country houses. Many of these not only defeated determined searchers armed with measuring rods, ripping up floorboards and wainscoting, but were so well hidden that as houses changed hands over the years and their locations were forgotten about, these hideaways weren't rediscovered for decades or even centuries afterwards.

Little John was arrested in the same raid in which Oldcorne and Garnet were caught. He emerged from his hiding place along with another Jesuit, Ralph Ashley, some days before Garnet. Ostensibly, he was trying to slip away when he thought the pursuivants had left – but it has been speculated that he deliberately allowed himself to be captured in order to make the searchers think they had found the only priest hole, and thus end the search.

Despite having an existing hernia, Little John was tortured by being hung from manacles. His hernia bulged so alarmingly that his torturers attempted to keep his innards in place by a fastening an iron plate to his abdomen – but it may well be that the edges of this plate led to his death by cutting into his flesh, because he died in agony from an open wound to his abdomen from which his bowels spilled out. The authorities claimed it was suicide. Their story was that he had been let down and given a knife with which to eat a meal and had used it to take his own life in order to avoid further torture. Few believed this story then or now, certainly not Father Gerard, who had experience of the manacles himself and who declared it would be impossible for someone just released from them to pick up a knife, let alone use one in that way. I believe that rather than being tortured to death deliberately, it is likely that it was the explanation provided by a panicked torturer who had bungled his work, thus robbing his masters of precious information.

Anne Vaux

Born in 1562, she came from a staunchly Catholic family. Her father, Baron Vaux, had been imprisoned for recusancy, and her aunt married Sir Thomas Tresham, father of plotter Francis.

Anne was a wealthy, intelligent and very courageous woman who (along with her sister Eleanor) put her own life in great jeopardy in support of the Catholic cause, especially in aiding and harbouring priests. She is particularly associated with Father Garnet, and there were rumours – which he vehemently repudiated – that they were in a relationship of some kind.

She even, like the Jesuits, went under assumed names, and acquired a large house known as White Webbs about thirty miles north of London, in the guise of Mrs Perkins. Sometimes referred to as 'Whitewebbs', on the edge of the royal hunting forest of Enfield Chase, the place was riddled with secret passages and hiding places and used as a Catholic 'safe house'. It also served as a meeting place for the plotters.

It is not believed that the plotters confided in her about their plans, but she was too shrewd not to realise that something big was in the offing and became very concerned. She supposedly implored Father Garnet, 'For God's sake to talke with Mr Catesbye and to hinder any thinge that possibly he might'. Like the others, she was eventually arrested and questioned, but remained composed and answered honestly enough without incriminating herself and was soon released.

Her loyalty to Garnet meant that when he was arrested she exchanged secret messages with him using invisible ink made from lemon or orange juice, but this was an old trick even then, and it wasn't long before she was arrested once more. This detention (in the Tower) lasted several months but didn't lead to any charges.

She was in her early forties at the time of the Plot. The last time her name appears in any known records is for 1637, but the date of her death has never been established.

One tantalising thing about Anne is the similarity between her surname and that of Guy Fawkes. When she featured as a character in a BBC dramatization of the Gunpowder Plot in 2017, her descendants made it known that the 'x' in their name wasn't silent and that their surname rhymed with 'Fawkes'. Furthermore, Fawkes' own surname itself is given as 'Faux' in some historical sources.

Chapter 4

The Official Story

The orthodox account of the Gunpowder Plot is relatively straightforward. After what almost amounted to a short 'reign of terror' by Mary Tudor in her attempts to return England to its Catholic roots, her successor Elizabeth, who herself had been arrested and had come close to losing her life as a suspected Protestant and intriguer against her sister, set the country onto a firmly Protestant path upon taking the throne. It is true that such punishments as those inflicted by Mary were not unusual for the period, and that Elizabeth went on to have twice as many people executed. But Mary's 300 heretics were burnt at the stake during a three month period (and included the Archbishop of Canterbury) whereas Elizabeth successfully pursued an expedient *via media*, a middle-way policy in religious matters, and her 600 executions came during the course of a forty-four year reign. (Both of their track records on capital punishment very much pale into insignificance when compared to that of their father, Henry VIII.)

During Elizabeth's long reign there was always a perceived threat from Catholics within England keen to overthrow her; this, heightened by a persistent and simmering threat from Spain, meant that the authorities were constantly on their guard, sifting evidence, assessing rumours, watching suspects. When, towards the end of Elizabeth's life, James VI of Scotland emerged as the front-runner among various candidates to succeed her, long-suffering Catholics allowed themselves a degree of optimism for the future. James was seen as being far more tolerant; there were Catholics in his Scottish court, and just a few years before his accession to the English throne his queen converted to that religion. We have already looked at how the early signs were good, but that it wasn't long before James was actively denouncing Papism, ordering Jesuit priests out of the country, and reinstating fines for recusancy. This proved all too much for a small group of English Catholics.

About a year after James came to the throne, Robert Catesby, a man with 'an extraordinary power of influencing others'[1] hatched a plan and gradually began to assemble the team of like-minded men needed to enable him to make his idea a reality. As we saw in chapter 2, Catesby's recruitment drive began when he summoned Thomas Wintour to a meeting at his house in Lambeth at which John Wright was present. Guy Fawkes' confession has it that 'these three first devised the Plot, and were the chief directors of all the particularities of it'. Probably as a result of the discussions at this meeting, it was decided that the services of Fawkes himself should be sought. Around Easter 1604, Tom Wintour was sent to Flanders to approach him, he being, according to Jardine, 'already well known to the discontented Roman Catholics in England as willing to engage in any enterprise for the restoration of the ancient religion'. At about the same time, Thomas Percy was invited to a meeting at the Duck and Drake on the Strand along with the above men. Even before this gathering he had expressed his disgust at James to his friend Catesby and had talked of killing the king himself. Now they were assembled, Percy is famously supposed to have said at one point 'Well, gentlemen, shall we always talk and never do anything?'

Catesby told him that they did indeed plan to do something, but insisted that they all took an oath of secrecy before revealing the full details of what he had in mind. The Strand was then London's principal street and the Dog and Duck was a popular inn, so in order to do this, they arranged to meet again in a house 'behind St Clement's', according to Wintour's later confession. After taking the oath, they went into another room, where they heard Mass and received the sacrament from Father Gerard. The idea, which seems to have been of Catesby's devising, was to find a place from which they could dig beneath the parliament building, stash a large amount of gunpowder there once the mining operation was complete, then wait till the king was due to attend the re-opening of parliament and blow the place up along with everyone in it.

Parliament wasn't due to reconvene till February of the following year, giving them around eight months to prepare. Conveniently, not long after the formation of their fellowship, Percy was made a Gentleman Pensioner. This nominally made him part of the king's bodyguard, and even though by this time the role was probably already more ceremonial than actual, it meant that Percy had a good excuse to look for a house in the Westminster complex which could not only serve as a base for the plotters but which was close enough to make a tunnel practicable. Also conveniently, there happened to be just such a place. It wasn't immediately available, however, so in the meantime they used Catesby's Lambeth house, which was on the other side of the Thames but, once again conveniently situated almost directly opposite the parliament buildings.

Two more men were brought into the plot before the end of 1604. The original group had decided they needed someone to look after the Lambeth house, since Catesby wasn't always going to be present and they were going to begin storing gunpowder and wood for the tunnel while waiting for the Westminster property to become vacant. For that purpose, they brought in Robert Keyes. It was at around this time that Catesby began to fear that his servant Thomas Bates knew something was afoot, and presumably realised that the situation was hardly likely to improve once the work got underway in earnest. Thus, Bates became the seventh man to be initiated into the group. The digging of the tunnel, so the story goes, now began in earnest.

Just before Christmas, the plotters heard that the re-opening of parliament had been postponed till October 1605, giving them more time to dig their way under the House of Lords – a task which was proving harder than they had envisaged. By Christmas, they had reached the foundations of their target building, but by around early February they were still only half way through the subterranean stone wall, said to be nine feet thick. So arduous was the work, in fact, that they decided that yet more manpower was needed, and Jack Wright's brother Kit was enlisted. Both John Grant and Tom Wintour's brother Robert were also added to their number.

There came a point when strange noises from above their heads caused the tunnellers some alarm, and Guy Fawkes was sent out to investigate. It was only now, we are told, that he and his fellow conspirators realised that they had made a big mistake. Rather than digging directly beneath the House of Lords chamber where the king was to lead the opening of the next session of parliament, they were, in effect, one 'floor' beneath that. There was another level between their mine and the Lords' chamber. Had their tunnel been successful, the gunpowder would have blown up a large ground floor room then being used as a coal cellar, the movement of which fuel had caused the hard-to-identify 'rushing' sounds above. It was decided that they would take advantage of yet another convenient occurrence. Like their rented house, that ground floor room beneath the Lords was available and, after some negotiating, it was rented out to Percy. Now they could abandon the tunnel and move the gunpowder directly into what has since become almost universally known as the 'cellar' (which it clearly wasn't – but we will come back to that in the next chapter).

Late in the day, around the end of September, Ambrose Rookwood and Everard Digby were enlisted – both being in a position to provide not only money but also horses and arms for the uprising which was to follow the death of the king. Another man whose wealth could be of use to the plotters was Francis Tresham, the last man to be admitted to the fellowship.

The gunpowder having been moved across the river to the rented house right beside the Lords, it was now surreptitiously transferred to the 'cellar' during the hours of darkness and hidden beneath a pile of wood. However, at around the same time that the last conspirators were enlisted, a mystery man delivered an enigmatic letter to the home of Lord Monteagle, Tresham's brother-in-law. The letter wasn't specific but spoke of a 'terrible blowe' being delivered 'this parleament', and beseeched Monteagle to retire to the country till it was all over. The letter perplexed Monteagle, who passed it first to Cecil. He and his fellow privy counsellors were equally bamboozled and brought it to the attention of the king, whose razor-sharp mind recognised an imminent threat:

> 'The King no sooner read the Letter, but after a little pause, and then reading it over again, he delivered his judgement of it in such sort, as he thought it was not to be contemned, for that the Stile of it seemed to be more quick and pithy, than is usual to be in…the superfluities of idle brains.'[2]

Cecil, who was one of several counsellors gathered round to examine the document, wondered whether the king might be making too much of it and 'told him that he thought by one sentence in it, that it was like to be written by some fool or mad man', since the letter said 'For the danger is past, as soon as you have burnt the Letter'. Cecil felt that this showed the writer up as a fool, but the king was more intent on the line about the 'terrible blow this Parliament', and he decided that:

> 'the danger mentioned should be some suddain danger by blowing up of Powder. For no other Insurrection, Rebellion, or whatsoever other private and desperate Attempt could be committed or attempted in time of Parliament, and the Authors thereof unseen, except only if it were by a blowing up of Powder, which might be performed by one base knave in a dark corner'.

Consequently, he ordered that a search of the buildings should be made before the opening ceremony. Even then, though, there was no rush to see whether they were all about to be blown sky high. Cecil, if the *King's Book* is to be believed, virtually humoured the king while secretly believing he was making a fuss about nothing:

> '…it was agreed that he should the next day, being Saturday, repair to His Highness: which he did in the same Privy Gallery, and renewed the memory thereof, the L. Chamberlain then being present with the King. At what time it was determined; that the said Lord Chamberlain should, according to his custom and Office, view all the Parliament Houses, both above and below, and consider what likelyhood or appearance of any such danger might possibly be gathered by the sight of them…'

But even then:

> 'as well for staying of idle rumours, as for being the more able to discern any mystery, the nearer that things were in readiness, his journey thither was ordained to be deferred till the afternoon, before the sitting down of the Parliament, which was upon the Munday following.'

It was then that the king's insistence that the letter to Monteagle be taken seriously paid off. The Lord Chamberlain, accompanied by Monteagle himself, commenced a search of 'the Parliament house', where:

> 'having viewed all the lower rooms, he found in the Vault, under the Upper House, great store and Provisions of Billets, Faggots and Coals: And enquiring of Whyneard, Keeper of the Wardrobe, to what use he had put those lower Rooms and Cellars: he told him, That Thomas Percy had hired both the House, and part of the Cellar or Vault under the same, and that the Wood and Coal therein was the said Gentlemans own provision. Whereupon the Lord Chamberlain, casting his eye aside, perceived a fellow standing in a corner there, calling himself the said Percy's man, and keeper of that house for him…'

For whatever reason – there were two of them, with presumably more to call upon if needed – Suffolk, the Lord Chamberlain, decided not to tackle or even question 'Percy's man' but to pretend that his suspicions hadn't been aroused and leave the stranger to his own devices while he went to report his findings to the king and his counsellors, announcing that:

'he no sooner heard Thomas Percy named to be the possessor of that house, but considering both his backwardness in Religion, and the old dearness in friendship, between himself, and the said Percy, he did greatly suspect the matter, and that the Letter should come from him. The said Lord Chamberlain also told, That he did not wonder a little at the extraordinary great provision of Wood and Coal in that house, where Thomas Percy had so seldom occasion to remain: As likewise it gave him in his mind, that his man looked like a very tall and desperate fellow.'

Now, the king insisted that 'the House was narrowly to be searched, and that those Billets and Coals should be searched to the bottom, it being most suspitious that they were laid there only for covering of the Powder'. Yet the privy counsellors were still, if this account is to be believed, close to being paralysed into inaction merely because of the fear that they were over-reacting to what they feared might turn out to be a nonsensical letter:

'they were all extream loth and dainty, that in case this Letter should prove to be nothing but the evapouration of an idle brain; then a curious search being made, and nothing found, should not only turn to the general scandal of the King and the State, as being so suspicious of every light and frivilous toy.'

In other words, it seemed they were almost more worried about the embarrassment that might be caused to the king and themselves if they were wrong, than they were at the thought that they might all be blown to kingdom come in the morning. Luckily for all concerned, goes the *King's Book* version of events, the king stuck to his guns as to the danger he perceived and gave them the ultimatum: 'either must all the parts of those rooms be narrowly searched, and no possibility of danger left unexamined, or else he and they all must resolve not to meddle in it at all, but plainly to go the next day to the Parliament, and leave the success to Fortune'.

Thanks to the James' perspicacity and determination, Guy Fawkes was discovered lurking with a lantern in the vicinity of a stash of gunpowder at around midnight, just hours before the great and the good were due to gather in the chamber above. Upon being challenged, Fawkes was open about his reason for being there, but gave them the false name of 'John Johnson' and little else. He was arrested and taken away for what might euphemistically be called 'questioning'. After enduring days of torture in the Tower of London, and with a manhunt already in progress for his accomplices, Fawkes' resistance, along with his body, were finally broken and he began to name names.

The rest of the conspirators were quickly tracked down. Some had already slipped away but a number of them made a last stand at Holbeche House, then within the county of Staffordshire, where they were surrounded and all either killed or arrested. Those plotters taken alive were questioned in the Tower, along with others who were associated with them. The surviving plotters were tried and found guilty. All faced the gruesome execution method of being hanged, drawn and quartered, the idea of which was to hang someone for as long as possible without them losing consciousness, after which they were disembowelled while still alive (sometimes also having their private parts cut off), before finally having their hearts cut out, heads cut off and the rest of their body cut into quarters. Two of the plotters attempted to hasten the process by jumping from the gallows in the hope that their necks would be broken, resulting in instant death. Robert Keyes' leap failed to kill him and he was forced to endure the full process; Fawkes, despite being visibly shattered by his tortures, did manage to summon up enough strength to make a 'death leap'. The only arrested plotter not to be executed was Francis Tresham, who had earlier died while in the Tower of supposedly natural causes.

So much for the orthodox account of the Gunpowder Plot. Much of fine detail of the tale as we know it comes from the confessions of the plotters themselves, but to what extent those statements can be trusted is very much open to doubt. There are lots of questions to be examined – the 'Monteagle letter' being the most famous – but perhaps the best illustration of how a seemingly established fact of the Gunpowder Plot can suddenly start to look less clear-cut when examined closely is the matter of the tunnel or 'mine'.

Not only does almost every aspect of that scheme stretch credulity to breaking point and beyond, but in all of the furore that erupted upon the arrest of Fawkes, the extensive manhunts, the subsequent investigations and detailed investigations, the enduring interest at the time and since regarding the plot and anything to do with it (Guy Fawkes' lantern is still said to exist in the Ashmolean Museum) there is not one single record of anyone actually having *seen* the tunnel, no report of it being examined, no report of it being filled in and blocked off as a security measure, no record of anyone finding it at any time in later years: not even centuries later when the building above it was finally destroyed, nor when the foundations for the new parliament buildings were being excavated. You don't have to be an archaeologist to know that even a filled-in tunnel would be obvious to anyone coming along in later years – and one with such historical significance would have been the cause of a national sensation almost on par with the discovery of the skeleton of Richard III beneath a Leicester car park. None of that happened. Might that not just be because there never was a tunnel in the first place? And if there are valid doubts over that part of the story, what about the rest of it?

Chapter 5

The Scene of the Crime

Although it is useful to get a good idea of the area and buildings we are talking about, there is a much more important reason for examining the plotters' target and its general vicinity. Doing so will help to bring to light anomalies, inconsistencies and unlikelihoods in the authorised version of events.

It is important to clarify first, for those in any doubt, that the buildings we know as the Houses of Parliament today are comparatively modern, having been completed in 1870 after the most of the old parliamentary buildings had been destroyed by fire in 1834. Today, apart from Westminster Hall and the Jewel Tower, little material remains from the time of the Plot.

The whole parliamentary estate comes under the heading of the Palace of Westminster, and the version which existed in Guy Fawkes' day was a ramshackle collection of buildings of various ages (but often ancient) and states of repair. It was an old royal complex, and there were no purpose-built chambers for the Lords and Commons as there are today. By 1605, the Commons were meeting in St Stephen's chapel, adjacent to Westminster Hall. The structure we are interested in was called the Queen's Chamber, a relatively small medieval hall lying to the south of Westminster Hall and the House of Commons. The building ran parallel with the Thames, which was about fifty paces away via a door or doors at the southern end which gave access to a passage known as Parliament Place, leading to Parliament Stairs – which in turn was virtually opposite the house across the river in Lambeth that Catesby had rented.

The other, much less well-known point, but one I briefly alluded to earlier, is that the famous 'cellar' beneath the old House of Lords, also sometimes referred to as an undercroft or vault, was no such thing in the strictest sense of any of those words. It was situated at street level and, at approximately 23 metres by 7 and with a ceiling over three metres from the floor, it wasn't at all the poky, cramped sort of place often portrayed or imagined. Nevertheless, we need a name for it, and, at the risk of contradicting myself, I shall refer to it as a cellar from now on, since plain old 'room' seems inadequate and 'cellar' has become the term of choice by so many historians.

The next most important building connected with the Plot is the house the conspirators settled upon as a base from which they could operate. The selection of this property, and the way in which the plotters went about its procurement, is pertinent to our questioning, sceptical take on this story.

In *The Gunpowder Plot – The Narrative of Oswald Tesimond alias Greenway* (1973) Francis Edwards describes it as 'not very far from parliament [sic] itself and as conveniently situated as could be desired... There was a garden adjoining the house so they rented this too, and built a fairly roomy outhouse (*casetta*) from which they began the mine'. This last point - that the tunnelling work didn't start inside the house itself, but the outhouse – is rarely mentioned. If true, it would surely have had thinner walls and consequently less soundproofing than the main house, increasing the likelihood of their lengthy labours being overheard – we are told that this is why they chose not to work at night.

Gerard says that the house Percy rented 'stood near the south-east corner of the old House of Lords', i.e. nearer to the river than that building, and adjacent to, if not adjoining, the Prince's Chamber.

Far from there being any attempt at secrecy or subterfuge, as there was in the way the Monteagle letter was delivered, the story is that Thomas Percy, one of the leading plotters, boldly presented himself, using his own name, to conduct the negotiations to wrest the lease from a current lessee reluctant to part with it. Negotiations became quite protracted and involved the dragging in by Percy of various other prominent people to help him fight his corner. It is true that his position as a Gentleman Pensioner at Court[1] meant that he didn't need an excuse to be seen at Westminster Palace nor to desire such a handy residence, but it seems strange that he didn't employ a go-between and remain anonymously in the background. In acting as he did, he was wilfully putting himself at the scene of the crime.

Gerard comes close to implying that Percy *deliberately* drew attention to himself and his object, and even that his chosen location was unsuitable. The plotters were renting not a whole house but part of a larger property, and more than one source has asserted that the building was only let out when parliament wasn't in session; when it was in session, the house was used by the Lords. This would presumably have meant that peers would have access to Percy's criminal headquarters, complete with tunnel, up to the very day that Fawkes was taken, since parliament had yet to reconvene.

Not only that, but it had only been recently that this very same building was being used by the commission which had been set up to thrash out the proposed union of England and Scotland. That was why the plotters weren't able to set up shop until December of 1604, several months after Percy had negotiated the lease.

The landlord's servant, questioned after Fawkes' arrest, stated that the part of the property rented by Percy was only used as a single-person letting, and that earlier in the proceedings Guy Fawkes had to move out in order to allow Percy to spend a night there. Yet according to Fawkes' own confession, not only did seven men live and sleep there, but they are supposed to have transferred and stored there twenty barrels of gunpowder from the house on the opposite bank of the Thames. This would represent a small mountain of barrels that are supposed to have been stacked up in either the room or the outhouse.

One of the stranger and harder to believe aspects of the Plot, as passed down to us from the official account via the questionable confessions of those who were taken alive when it all came crashing down on their heads, is this somewhat bizarre scheme to tunnel from beneath the house Percy procured next to the cellar beneath the Lords' chamber. It just doesn't add up. It would entail breaching the foundations of the Lords' building and, once there, digging out a cavity large enough to hold the eventual total of thirty-six barrels of gunpowder. 'The floor above', as Gerard points out, '… must, according to all rules of calculation, have collapsed'.

Ultimately, as we shall see, the scheme failed and the barrels were simply carted directly to the famous 'cellar' beneath the Lords' chamber, supposedly without ever attracting attention. The fact that they achieved this with ease makes the whole mining plan, devised and effected by men who weren't even used to physical labour, let alone knowing how to excavate and make secure such an underground passage, even harder to swallow.

Work is said to have begun on 11 December. We are required to believe that these novice excavators had dug their tunnel all the way to the foundations of the cellar within two weeks, taking a Christmas break before launching their attack on the buried wall, continuing till they were right beneath the Lords. Tom Wintour is supposed to have said when later questioned that the wall was nine feet thick, but this is another suspicious circumstance since even after over three months' work they hadn't even come close to smashing their way through it (unsurprisingly) despite bringing in more manpower. How then, could Wintour or any of the others have known how thick the wall was?

The big question here is how, at the heart of governmental power, thronging with people – both those who lived in the immediate area and those whose business it was to visit, and where dwellings of all kinds stood cheek-by-jowl, could these men have hacked away with their implements, smashed at the stone foundations for weeks on end, and regularly emerged to dispose of vast amounts of spoil, without attracting even the slightest bit of attention? How could they even believe such a feat would be possible in the first place? Gerard says that:

> 'This, it must be remembered, was most populous. There were people living in the very building, a part of which sheltered the conspirators. Around, were thickly clustered the dwellings of the keeper of the Wardrobe, auditors and tellers of the Exchequer, and other such officials.'

And even though Parliament wasn't sitting for most of this time, he points out that:

> 'it is quite certain that the Lords actually met on February 7th – that is while the mining operations were going on – and not only went through the ceremony of prorogation, but transacted some little business besides, Lord Denny being introduced and his writ of summons read.
>
> '[He found it] incomprehensible that the miners should have known nothing of so startling an occurrence, or that knowing of it they should never have made the slightest mention thereof. It is even more difficult to explain how the Peers thus assembled, and their attendants, could have failed to remark the mine, then actually open, in premises belonging to themselves, or any suspicious features of earth, stones, timber, or barrels.'

Fawkes is supposed to have said in one of his confessions:

> 'I stood as sentinel to descry any man that came near; and any man came near to the place, upon warning given by me, they ceased until they had again notice from me to proceed...'

But in such a busy place it is almost impossible to believe not only that such a stop-start plan could ever be practicable or be believed to be so by the plotters, but that our 'tall, desperate-looking fellow' could loiter about the place day after day, passing on warnings or suddenly darting indoors whenever anyone passed by, without becoming a figure of suspicion himself.

In the original draft of his confession of 8 November, Fawkes says that the 'masse of earth that came out of the myne' was deposited in the garden of the house Percy had rented (bear in mind that they were only the tenants of part of the house). Interestingly enough, this far-fetched scenario, considering the amount of spoil that must have come out of the ground, was omitted from the published version of the confession. On top of this, Fawkes claims they hacked their way about half way through a wall which we have seen was described as nine feet thick, so in addition to the excavated soil there must have been a considerable amount of rubble. We are presumably expected to believe that someone was employed in the extremely noisy and challenging task of breaking the larger pieces up into smaller, more manageable and less obvious ones, or that great chunks of broken stone were scattered about the garden.

Alerted to a noise above, they eventually discovered that the 'cellar' was being used to store and sell coal – meaning that right above where they were smashing at the stone foundations, and from where they could clearly hear coal being moved about, people were supposedly going about their business oblivious to what was happening beneath their feet. They also finally discovered that it wasn't a cellar, and that it was could be hired out – which they duly did.

Thus we have the almost farcical situation of a group of men spending months tunnelling from one place to another in 'secrecy'; one of them who had spent the time keeping an eye on the lie of the land then saunters into the place they thought they were going to blow up and finds it wasn't that place at all but a floor below it; he finds it available to let, and his master duly rents it out! This would be rather like Colditz tunnellers toiling and failing to execute a carefully hatched plan, only to step outside their hut and discover it was actually outside the perimeter fence. How credible is it that Fawkes the lookout and Percy, at least (who must have visited the House of Lords any number of times) failed to realise that the place they were trying to tunnel beneath just yards away was not the House of Lords but a half-empty coal storage area?

Either Fawkes or Percy negotiated the letting of the cellar (Fawkes' draft and published confessions differ on this) from one Bright, but this throws up yet more contradictory evidence, because Mrs Whynniard, the wife of the landlord, stated that it wasn't Bright's cellar to dispose of; it was currently being rented by a man called Skinner.

Whoever they rented it from, still in supposed secrecy, the plotters now purportedly manhandled thirty-six barrels of gunpowder into the cellar (calculated to weigh around four tons); to hide these, they also transferred 500 'faggots' (bundles of twigs), 3,000 billets (small pieces of wood), numerous 'great bars of iron', and 'massy stones'. These last two were added to the top of the pile in order to cause maximum damage when the powder went up. They brought in outsiders to do the donkey work for them, and it seems strange that men who are supposed to have been prepared to labour as miners for months chose not to quietly move these loads into the cellar surreptitiously themselves, but to take the quite unnecessary step of bringing in strangers. Fawkes even has Percy arranging to have a 'new dore' knocked through into the medieval cellar – bearing in mind that he was only renting the place – to make it easier for all the materials to be carried into it. It is tempting to think that they might just as well have put a sign up outside the Lords declaring *Danger – Demolition in Progress*.

Readers might be surprised to learn that the plotters considered it necessary to hide the barrels of gunpowder under piles of wood not just in case of a random search by the authorities, *but because this cellar directly beneath the House of Lords was open to the public*. There was the buying and selling of coal, and Wintour's later statement that the gunpowder was hidden beneath the woodpile so that 'we might have the house free, to suffer anyone to enter that would'. Gerard asserts that 'it is highly probable that the cellar was used as a public passage'.

Of all the confessions, testimonies and witness statements, only Guy Fawkes and Thomas Wintour mention the tunnelling episode. Cecil, when writing to ambassadors four days after Fawkes' arrest, makes no mention of any subterranean passage. 'It is,' Gerard commented, '…almost impossible to believe that the important and dramatic episode of the mine ever, in fact, occurred.' There is no mention in any account of anyone having actually seen either the tunnel or the half-breached wall (or of the damage to the foundations being repaired, as they surely must have been if the story is true), yet they would surely have been sites of great curiosity. Gerard added this regarding the evidence for the mine, which:

> 'is not even mentioned, either in the other numerous confessions of Faukes and Winter themselves, or by any of the other confederates. Save for an incidental remark of Keyes, that he helped to work in the mine, we hear nothing else of it; while not only is this confession quite as strange a document

as the two others, but, to complicate the matter still more, Keyes is expressly described by Cecil himself as one of those that "wrought not in the mine". It is hard to understand how so remarkable an operation should have been totally ignored in all the other confessions and declarations, numerous and various as they are; while, on the other hand, should this striking feature of the Plot prove to be a fabrication, what is there of which to be certain?'

How could the plotters have known the thickness of the foundation wall they were trying to break through? The only way, surely, was to assess it by eye, either from the outside or by gaining access to the other side of the wall from within, remembering that the tunnel was abandoned before Fawkes was sent to see what was causing the noises from above. Both methods would have instantly revealed to them that they were in fact attacking the foundations of a cellar, not digging their way directly beneath the Lords' chamber itself.

The bulk of the gunpowder was in place by spring 1605, the remainder around September; the re-opening of Parliament was first scheduled for 3 October, and then put off till 5 November. Thus, according to the story as it is usually told, the plotters dispersed for around six months once the main supply of powder was in place, leaving enough gunpowder to blow up half London stored beneath the House of Lords, covered by bundles of wood. Cecil wrote to ambassador Sir Thomas Parry telling him that access to the vault was possible without the need to go through Percy or any of the other plotters. With everything in place, all the conspirators could do was keep their heads down and await their big moment.

Chapter 6

Spymasters, Subterfuge & Set-Ups

Depending on your take on these things, whether the Gunpowder Plot was allowed to proceed after the government knew about it, was stoked up by agent provocateurs, or was even set in motion in the first place by agents of Cecil, is either conspiracy theory paranoia or just the kind of thing governments did then and still do today. Whatever the truth behind the Plot itself, there is ample evidence to show that both Cecil, and Walsingham (whose mentor was Cecil's father) before him, were not averse to Machiavellian practices.

The role of Walsingham, Elizabeth's famous spymaster, in what became known as the Babington Plot is a case with parallels to our story. That case also featured the mysterious forger and code-breaker Thomas Phelippes, whose name is also associated with the Gunpowder Plot.

Mary Queen of Scots, Elizabeth's cousin and rival to the throne, was being held under a sort of house arrest at various stately homes in England after fleeing a Scottish rebellion. A plot to rescue her and place her on the throne in Elizabeth's place (allied with a Spanish invasion) came to be named after a rather naïve young man called Anthony Babington, who had initially been recruited by others to act as a secret messenger between Mary and her supporters. The problem for Walsingham in exposing such schemes was that correspondence between Mary and the outside world had been halted by his own employer, Elizabeth. His way of circumventing this security measure and actively facilitating the passing of messages between his queen's enemies and Mary, was to employ a double agent to provide Babington with a 'secret' method of exchanging letters. This was done by way of waterproof packages within the stopper of beer barrels delivered to Chartley Hall, where Mary was then being held. It was close to being what might be called 'entrapment' in modern parlance.

Babington embarked upon a correspondence with Mary using this method. As an added layer of security, he composed his messages using a cipher. The problem was that it was a pretty basic system, one well-known to anyone experienced in the dark arts of clandestine correspondence. Thus it was a straightforward task for the messages to be opened, deciphered, then allowed to continue on their way without arousing the suspicions of Mary, Babington or any of the other conspirators, who had no idea that their scheme had been fatally compromised from the start. Walsingham allowed the correspondence to continue until he had all the written proof he needed, then pounced. Torture, confessions and executions followed. This whole process is similar to the one which many believe led to the arrest of Guy Fawkes and everything that followed.

The Gunpowder Plotters' nemesis was not Walsingham but Sir Robert Cecil, though he was just as formidable an enemy, a man at the top of his game. Sir Robert Naunton, a member of parliament during Cecil's reign, described him as being 'a product of the academies of Art and Cunning', referred to the 'perfection of his memory and intellectuals' who was 'his crafts-master in foreign intelligence, and for domestic affairs'. Through his network of informers and spies and his ability to intercept private correspondence, Cecil was aware of what was happening not just in Britain but in Europe at any given time. His agents told him which interesting characters were newly arrived in London from abroad, who was talking to whom, and quite often what they were talking about. One of, if not the, least plausible scenarios of the whole unconvincing official story is that Cecil was in the dark until the last minute regarding the machinations of Catesby and his ever-growing band of very well-known Catholic conspirators.

What writings we have from Cecil in relation to any of the darker arts he was involved in tend to be vague, probably deliberately. An example is a letter he wrote to James I's secretary on 24 October 1605, just over a week before Fawkes was caught:

> 'I spend my time in sowing so much seed as my poor wretched fingers can scatter, in such a season as may bring forth a plentiful harvest. I dare boldly say no shower or storm shall mar our harvest except it should come from beyond the middle region.'

We can be sure he wasn't talking about gardening. There must be little doubt that if there was a credible plot against the monarch, Cecil was the man with the wit and the intelligence resources in place to uncover it; if there wasn't a plot against the monarch but he believed that one would suit his own or the nation's ends, Cecil possessed the cunning and required level of ruthlessness needed to rustle one up and then 'discover' it.

Gerard quotes the French author Cyrille Jean Destombes, who pointed out that:

> 'The plots undertaken under Elizabeth and James I have this feature in common, that they proved, one and all, extremely opportune for those against whom they were directed. To this law the Gunpowder Plot was no exception'.

Roger Palmer (Lord Castlemaine) who, like his contemporary Samuel Pepys, fell victim to a trumped up Catholic witch hunt known as the Popish Plot, wrote in *The Catholique Apology* (1674, third edition): 'It was a piece of wit in Queen Elizabeth's days to draw men into such devices,' and that 'making and fomenting plots was then in fashion...'

Father John Gerard, who knew some if not all of the plotters, had personal experience of the means by which 'confessions' and useful information could be extracted. He was staying in a house recommended to him by Nicholas Owen which was raided after they were betrayed to the authorities. Gerard and Owen found themselves surrounded by men wielding 'swords and staves', before being taken away and interrogated by the infamous Richard Topcliffe, 'a man of cruelty, a thirst for the blood of the Catholics...crafty and cunning'. After an initial attempt to intimidate Gerard failed, and before examining him further, Topcliffe proceeded to write out an incriminating confession of his own invention in which Gerard more or less admitted to treason, and then demanded that the priest sign it. Instead, Gerard offered to write out his own explanation of his recent activities. He knew that Topcliffe would be delighted by this suggestion, because it would provide him with handwriting which could be compared to letters found in the homes of other Catholics which had been raided. Gerard, though, circumvented this possibility by writing in a 'feigned hand' a much less incriminating statement than Topcliffe had in mind, denying some specific accusations and focusing on his quest to save souls. As Gerard relates in his book *During the Persecution*, upon seeing what he was doing 'the old man waxed wroth. He shook with passion, and would fain have snatched the paper from me'. Gerard resisted:

> '"If you dont want me to write the truth," said I, "I'll not write at all."
> '"Nay," quoth he, "write so and so, and I'll copy out what you have written."

41

> "'I shall write what I please," I answered, "and not what you please. Show what I have written to the Council, for I shall add nothing but my name."'

Furthermore, knowing Topcliffe's reputation, Gerard signed his name so close to the bottom line of the confession that nothing could be slyly inserted at a later date. Topcliffe 'broke out into threats and blasphemies' at this, crying, 'I shall get you into my power, and hang you in the air, and show you no mercy; and then I shall see what God rescues you out of my hands.'

The memoirs of Godfrey Goodman, Bishop of Gloucester, a young man at the time of the Plot, describes the atmosphere at this time:

> 'The Roman Catholics seem to have made just complaints of the subtle and unworthy artifices of Leicester and Walsingham, by whom they were entrapped into the guilt of high treason. "And verily," as [Camden] expresses it, "there were at this time crafty ways devised to try how men stood affected; counterfeit letters were sent in the name of the Queen of Scots and left at papists' houses; spies were sent up and down the country to note people's dispositions and lay hold of their words; and reporters of vain and idle stories were credited and encouraged."'[1]

A fascinating glimpse into the behind-closed-doors world of espionage of this era is available in the form of one Arthur Gregory. He was a spy, forger, and an expert in breaking open letters bearing wax seals and repairing or re-creating them with such skill that his work went undetected by the recipient. He is almost certainly the man of the same name whose talents allowed Mary's correspondence to be read surreptitiously. He is probably typical of many other such shadowy figures in that he was never officially a paid employee of Walsingham or Cecil, but, like a modern underworld informant, was apparently rewarded on an ad hoc basis for work done and information received. This meant that although he seems to have served for a time as a customs officer in Poole, for the most part he couldn't carry out his secret duties and also hold down a 'proper' job. As a consequence, he was always short of money and gently hinting at the same to Cecil. Here is a flavour of the correspondence.[2] In one letter he reminds his sometime employer of his ability to 'write in another man's hand'. A later hand adds:

'Mr Lieutenant expecteth something to be written in the blank leaf of a Latin Bible, which is pasted in already for the purpose. I will attend it, and whatsoever else cometh.'

'I have in myself, [says Gregory] to do her Majesty especial service in such sort as all our ingeners [engineers] never dreamed of the like...'

'To be the better able to perform my promise touching the safe making of my sealing metal, I have so well practised therein that I can show you a way to work it cold like wax; and for any other mystery that belongeth thereto, I will most frankly discover [ie reveal] the depth of my skill and deliver to you the box with the perspective glass, furnished with all these subtleties, and instruct you in the secret use thereof. 29 Feb. 1594.'

Here, he reports back to Cecil after having intercepted and opened some letters:

'The breaking of the covering and folding it after in other crests caused me to have much trouble, which I little regard did not the same enforce suspicion also, which I presume to note that some care may be had hereafter upon the like occasion... From my poor lodging, 12 October, 1594.'

'1596, Aug. 1 I am sorry that among so many seals upon the out cover there is no choice of one perfect print. I wish it had been better, nevertheless I will proceed as I may and do my best. But if your Honour hath had any other letters that could help it, I humbly desire you to send the bare seal, for it importeth greatly.'

More examples of Gregory at work:

'There is an honest merchant of this place, lately arrived from Seville, who being familiar with an Englishman there told him in secret that one Sr. Davis, a seminary, comes once a month to a place called Hamme, and to Parley, some four miles from this town, to the house of one Owen Martin and goes in a long russet cloak, a broad brimmed hat, wears a sword, and rides a bay nag with a white star in the forehead... And further

the said merchant was certainly advised that there are twenty seminaries appointed to be sent into these parts to win souls…
29 March 1605'

'I wrote unto your secretary long since of a seminary priest, one Nicholas FitzJames, that was at Careye's house at Hame, near to this place, the 24th of the last month, in company of Jesley his son-in-law, who rode with the priest from thence in view of some that had known him to have said mass in that house, and there the last year married one Mr Perham, uncle to Sir Edward Perham…
Poole, 24 May, 1606'

In general, Gregory seems to have been something of an inventor and an opportunist, always on the lookout for money-making ideas:

'Arthur Gregory hath a device to make a ship go alone for a mile or two, which striking on any other ship shall take fire and burn both, and so to burn a whole fleet. He hath also a means to make a ship go much faster than she did and better by mending her sails. Also he hath a way to make ten men able to manage a cannon in a ship better than the other that Mr Platt told you of…'

More indications as to the atmosphere and practises of the era come from a book attributed to Sir Anthony Weldon, who served in the court of James I, which refers to the trials of Sir Walter Raleigh and Henry Brooke (Baron Cobham). The latter denounced the written confession of his which was presented to the court as being a forgery. He said that 'that villain Wade… got me, by a trick, to write my name upon a piece of white paper, which, I thinking nothing, did; so that if any charge came under my hand, it was forged by that Villain Wade, by writing something above my hand, without my consent or knowledge'.[3]

Wade (more usually known as 'Waad') was part of Cecil's inner circle and Lieutenant of the Tower of London at the time of the Plot. Even his own biographer[4] says that the veracity of this accusation is 'highly likely', and that Waad was well known for his devious practices during interrogation. He was also known to open prisoners' letters, and make copies…before resealing them. Waad had confessed as much in 1602 when pursuing the Jesuits. Such practices were routinely used in the intelligence services.

This is of particular interest to our story, because whereas Topcliffe's attempt to trick Gerard into signing a false confession happened during the reign of Elizabeth, and he died just before the Gunpowder Plot got underway, Waad's activities not only add to the overall pattern of such deceitful activity but were also contemporaneous with the Plot. The trial of Sir Walter Raleigh for treason took place only two years before Guy Fawkes' arrest, and Waad himself was heavily involved with the interrogations of the plotters in the Tower.

Regarding Raleigh's trial and death sentence, the writer Christopher Lee[5] says 'The whole thing was of course nonsense…'. The details of the charges against Raleigh were only revealed to him on the morning of the trial and the case was largely based on the claims of his friend and supposed co-conspirator Cobham, who, unknown to Raleigh had been presented with the lie that Raleigh had accused *him* of treason. Sir Walter Raleigh was destroyed in this way despite being one of the greatest men of his time. What chance did people like Catesby and Fawkes stand?

Chapter 7

The Monteagle Letter

The way the Plot unravelled has long been one of the most talked about and written about aspects of the affair, because of the way it is tied in with what is usually seen as its biggest and most intriguing mystery: the Monteagle letter. This is the version as transcribed by Spink in its original, unpunctuated form:[1]

> 'My lord out of the loue i beare yowe to some of youere frends i haue a caer of youer preseruacion therfor i would aduyse yowe as yowe tender youer lyf to deuys some exscuse to shift of youer attendance at this parleament for god and man hath concurred to punishe the wickednes of this tyme and thinke not slightlye of this aduertisment but retyere youre self into youre contri wheare yowe maye expect the euent in safti for thowghe theare be no apparance of anni stir yet i saye they shall receyue a terrible blowe this parleament and yet they shall not sei who hurts them this councel is not to be contemned because it maye do yowe good and can do yowe no harme for the dangere is passed as soon as yowe have burnt the letter and i hope god will give yowe the grace to mak good use of it to whose holy proteccion i comend yowe.'

For the convenience of readers, here is a version in a punctuated, more modern form of English:

> 'My lord, out of the love I bear you to some of your friends I have a care of your preservation. Therefore, I would advise you as you tender your life to devise some excuse to shift of your attendance at this parliament, for god and man hath concurred to punish the wickedness of this time; and think not slightly of this advertisement but retire yourself into your

country, where you may expect the event in safety. For though there be no appearance of any stir, yet I say they shall receive a terrible blow this parliament and yet they shall not see who hurts them. This counsel is not to be condemned, because it may do you good and can do you no harm, for the danger is passed as soon as you have burnt the letter, and I hope god will give you the grace to make good use of it to whose holy protection I commend you.'

Gerard outlines the story of the letter as it is has been told for centuries:

'…we are assured – and this is the crucial point of the whole story – the government of James I had no suspicion of what was going on, and, lulled in false security, were on the verge of destruction, when a lucky circumstance intervened. On October 26th, ten days before the meeting of Parliament, a Catholic peer, Lord Monteagle, received an anonymous letter, couched in vague and incoherent language, warning him to absent himself from the opening ceremony. This document Monteagle at once took to the king's prime minister, Robert Cecil, Earl of Salisbury, who promptly divined its meaning and the precise danger indicated, although he allowed King James to fancy that he was himself the first to interpret it, when it was shown to him five days later. Not for four other days were active steps taken, that is, till the early morning of the fatal Fifth. Then took place the discovery of which we have already heard.'

Such is, in brief, the accepted version of the history.

He also emphasises the importance of the Monteagle letter:

'The government account clearly stands or falls with the assertion that this was in reality the means whereby the impending catastrophe was averted. That it was so, the official story proclaimed from the first with a vehemence in itself suspicious, and the famous letter was exhibited to the world with a persistence and solicitude not easy to explain.'

He makes the reasonable point that a letter trying to tip off a friend or relative in order to save their skin would hardly be a remarkable or surprising thing.

That the uncovering of the plot was due to the interception of a letter is something the authorities were bound to mention, but to copy it out verbatim to foreign ambassadors and others, as well as reproducing it in full in the *King's Book*, does smack of an attempt to 'sell' the idea to the public at large. An official account of the Plot supposedly written by the king himself, the *King's Book* was rushed into print before the end of November 1605 and is now widely viewed as a piece of government propaganda. Jardine says that the idea was to 'surround fictions by undoubted truths with such apparent simplicity and carelessness, but in fact with such consummate art and depth of design, that the reader is beguiled into an unsuspecting belief of the whole narration', and Spink remarked upon the 'comical, side-glance, slantingdicular, ninny-pinny way in which the *King's Book*, for the most part, is drawn up'.

There is also something about the way Monteagle was treated by Cecil which is worthy of closer examination. Just about anyone who had any sort of contact or connection with the plotters was treated as a potential suspect and at the very least questioned. Monteagle, the recipient of an enigmatic and sinister letter from a mystery source was in fact given a special sort of treatment that wasn't extended to others even remotely connected to the Plot and to those involved. Monteagle *was* connected to those involved, and moreover had, like many of the plotters, taken part in the Essex rebellion. Not surprisingly, when it fell to him to pass the warning letter to Cecil he was feeling a little nervous, as the *King's Book* tells us:

> '...whereof my L. Mountegle...only adding this request by way of protestation, That whatsoever the event hereof might prove, it should not be imputed to him, as proceeding from too light, and too suddain an apprehension, that he delivered this Letter, being only moved thereunto for demonstration of his ready devotion, and care for preservation of His Majesty and the State.'

He need not have worried, because, despite the suspicious manner by which he had been the means of alerting the authorities, Cecil went to great lengths to keep Monteagle's name from being associated with the outrage. Whenever it appeared in subsequent accounts by the plotters it was removed – even to the extent of sticking blank pieces of paper over his name or excising whole passages. This would make more sense if the government had had prior knowledge that he was 'onside' – which in turn would mean that they had prior knowledge of the Plot itself.

Monteagle was also awarded a handsome annuity, and a surprising amount of care went into the wording of such a straightforward grant.

In particular, at a point where the letter describes the Monteagle message as providing the first means to discover that most wicked and barbarous plot, Cecil himself added *and only* after *the first*. It clearly mattered to him that no one was left in any doubt on this point; his department had no knowledge of what was going on before Monteagle received the letter. It strikes one as strange that the busy Cecil should feel the need to micromanage a simple piece of bureaucracy in that way – especially considering that in a sense he was going out of his way to draw attention to the failings of his own far-reaching intelligence network, whose role was the discovery and prevention of exactly such threats to the state.

Most historians and commentators, from soon after the exposure of the Plot right up to modern times, doubt the veracity of the official stance on the Monteagle letter. Sir Edward Hobart, writing to the English ambassador in Brussels, Sir Thomas Edmondes, just a few weeks after the arrest of Fawkes, felt sure that cynics, at least, would be bound to suspect that Monteagle himself was behind the letter, and that Thomas Ward, Monteagle's man, 'is suspected to be accessory to the treason'.[2] It is interesting to note that Hobart also reports a rumour that there were in fact *two* letters – an identical one having been sent to Northumberland, who concealed the fact.

Moving forwards to the Victorian era, when there seems to have been a resurgence of interest in the subject, David Jardine said it was 'hardly credible that the letter was really the means by which the plot was discovered' and subscribed to the view that it was in fact a smokescreen devised by Cecil to draw attention away from the true means by which he had obtained his information. The historian John Sherren Brewer, who edited Goodman's *Court of King James* volumes, held a similar view.

In the present day, Antonia Fraser, whose *Gunpowder Plot: Terror & Faith in 1605* has become a classic work on the subject, was of the opinion that it is 'difficult, if not outright impossible' to believe that the letter was the warning of a concerned well-wisher that it was purported to be; she is of the opinion that there is 'something very fishy' about the whole episode. She calls Monteagle's sister, Mary Habington of Hindlip Hall, a prime suspect, but ultimately suggests that Tresham wrote the letter. It was 'a fake and not only Monteagle but Salisbury knew it was a fake. It was brought into being for a special purpose.' This, though, raises the question of what might have been behind Cecil's desire to manipulate the story in this way. If the Plot *had* been foiled at least in part by the brilliance of Cecil and his spies, why would he be so coy about it? It is possible that taking the credit would have led to a need for explanations, which in turn might have exposed methods and strategies Cecil preferred to keep in the dark so they might be used on future unwitting suspects. But as well as that, or instead of it, what if his desire to stay out of the limelight was because there was something unsavoury involved in the uncovering (and even creation of) the Plot, something less than heroic; something that conceivably even the king couldn't be allowed to know about?

As we have seen, Monteagle had already gone as far as involving himself in not just a plot, but an actual armed uprising against the government less than five years earlier. Moreover, he was a personal friend of Catesby and other conspirators (Gerard describes it as an 'intimacy with the principal conspirators'[3]), and also like so many of the other plotters, was related by blood or marriage – in his case to Tresham's sister. One of his servants (the man Monteagle asked to read the mystery letter out loud for him) was said to be a friend of Tom Wintour. According to one of Wintour's confessions, Monteagle was in touch with Catesby just days before 5 November, informing him that the Prince of Wales would not be attending the opening ceremony.

Is it possible that Cecil had some sort of hold over Monteagle, and/or that he felt he could be more useful to him alive than dead? The author of a Gunpowder Plot Society article has suggested that Catesby must have had his doubts about Monteagle, whom he knew well, not to have tried to involve him in the Plot the way he did with virtually everyone else he knew.

So, for someone who had in effect taken up arms against his country in the recent past, Monteagle was surprisingly well regarded and trusted, having been made a commissioner for the prorogation of 3 October. Gerard points out that this was 'a most unusual distinction for one in his position', and when his brother was imprisoned in Calais, King James personally intervened to secure his release.

There are also question marks over when and how the letter was delivered in the first place. The *King's Book* says Monteagle got it on 26 Saturday October:

> 'The Saturday of the week, immediately preceding the King's return, which was upon a Thursday (being but ten days before the Parliament.'

Cecil informed British ambassadors that it was about 'eight days before the Parliament should have begun', while informing Henri IV of France that was delivered 'some four or five days before'.

We do know that it was delivered to him at a house he owned in Hoxton (in modern Shoreditch, but then a rural setting about a mile outside London) by 'an unknown man' just as he was about to eat at 7pm. The manner of its delivery is described thus in the *King's Book*:

> 'For the Saturday of the week, immediately preceding the King's return, which was upon a Thursday (being but ten days before the Parliament) The Lord Mountegle, Son and Heir to the Lord Morley, being in his own Lodging, ready to goe to supper, at seven of the clock at night, one of his Footmen (whom he had sent of an errand over the street) was met by an unknown man, of a reasonable tall personage, who delivered him a Letter, charging him to put it in my Lord his Masters hands: which my Lord no sooner received, but that having broken it up, and perceiving the same to be of an unknown, and somewhat unlegible hand, and without either Date or Subscription; did call one of his men unto him for helping him to read it. But no sooner did he conceive the strange contents thereof, although he was somewhat perplexed what construction to make of it (as whether of a matter of consequence, as indeed it was, or whether some foolish devised Pasquil, by some of his enemies to scare him from his attendance at the Parliament) yet did he, as a most dutiful and loyal Subject, conclude not to conceal it, whatever might come of it.'

Many accounts say that Monteagle got a servant to read it out loud, but the account in the *King's Book* actually says it was written in a 'somewhat unlegible [sic] hand...' and that he 'did call one of his men unto him for helping him to read it', which isn't quite the same thing. The man may simply have helped him decipher certain hard-to-read words; but the letter still exists, and given its great age and taking into account the writing style of the period, it is in fact written in a bold, clear hand, and apart from the lack of punctuation it strikes one has being relatively easy for a literate man of that era to read.

Whatever the significance of this may be, Monteagle allegedly blithely allowed a servant to read this enigmatic and surreptitiously delivered document without troubling to first ascertain what secrets or even embarrassments it might contain.

A further interesting fact is, as Father Oswald Tesimond points out, that Monteagle rarely dined at the Hoxton house, and hadn't done so for more than a month before the letter was delivered:

> 'Whoever took the letter to him was, therefore, [says Tesimond], someone who knew the Baron intimately, and

consequently was well known to his household. How was it, then, that the page did not know the man to whom he spoke and gave the letter? One could add to this the incredible foolishness of anyone who entrusted a letter of this kind, being of such importance, to the hands of a page. It also showed monumental carelessness on the part of the baron to have such a letter read out in the presence of all who were at supper. This letter had been sent to him confidentially, and as something of the utmost significance. The secretary was at least right when he said that whoever wrote it showed great stupidity, if only for having written so openly of a secret so enormous.'

Another point here is that, as the *King's Book* tells us, the letter was not delivered directly to the house but was handed over to one of Monteagle's men in the street outside who had been sent on an 'errand'. Now, it may be that the mystery man was intending to visit the house, perhaps discreetly at a back door, and that on his way he fortuitously noticed the footman emerge. But it is also possible that he was lurking outside, waiting. That in turn might indicate that our messenger *knew* that someone would be venturing out, i.e. it was a planned transaction and Monteagle was aware that at 7pm (a suspiciously precise, on-the-hour time) he must send someone out to 'bump into' the visitor. A ploy like this would ensure that Monteagle was one small step further removed from what happened that night.

A rather startling story which, if true, would show Monteagle and his letter in a different light, was uncovered by antiquary William Fulman in Corpus Christi library, Oxford. It was a document concerning an unknown correspondent of fellow antiquary Anthony Wood. On coming across this find, William Fulman queried several points and received unequivocal replies from Wood. The results of his enquires were as follows:

- The November 5th business was without all peradventure, a State Plot. I have collected many pregnant circumstances concerning it.
- 'Tis certain that the last Earl of Salisbury confessed to William Lenthal[4] it was his father's contrivance, which Lenthal soon after told one Mr Webb…and his kinsman, yet alive.

- Sir Henry Wotton[5] says 'twas usual with Cecil to create plots, that he might have the honour of the discovery, or to such effect.
- The Lord Mounteagle knew there was a letter to be sent to him before it came. (Known by Edmund Church, Esq., his confidant.[6])
- Sir Everard Digby's[7] sons were both knighted soon after, and Sir Kenelm[8] would often say it was a State design, to disengage the king of his promise to the Pope and the King of Spain, to indulge the Catholics if ever he came to be king here; and somewhat to his purpose was found in the Lord Wimbledon's[9] papers after his death.
- Mr Vowell,[10] who was executed in the Rump time, did also affirm it so.
- Catesby's man (George Bartlet) on his death-bed, confessed his master went to Salisbury House several nights before the discovery, and was always brought privately in at a back door.

In response to a query by Fulman, the unknown author stated that:

'Catesby, 'tis like, did not mean to betray his friends or his own life—he was drawn in and made believe strange things. All good men condemn him and the rest as most desperate wretches; yet most believed the original contrivance of the Plot was not theirs.

Samuel Rawson Gardiner, in his rebuttal of Gerard's case[11], isn't able to do a very effective job of countering this evidence. He makes one or two pedantic points, such as the fact that Sir Everard Digby's sons weren't knighted 'soon' after, but a number of years later (thirty in the case of one), but all he can really say in protest is that the story 'was produced long after the event', which is perfectly true but not necessarily damning. Gardiner points to the sheer 'inherent improbability' of these assertions:

'Whatever else a statesman may communicate to his son, we may be sure that he does not confide to him such appalling guilt as this.'

But at least as strong a case could be made for the *opposite* being true: that a dying man would want to get it off his chest.

We are told that Monteagle wasn't sure whether it was either some sort of hoax intended to 'scare him from his attendance at the Parliament' or something more ominous. But what would be the point of preventing his attendance? What could anyone, enemy or otherwise, gain from tricking Monteagle, specifically, to miss the ceremony to open a new session of Parliament? He decided that as a 'loyal subject' (since the Essex Rebellion, at least!) he needed to take it to the king that very evening:

> 'notwithstanding the lateness and darkness of the night in that season of the year, he presently repaired to His Majesties Palace at Whitehal, and there delivered the same to the Earl of Salisbury, His Majesties Principal Secretary.'

When he arrived at Whitehall, Monteagle discovered James was away on a hunting trip. This could also be seen as yet another convenient piece of timing, because it meant that Cecil, to whom the letter was handed, could now take control of it and stage-manage its delivery to the king. Furthermore, he could see to it that when the king did get it they would be that bit closer to 'D Day' – because after consulting others, Cecil decided, even though the *King's Book* declares that both Cecil and the king were already aware of 'some business the Papists were about…making preparations for some combination amongst them against this Parliament time', not to hasten to the king with the news or even send a messenger, but to wait until 1 November, the day after James returned from the hunt.

In fact, the initial reaction of the king's ministers to the contents of the letter was surprisingly sanguine. The *King's Book* tells us that Cecil and the Lord Chamberlain (the Earl of Suffolk), the first two men to read the letter, thought fit to summon three more privy counsellors: the Lord Admiral (the Earl of Nottingham) and the earls of Worcester and Northampton. Those five, 'having all of them concurred together to the re-examination of the Contents of the said Letter, they did conclude that how slight a matter it might at the first appear to be', despite the rider that it shouldn't 'absolutely be contemned [sic]'

One reason given – at least for Cecil consulting the king rather than immediately investigating the matter himself, if not for the delay in informing him – was that Cecil and the other king's ministers were apparently perplexed by this letter. They needed 'His Majesties fortunate Judgement in cleering and solving of obscure Riddles and doubtful Mysteries'. Perhaps even more surprising was that the delay meant that 'more time would in the mean while be given for the Practise to ripen…whereby the Discovery might be the more clear and evident…'[12]

In other words, five days before the opening of parliament, rather than sending out searchers, contacting informants, looking into the whereabouts of prime suspects, James' renowned and ruthless spymaster felt it would be easier to catch them just as they were about to strike. But does this make sense? Even without the benefit of hindsight, isn't it more likely that any plotter or plotters would by now have completed their preparations and be lying low, waiting for the moment to strike? If Cecil and the king didn't know in what form the 'blowe' was to come, it could have been an assassin, perhaps even someone on the inside. Catesby had been due to join the king on his hunting trip. If he had done so, how many opportunities must there have been for him to run His Majesty through? There might have been an armed gang lurking and waiting to pounce. Waiting till the attack was launched, depending on the assailants' strength, might have been too late. If, however, Cecil already expected an explosive event of some kind and there was gunpowder lying around waiting to be ignited, the king and his senior ministers were already meeting to discuss the letter, how did he know he could afford to be so calm and patient? How could they be sure that *they* were not the target, and that the villains (especially if they knew about the letter, as Cecil probably expected they did) wouldn't decide to blow them up at any moment? In the event, the apprehension of Guy Fawkes himself involved a fair degree of luck and bad timing on his part, if the official account is to be believed. Furthermore, if Fawkes had had any inkling at all that a search was underway, he could easily have ignited the gunpowder prematurely, taking Cecil, the king and many others with him.

The editor of the Folio edition of Father Tesimond's account draws attention to Cecil, writing to Sir Charles Cornwallis on 9 November, that the Monteagle letter was 'in a hand disguised' and points out that this raises the question of how he could possibly know this if he didn't know who its author was.

As we have seen, for whatever reason the letter was not in the king's hands until 1 November, after which, even though James supposedly employed his superior intellect in working out what terrible deed the message was alluding to, nothing was done until the afternoon of the day before Parliament was due to open. The version we have already heard from the *King's Book* – that James sent the Lord Chamberlain (Thomas Howard, the Earl of Suffolk) and Monteagle himself, to see what was going on and, lulled in false security, were on the verge of destruction, when a lucky circumstance intervened. The *King's Book* says that Suffolk noticed the 'billets, faggots, and coals' stored in the cellar, together with 'a very tall and desperate fellow' (i.e. Fawkes) lurking in a corner. Still no action was taken. Suffolk, says the *King's Book*, left the desperate fellow to his own devices and went to report his findings to His Majesty. This is notably at odds with the version of events sent to ambassadors, in which Suffolk found only the pile of faggots. There was no mention of any tall, desperate fellow – a surprising detail to omit in an honest, open account.

Now, says the *King's Book*, His Majesty insisted that the House was to be 'narrowly' searched (implying that the first search – instigated on the suspicion that someone was about to blow parliament up, only needed be a superficial one) and had the genius idea that the pile of faggots might conceal something and so should be searched 'to the bottom'. To this end, he sent Sir Thomas Knyvet, a Gentleman of the Privy Chamber, together with a party of men comprising 'such a small number, as was fit for that errand'. This was around midnight, which again implies that several more hours were allowed to elapse since Suffolk's highly suspicious discovery. But this is almost the polar opposite of what Britain's ambassadors were told, which was that the 'insisting' was done by the lords 'in spite of the king'.

The *King's Book* story has it that before they could enter the building they came across and arrested the man whom Suffolk had spotted earlier, whereas James' letter to Henri IV of France says he 'found Faukes within'. Whether Fawkes was inside or out, the problem is that there is no indication that Suffolk was with them now – indeed, the impression is that he wasn't – so how did they know it was the man he'd seen? Because he was tall? Because he looked 'desperate'? Whether Fawkes was arrested in his own room (see elsewhere), inside or outside the vault where the powder had been amassed, it was now that Knyvet decided to poke around, and duly uncovered the first barrels of gunpowder.

'Never, assuredly,' says Spink, 'was a true story so hard to tell.'

Historians and writers have been conjecturing for years – centuries – as to the true identity of author of the Monteagle letter, and the list of suspects is long. They include Monteagle himself, Cecil, Tresham, Father Oldcorne, and (according to Jardine) Anne Vaux, the woman who knew many of those involved and who had long played a crucial role in harbouring Jesuit priests. Sir William Waad suspected Percy, on the basis that saving Monteagle's life would ensure that he could continue to repay money he owed Percy's wife. According to Thomas Lathbury,[13] Lord Monteagle himself is also said to have expressed a suspicion that it was Percy when he was accompanying the Earl of Suffolk in the search of the cellar. Spink[14] rules Tresham out on the basis that:

> 'when a prisoner in the Tower of London, and even when in the act of throwing himself on the King's mercy, [he] never gave the faintest hint that the Letter was attributable to him. But, on the contrary, actually stated first that he had intended to reveal the treason, and secondly that [he had been guilty] of concealment.'

Spink rules out Tresham partly on the basis that if he had sent the letter he would have said so when he was arrested. This is a good point, because it would have been in his favour to have admitted to something which ostensibly at least brought the Plot to a halt just in time. He examines the possibility that it was Kit Wright with the aid of Monteagle's man Thomas Ward (who was the man intercepted by the stranger outside Monteagle's house when delivering the letter), and finds evidence that the two were connected. But his eventual choice is an outsider – Father Oldcorne, who was Digby's priest. He was arrested as part of the general manhunt and executed despite there being no evidence against him.

Antonia Fraser similarly casts doubt on Tresham as the author of the letter because he, like his fellow plotters, met a grisly end precisely *because* of it. But with respect, I wonder whether this is too simplistic a view. For one thing, if the writer had been a plotter or even a double agent working for Cecil, he could well have been double-crossed, i.e. he was acting on a promise that his skin would be saved, while Cecil all along planned to get rid of someone who could one day expose the truth. Melodramatic though it might seem, Cecil seems to have been perfectly capable of such skulduggery. But what if Cecil *did* save Tresham's skin? The other equally intriguing thing about him specifically and not the other plotters, is that he was *not* executed or killed in the Holbeche raid, but died in the Tower from 'natural' causes. There is a school of thought which has this as a cover for his escape to Europe, facilitated by Cecil himself – a sort of proto-witness protection scheme. Again, we are in melodrama territory here but there is evidence to back it up which, while a long way from being conclusive, is at least worthy of serious consideration. This theory is examined in more detail in the final chapter.

Tresham, Monteagle's brother-in-law, wasn't the only one of the conspirators who advocated providing potential Catholic victims (including

Lord Stourton, who was married to another of his sisters) with advance warning to stay away from Parliament. Keyes, Percy and Fawkes all had their own pet causes – but Tresham appears to have been the more agitated on this issue, and the one whom Catesby and Tom Wintour subsequently accused of having sent the Monteagle letter; and it was those two who resisted the move. But then Tresham arrived uninvited to a meeting at White Webbs and according to Fawkes, had what seems to have been, reading between the lines, a serious fall-out with Catesby and Tom Wintour. It would appear that he got cold feet over the whole business, which might explain why he didn't fly from London. Perhaps in his eyes he had washed his hands of it on grounds of conscience, and no longer even thought of himself as a 'plotter'.

Jardine goes so far as to suggest that as well as Tresham warning Monteagle, other plotters probably surreptitiously and individually took similar measures concerning their own friends. After his arrest, Digby wrote to his wife to tell her that several others were to have been warned, and that 'you may guess I had some friends that were in danger, which I prevented'. No other letters have come to light – but then, it would not have been in the interests of any recipient to associate himself or herself, however innocently, with knowledge of the Plot of any kind. If such communications existed, they were no doubt burnt immediately after being read:

> 'Who [wonders Tesimond] can really believe that the Earl of Salisbury and his friends, men who showed the utmost astuteness in everything else, would have proved so dense when interpreting a letter that was clear enough? Even a schoolboy would have found it easy enough to guess at, without taking it to the King as if he were some prophet...'

And Gerard:

> 'It is impossible to say more than this, that the accounts handed down cannot by any possibility be true, inasmuch as on every single point they are utterly and hopelessly at variance.'

Chapter 8

The Arrest of Guy Fawkes

Guy Fawkes' importance to the Gunpowder Plot has been greatly exaggerated by history almost solely because he was the shadowy figure caught, metaphorically if not quite literally, with his hand hovering over the fuse. It is a captivatingly melodramatic image and, as far as it goes, close to the truth. Fawkes was going to do what many have wanted to do before and since; sort that lot in parliament out. There is even a Guido Fawkes blog by a political activist, supposedly uncovering political wrongdoings. It should really, however, be the Robert Catesby campaign – but then that would almost certainly mean nothing to the vast majority of the general public. I'm sure that even today many people assume Fawkes to have been the Plot's ringleader. He was an intelligent, literate man and a successful military officer – but as we have seen, as far as the Plot was concerned he was the bagman, the lookout, the hired muscle. The truth is that any of the conspirators could have ignited the powder, and most could have procured it in the first place or at least have found someone else who could. Without Catesby, the plot would have eventually faltered – if it would have even been initiated in the first place, which is far from certain; without the money-men he enlisted, it could never have got off the ground, at least not in the form it eventually took.

But the fact remains that Fawkes is the man whose name is synonymous with the Gunpowder Plot, and whatever jiggery-pokery lay behind the story, only the most zealous conspiracy theorists would deny that he is the man who would have lit the fuse given the chance.

What were the actual circumstances of Guy Fawkes' arrest?

There are several variations on the story of the way in which Fawkes was apprehended. Although they only differ in what might seem like relatively minor detail, those details all add to the picture of the way facts (and quite possibly the confessions) may have been manipulated to suit the story.

The King's Book

With a full title of *THE Gunpowder-Treason: With a Discourse of the Manner of its Discovery; AND A PERFECT RELATION OF THE Proceedings against those horrid Conspirators; Wherein is Contained their Examinations, Tryals, and Condemnations: LIKEWISE KING JAMES's SPEECH To Both Houses of PARLIAMENT, On that Occasion*, it is not hard to see why the publication has become abbreviated. This official, published account of the affair places Guy Fawkes outside Parliament – perhaps in Parliament Place – at the moment of his arrest, after having previously been seen in the cellar. We have already come across most of this information. Lord Suffolk, the Lord Chamberlain, was first sent with none other than Monteagle on the afternoon of the 4th to see what he could find in the cellar, whereupon he discovered the pile of faggots (which must have been pretty mountainous, bearing in mind the supposed number of barrels of gunpowder it was concealing). He didn't think fit to examine the pile, and when he also caught sight of Fawkes lurking in a corner he neither arrested or even questioned him. The *King's Book* implies that Suffolk wanted to avoid arousing Fawkes' suspicions. It seems strange that he should feel the need to act in so furtive a manner, considering his position of authority, the importance of his mission and the possible consequences of failing to act there and then. For all he knew, Fawkes might have realised (or feared) that the game was as good as up and so have proceeded to light the fuse as soon as Suffolk left.

Another peculiarity about the *King's Book* scenario, and one that seems rarely to be queried, is that according to this account not only was Fawkes present on the afternoon of 4 November but also Whynniard, from whom the place had been rented. We have already learned that when James sent Suffolk to see what was going on beneath parliament he found the great pile of faggots, coals and other materials. He asked Whynniard, who must, then, have been there or thereabouts, what the cellar was being used for and was told that they had been rented out to Percy, and that the wood and coal belonged to him. It was at this point that Suffolk first set eyes on the man who would prove to be Guy Fawkes.

> '[Suffolk] found in the Vault, under the Upper House, great
> store and Provisions of Billets, Faggots and Coals: And
> enquiring of Whyneard, Keeper of the Wardrobe, to what use
> he had put those lower Rooms and Cellars: he told him, That
> Thomas Percy had hired both the House, and part of the Cellar
> or Vault under the same, and that the Wood and Coal therein
> was the said Gentlemans own provision. Whereupon the Lord
> Chamberlain, casting his eye aside, perceived a fellow standing
> in a corner...'

But that deal to hire out the cellar to Percy had been concluded around seven months previously. What was Whynniard doing in there just hours before Fawkes was to blow the place up? Was he still able to come and go as he pleased while the barrels of gunpowder were being amassed? With so little time to go before the big event and Fawkes allegedly armed with the necessary tools to ignite the powder, would he not have found a way of getting Whynniard out of the place he and his colleagues were paying for the use of?

In any event, Suffolk reported back to the king, who seemed to be the only one capable of deciding that the pile of wood should be inspected more closely in case it concealed something nasty. And here we get the description of the arrest and where it took place:

> 'Sir Thomas Knevet, (a Gentleman of His Majesties Privy
> Chamber)... went about the midnight next after to the
> Parliament house, accompanied with such a small number, as
> was fit for that errand. But [before his entry into the house],
> finding Thomas Percy's alledged man standing without the
> doors, his Cloaths and Boots on, at so dead a time of the night,
> he resolved to apprehend him as he did, and thereafter went
> forward to the searching of the house, where after he had
> caused to be overturned some of the Billets and Coals, he first
> found one of the small Barrels of Powder, and after all the
> rest, to the number of thirty six Barrels, great and small: And
> thereafter searching the fellow, whom he had taken, found
> three Matches, and all other instruments fit for blowing up the
> Powder, ready upon him, which made him instantly confess
> his own guiltiness, declaring also unto him, *That if he had
> happened to be within the house when he took him, as he was*

immediately before (at the ending of his work) he would not have failed to have blown him up, house and all.'

I've drawn attention to the last part of Fawkes' supposed statement because I take it, if authentic, to mean that he had just come out of the cellar (having readied the barrels), which would take him even further away from the claim that he was arrested in his own rooms and had time to throw some of his equipment away, as outlined in our next piece of evidence.

Guy Fawkes' Confession of 5 November

'[Fawkes] saith that he hadd touchwood and match also about eight of nine inches long about him, and when they came to apprehend him, he threwe the touchwood and match out of the window in his chamber neare the parliament house towards the water stair.'

So here, Fawkes is peering out of the window of the rented house next to the Lords' chamber. Remember that it is nearly midnight in the days before street lighting, and the house is situated among taller and grander buildings in the crowded Westminster complex. He sees shadowy figures approaching, somehow knows they have come to arrest him, and throws his incriminating items away. One problem with this is that they could only have known he was in the house if they knew much more about the Plot than was ever admitted to. That this account is completely at odds with every other version of his arrest yet it is supposedly from his own mouth, gives us further cause for concern regarding any of the confessions obtained by Cecil's interrogators.

King James

The king, in a speech to Parliament on 9 November, declared that Fawkes was caught 'but new come out of his house...having his fire-work for kindling ready in his pocket'.

So in this variant on the facts of the arrest, Fawkes has left the security of the house. If the previous version also contains any truth it would mean he saw the search party on its way, but rather than assume they would go to the cellar looking for him, he came out to give himself up. Either way, he could not have thrown his vital equipment for igniting the powder out of the window first if they found it in his pocket.

Cecil to Ambassadors

The king's chief minister sent an account of the events to English ambassadors abroad in which he says the initial search found the faggots but not Fawkes. Fawkes was seized when he was newly come out of the vault. This is obviously at odds with both the confession *and* the king's account but ties in with what Fawkes allegedly said according to the *King's Book* about having been in the house 'immediately before' his arrest. However, Gerard tells us that Cecil's earliest draft of the story has Fawkes arrest occurring in the place itself, as he was busy to prepare his things for execution. Things are getting complicated – but there's more.

Cecil to Henry IV of France

This version differs in some small but significant details. Knyvet was given the task of making a search of the Old Palace and keeping an eye out for whoever was coming and going. The initial observation of the faggots and Fawkes in the afternoon is not mentioned, and Knyvet is described as going into the vault 'by chance' and finding Fawkes inside. Only then were the faggots moved to reveal the gunpowder.

Earl of Suffolk

In a letter to Dudley Carleton (who had helped Percy obtain the lease of the house), the Earl of Suffolk says that Fawkes was actually engaged in making his trains (i.e. laying a trail of gunpowder to act as a fuse). In other words, we have moved from Fawkes tossing his essential items away in a panic to him being in position, having set everything up, and being virtually ready to set off the powder whenever he wants to.

There is a theory that the plotters always cynically intended to leave Fawkes, the outsider, to take the blame, which seems unlikely though not impossible. The most detailed story went that there was a man called

Pickering of Titchmarsh in Northamptonshire who was known to own a particularly fast horse, and that this was obtained by Robert Keyes. So far, so good. Keyes did have a Northamptonshire connection. Although he was probably from Derbyshire, the home county of his father, his wife was a governess to the Mordaunt family in Northamptonshire and Keyes himself lived there for a time and worked for Lord Mordaunt. More importantly, if this story is to be believed, Pickering was brother-in-law to Keyes. The biggest problem with this idea is that the man usually named is Sir Gilbert Pickering, but the Titchmarsh person of that name and title wasn't born until six years after Fawkes was hanged, and the only other Gilbert Pickering of Titchmarsh I have been able to trace would have been sixteen at that time.

Perhaps it was a relative. In any event, the claim (the main source of which is Caulfield's *History of the Gunpowder Plot*) was that Guy Fawkes was to light the fuse to the gunpowder beneath the House of Lords and immediately flee to a prearranged spot at St George's Fields, across the Thames in Southwark and make his escape. The story then takes something of a melodramatic turn. Pickering was said to have been a Puritan, a group whose existence troubled King James as much as the Catholics, if not more, and the aim of the plotters was to lay the blame for the terrible explosion at their door. Thus, Pickering was to be killed by the plotters and his body secretly disposed of; Fawkes himself would be killed upon his arrival at the rendezvous point across the river and his body so badly mutilated that he could not be identified. The plotters would then put it about that this was Pickering, who had blown up Parliament in the name of the Puritans and then attempted to escape on the famously fast horse that he had brought along for that very purpose. However, he had been intercepted by an angry mob and beaten to death on the spot, before the authorities could arrive on the scene. This version of events further goes on to claim that the reason Fawkes named other plotters after his arrest was not that he had been broken under torture but that he had either realised, or been informed, that he was to have been so treacherously used by the men whom he had assumed were his friends.

While this story is not impossible, there is little evidence for it and it seems to be based solely on hearsay. It is, admittedly, an elaborate and surprisingly imaginative tale for anyone to have concocted, and it is hard to see what anyone would have had to gain from doing so. Fawkes is said in a letter from Cecil to have been 'booted and spurred' when arrested, which would fit in with the idea of the speedy getaway horse, but would he have had time to cross the Thames in a boat before the mighty explosion would have sent stone and other debris flying in all directions like bullets and cannon balls? Spink says that a slow-burning match would have given Fawkes about fifteen minutes to get to a ship moored in the Thames, though not to the south bank but ready to take him to Flanders. If the blast had been as great as most commentators assume, then such a ship would probably have been dismasted by the explosion, or at the very least had its sails and rigging badly damaged, before it could have got very far. (If it could have gone anywhere at all, which would have depended on current and wind.) Some even assert that Fawkes, with his military and explosives expertise, *knew* he would never have had the time to get clear of the blast area, and that he was on a suicide mission.

It is not beyond the bounds of belief that a story of a sinister plan to murder Fawkes would be devised by someone like Cecil or Waad, fearing that their brave captive might either endure his torture without giving anything away or hold out for so long that he died before getting the chance. Making him believe he would have been betrayed by those he trusted might just tip the balance in their favour. The Pickering tale does have a hint of sophistication or at least ingenuity about it, of the kind that Cecil or one of his underlings might have cooked up. But if this had been the case and Fawkes believed the tale, surely his anger at the attempted treachery of his fellow conspirators would have been such that he would have exposed their duplicity either at his trial or at some point before his execution?

He wasn't a gentleman, 'a man of blood', but a foot soldier, and foot soldiers are expendable in war. But this overlooks his childhood friendships with the Wrights; and anyway, they must have realised that no matter how brave he was, there was a good chance he would eventually name names under torture (as, indeed, he did). It is just about feasible that someone like Catesby alone might set Fawkes up as a sort of patsy, in the way some see Lee Harvey Oswald's role in the shooting of John F Kennedy, and even that he might endeavour to do so without telling the others; but again there is little evidence for this. What is of interest is that the variations and inconsistencies in the account of Fawkes' arrest from the different official accounts and from those who were in a position to know the true facts, fit in with the overall pattern of inconsistencies and improbabilities in this story, and provide more weight to the conspiracy angle.

But Fawkes was not the only one to fall into Cecil's net, as we shall see.

Chapter 9

The Published Confessions: Guy Fawkes

'Amongst all the confessions and 'voluntary declarations' extracted from the conspirators, there are two of exceptional importance, as having furnished the basis of the story told by the government, and ever since generally accepted. These are a long declaration made by Thomas Winter, and another by Guy Faukes, which alone were made public, being printed in the "King's Book," and from which are gathered the essential particulars of the story as we are accustomed to hear it.'

John Gerard SJ, *What Was the Gunpowder Plot?*

A great deal of what we know, or think we know, about the Plot comes ostensibly from pens or out of the mouths of those plotters who survived the rounding up phase following the arrest of Guy Fawkes, and others on the fringes. Various people who were associated with the gang or had dealings with them were interviewed, such as Mrs Whynniard, wife of the man from whom the house and vault were hired and John Shepherd, their servant. Mrs Whynniard's husband couldn't be spoken to because he had died just hours after Fawkes was arrested. His wasn't the only potentially convenient death, and we will come back to this subject later. But it is what the plotters themselves are supposed to have said which is of the main interest to us.

Of the thirteen main Gunpowder Plot conspirators, four were killed in the raid on Holbeche House and three were taken alive; three were captured during their flight from Holbeche; one remained in London and was soon arrested; one went to ground but was finally caught the following January. Fawkes we already know about.

John and Kit Wright, Catesby and Percy were shot dead at Holbeche. Tom Wintour was wounded and arrested, as was Ambrose Rookwood.

John Grant, blinded in the 'explosion' (see next chapter) was also apprehended there. Thomas Bates managed to get away from the Holbeche raid but was caught a few miles away; Robert Wintour had fled before the attackers arrived and was caught two months later at Hagley Park, Worcestershire after having been given away by a servant. Robert Keyes went on the run but didn't last so long, being caught in Warwickshire after less than a week. Everard Digby is another who slipped away from Holbeche but he was captured close by. Francis Tresham is the only man who made no attempt at either fight or escape, an apparent display of insouciance highlighted by those who see him as the author of the Monteagle letter. 'Acting as a man very sure of himself', says Tesimond. He was arrested in London a week after the plot had been exposed, but Tesimond also points out that the authorities promulgated the idea that Tresham 'had confessed all he knew', yet his confession wasn't published, nor was he publicly vilified in the same way that the other plotters were. A murky cloud of suspicion hangs over his subsequent 'illness' and death in the Tower, as we shall see later.

Guy Fawkes was obviously the first to be caught, and so the first man to be questioned. Torture was to be a feature of his and other interrogations, but not at first. He was quizzed several times, initially sticking to his John Johnson identity. It sounds like an alias which is not only unimaginative, but one so phoney-sounding in such circumstances as to almost guarantee suspicion. However, it is just possible that he 'borrowed' it from someone on the fringes of the plot. In April 1605, after Fawkes had been put to death, one 'John Johnson, servant to Mr Bartlet' was one of the many people examined to see what information they might provide. Robert Catesby's servant was George Bartlet, so could this be another case of a 'servant' having a servant, as with Thomas Bates, who is often referred to as Catesby's servant but who also had a servant of his own? If so, this might this be where Fawkes got the idea for the name from.

The other problem with Fawkes' false identity was that he was carrying a letter in his pocket which addressed him by his real name. He was first taken to James I's private apartments where the privy council had gathered. This was still on 5 November, early on the morning after his arrest, and Fawkes was in no mood to co-operate. Consequently, James issued an order on the following day which explicitly required that 'If he will not other wayes confesse' the prisoner be tortured in order to loosen his tongue, commencing with the 'gentler' methods, and building up 'by degrees to the worst... God speed youre goode worke'. This unsavoury work went on throughout that day and into the next when Fawkes finally broke and named some of his fellow conspirators. He left several names out, but it was enough to end his agonies and for the investigation to move forward in earnest.

It is generally accepted that the 'gentler' torture was to be hung by iron manacles (or rope) attached to the wrists. We are used to seeing cartoons and comedy sketches of men chatting to each other while being suspended in this way, and we might be forgiven for thinking that it seems very uncomfortable but perhaps on the whole bearable. In fact, it was a far more agonising and debilitating ordeal than one might think. The pain could lead to loss of consciousness, and lengthy sessions could result in permanent physical damage. Prisoners were not usually chained to the wall, but suspended from the ceiling or a high beam, so that all of the bodyweight was supported by the wrists, arms and shoulders. This could go on for hours at a time, as seems to have happened in Fawkes' case. Father Gerard described his own experience of the manacles in some detail. Even if he had wanted to answer his 'inquisitors' questions, he was in too much pain to reply, and the sensation of the build-up of blood pressure in his arms and hands was such that he believed, wrongly, that the blood was 'bursting forth' from his fingers. He passed out several times. Each time this happened his captors put steps beneath his feet or supported his body till he came to – then took the steps away again when he did. He was unchained for the night, and when he was brought back for another session his arms were still so swollen that the only place the manacles would fit was the squashed down area of flesh where they had been fastened the previous day. Despite all this, he didn't break (they wanted him to renounce his religion) and when it was finally over he couldn't hold a knife to eat with for days and could barely use his hands and fingers at all for many days afterwards. It was months before he regained the use of his hands properly, and a feeling numbness persisted longer still.

But the 'worst' sort of torture James was referring to was the rack. Just as with the manacles, when I was a child and we were told the Guy Fawkes story it always surprised me a little that this was the worst they could come up with. Having your arms and legs stretched must have hurt, I thought, but it was hardly like being poked with hot irons or having your fingernails pulled out, and I always liked to fancy that I could have withstood someone pulling at my limbs with a bit of rope. In fact, the rack method was taken to extremes I never dreamt of; eventually all four limbs could be dislocated –

literally pulled from their sockets – and even, in extreme cases, ripped from the body completely. We don't know what specific injuries Fawkes suffered, but the fact that his suffering was great is evidenced by the famously faint and illegible squiggle of the signature he appended to one of his confessions during this time when compared to his usual hand. He was, though, able to scale the ladder on his way to being hanged when the time came, albeit with help, which might indicate that his lower limbs either didn't suffer dislocation. However, it is quite possible that those experienced and skilled in torture were equally adept at reducing dislocations once they had the information they were seeking.

There were eleven separate statements relating to Guy Fawkes' part in the Plot, beginning with a confession on the morning after his arrest on 5 November, including a list of questions drawn up by James I on the 6th and his responses furnished on the same day, and concluding with Fawkes' declaration of 25 January 1606. The only words of Fawkes' the public got to hear were from his signed confession of 17 November, which itself was based on a draft of 8 November. It is the differences between the 'original' document of the 8th and the final, published version of the 17th which are of interest to us here.

A Comparison of the Two Documents

The draft confession document is not handwritten by Fawkes (an educated, literate man), isn't signed by him, names no co-conspirators, and is in fact written in the third person. As Gerard says (my italics):

> 'The document thus described is manifestly a draft, and not a copy of a deposition actually taken… What, however, is most remarkable is the frank manner in which this document is treated as a draft. *Several passages are cancelled and others substituted, sometimes in quite a contrary sense, so that the same deponent cannot possibly have made the statements contained in both versions.* Other paragraphs are "ticked off", as the event proves, for omission.'

In other words, what we have is as much a construction of what the authorities wanted their man to have said as it is a verbatim confession by Guy Fawkes himself. The document Fawkes did eventually sign on

17 November is now in the first person. Those parts of the confession entered into the first version but 'ticked off' have now disappeared, but the names of the fellow plotters are added. It is now time to compare the two versions. We will take it a sentence at a time, which might be rather laborious but which will hopefully prove quite enlightening. The version drawn up on the 8th, unsigned but supposedly based on information provided by Fawkes, is in italics and the the comparable passage from the signed, published confession follows:

'He confesseth that a Practise in generall was first broken unto him, agaynst his Majesty, for the Catholique cause, and not invented or propounded by himself, and this was first propounded unto him about Easter last was twelvemonth, beyond the seas in the Low countreyes, by an English Lay-man, and that English man came over with him in his company into England '

'I confesse that a practise in generall was first broken unto me against his Majestie, for releife of the Catholique cause, and not invented or propounded by my self. And this was first propounded unto me about Easter last was twelvemonth, beyond the Seas, in the Low countries of the Archdukes obeysance by Thomas Wynter, who came thereupon with me into England.'

The 'English Lay 'Man' has now become Thomas Wintour. It is important to bear in mind that additions like this are not the result of further interrogation. This second document is supposedly no more than an edited or tidied up version of the first.

'… and they tow and three more weare the first five mencioned in the former examination.'

'… and there wee imparted our purpose to three other Englishmen more, namely Robt Catesby, Thos Percy, and John Wright.'

Three further plotters are now named.

'And they five resolving to do some thinge for the Catholick cause,—a vowe being first taken by all of them for secrecye,— one of the other three propounded to perform it with Powder, and

resolved that the place should be,—where this action should be performed and justice done,—in or neere the place of the sitting of the Parliament, wherein Religion had been uniustly suppressed. This beeinge resolved the manner [of it] was as followeth.'

'who all five consulting together of the meanes how to execute the same, and taking a vowe among our selves for secresie Catesby propounded to have it performed by Gunpowder, and by making a myne under the upper house of Parliament, which place wee made choice of the rather, because Religion having been unjustly suppressed there, it was fittest that Justice and punishment should be executed there.'

Catesby is named as the proposer of using gunpowder in the latest version.

'First they hyred the Howse at Westminster of one Ferris, and havinge the howse they sought to make a myne under the upper howse of Parliament,'

'This being resolved amongst us, Thomas Percy hired a howse at Westminster for that purpose, neare adjoyning the Parlt howse.'

Ferris's name has been cut; Gerard says it appears to have been 'tampered with' even in the original. Percy is now named as the one procuring the house.

'...and they begann to make the myne in or about the xi of December, and they five first entered into the worke.'

'... and there wee beganne to make a myne about the xi of December 1604. The fyve that entered into the woorck were Thomas Percye, Robert Catesby, Thomas Wynter, John Wright, and my self.'

The miners are named in the second version.

'... and soone after toke an other unto them, havinge first sworne him and taken the Sacrament, for secrecye.'

'... and soon after we tooke another unto us, Christopher Wright, having sworn him also, and taken the Sacrament for secrecie.'

Now the new addition is also named.

> *'And when they came to the wall,—that was about three yards thicke,—and found it a matter of great difficultie, they tooke to them an other in like manner, with oath and Sacrament as afore sayd.'*

'When wee came to the verie foundation of the Wall of the house, which was about 3 yeards thick, and found it a matter of great difficultie, we took to us another gentleman Robert ~~Wynter~~ Keys in like manner with our oathe and Sacrament as aforesaid.'

We now have yet another named conspirator – but in this case the surname 'Wynter' has been deleted and replaced with 'Keys'. This change is in Cecil's own hand according to Gerard – who points out that in a letter of 14 November – much closer to the time of the arrest – he had told Edmondes, England's ambassador in Brussels, that Keyes 'wrought not in the myne' and included Robert Wintour as one who had so done.

> *'All which seaven, were gentlemen of name and bloode, and not any man was employed in or about that action,—noe not so much as in digginge and myning that was not a gentleman.'*

This declaration disappears altogether in the second version.

> *'And having wrought to the wall before Christmas, they reasted untill after the holydayes, and the day before Christmas,—~~having a masse of earth that came out of the myne,—they carryed it into the Garden of the said Howse, and after Christmas they wrought on the wall till Candlemas, and wrought the wall half through, and sayeth that all the tyme while the others wrought he stood as Sentynell to descrie any man that came neere, and when any man came neere to the place, uppon warninge given by him they rested untill they had notyce to proceed from hym, and sayeth that they seaven all lay in the Howse~~, and had shott and powder, and they all resolved to dye in that place before they yeilded or weare taken.'*

'It was about Christmas when wee brought our myne unto the Wall, and about Candlemas we had wrought the Wall half

72

through. And whilst they were a working, I stood as sentinell, to descrie any man that came neare, whereof I gave them warning, and so they ceased untill I gave them notice agayne to proceede. All wee seaven lay in the house, and had shott and powder, being resolved to dye in that place before we should yeild or be taken.

The unlikely story that huge amounts of spoil were deposited in the garden of a house they only shared the use of is deleted from the original.

> *'And as they weare workinge, they heard a rushinge in the cellar which grew by one Brights selling of his coles whereuppon this Examinant, fearinge they had been discovered, went into the cellar and viewed the cellar,'*

> 'As they were working upon the wall, they heard a rushing in a cellar of removing of coles; whereupon wee feared wee had been discovered, and they sent me to go to the cellar,'

Just a minor, probably inconsequential difference here: in the first version Fawkes takes it upon himself to investigate the cause of the sounds above, in the second he is sent by the miners.

> *'... and perceivinge the commoditye thereof for their purposs, and understandinge how it would be letten his maister, Mr Percy, hyred the Cellar for a yeare, for 4 pounds rent. And confesseth that after Christmas 20ty barrells of Powder weare brought by themselves to a Howse which they had on the Banksyde in Hampers, and from that Howse removed the powder to the sayd Howse, neere the upper Howse of Parliament. And presently upon hyringe the cellar, they themselfs removed the powder into the cellar, and couvered the same with faggots which they had before layd into the sellar.'*

> '... and that the Cellar was to be lett, viewing the commoditye thereof for our purpose, Percy went and hired the same for yearly Rent. Wee had before this provyded and brought into the house 20 barrells of Powder, which wee removed into the Cellar, and covered the same with billets and fagots, which we provided for that purpose.'

There is little of material difference between the two accounts here.

> *'After, about Easter, he went into the Low Countryes,—as he
> before hath declared in his former examination,—and that the
> trew purpos of his goinge over was least beinge a dangerous
> man he should be known and suspected, and in the meane
> tyme he left the key* [of the cellar] *with Mr Percye, whoe in his
> absence caused more Billetts to be layd into the Cellar, as in
> his former examination he confessed.'*

> 'About Easter, the Parliament being proroged tyll October next,
> wee dispersed our selfs and I retired into the Low countryes,
> by advice and direction of the rest, as well to acquaint Owen
> with the particulars of the plot, as also lest by my longer staye
> I might have grown suspicious, and so have come in question.
> In the meane tyme Percy, having the key of the Cellar, layd in
> more powder and wood into it.'

One minor and two possibly significant alterations here. Fawkes is initially only made to say that more billets were brought in, but yet more powder is added to the published statement. Then, the first version has Fawkes leaving the country because he was a 'dangerous man' who should be 'known and suspected'. But Fawkes had been out of the country for around thirteen years, and although he was probably under some sort of observation by Cecil's overseas spies, this pales into significance compared to Catesby and the others involved in the Essex rebellion who had actively risen up against the state just four years previously. They were the 'dangerous men', known to the authorities, yet they were openly moving around London and the rest of the country right up until the mining commenced (and during their break from it). Fawkes' daily sentry duties are what would have been most likely to drawn attention to him, not his subsequently living quietly in heavily populated London. The other change is to bring in the name of Hugh Owen, a Welsh spy living in Flanders who had originally pointed Tom Wintour in Fawkes' direction when he was looking for someone who could deal with the gunpowder. Cecil seemed intent on drawing Owen, who had long been a thorn in the side of the English government through his machinations, into the net he was casting, and opened negotiations to have him extradited before he is named in any of the confessions attributed to Fawkes. This is one of numerous indications that Cecil knew much more than we are led to believe before the Plot was officially rumbled. It is only after an exchange of messages took place between London and Flanders that Owen's name suddenly appears in the edited version of 17 November.

> *'... and retourned about the end of August or the beginninge of September, and went agayne to the sayd howse, nere to the sayd cellar, and received the key of the cellar agayne of one of the five. And then they brought in five or six barrells of powder more into the cellar, which all soe they couvered with billetts, saving fower little barrells covered with ffaggots, and then this examinant went into the Country about the end of September.'*

> 'I returned about the beginning of September next and then receyving the key againe of Percy, we brought in more powder and billets to cover the same againe. And so [I] went for a tyme into the country, till the 30 of October.'

Percy's name is again added to the published account.

> *'It appeareth the powder was in the cellar, placed as it was found the 5 of November, when the Lords came to proroge the Parliament, and sayeth that he returned agayne to the sayd Howse neare the cellar on Wednesday the 30 of October.'*

This is marked for deletion, and does not appear in the final version apart from the date of Fawkes' return.

> *'He confesseth he was at the Erle of Montgomeryes marriage, but as he sayeth with noe intention of evill, havinge a sword about him, and was very neere to his Majesty and the Lords there present.'*

Also kept out of the published document. Was it to keep the name of the Earl of Montgomery (a friend of the king) out of it?

> *'Forasmuch as they knew not well how they should come by the person of the Duke Charles, beeinge neere London, where they had no forces,—if he had not been all soe blowne upp,— He confesseth that it was resolved amonge them, that the same*

day that this detestable act should have been performed, the same day should other of their confederacye have surprised the person of the Lady Elizabeth, and presently have proclaimed her queen (to which purpose a Proclamation was drawne, as well to avowe and justify the Action, as to have protested against the Union, and in no sort to have meddeled with Religion therein. And would have protested all soe agaynst all strangers) and this proclamation should have been made in the name of the Lady Elizabeth.'

'Concerning Duke Charles, the Kings second son, we hadd sundrie consultations how to sease on his person, but because wee found no meanes how to compasse it,—the Duke being kept near London,—where we had not forces enough, wee resolved to serve ourselves with the Lady Elizabeth.'

The official version is little more than a condensed version of the first in this case. Even so, it does go to show how the authorities were prepared to paraphrase where it suited them – the corollary of which being that the published declaration of Guy Fawkes can in no way be considered a verbatim confession, even in 'innocent' matters.

'Beinge demanded why they did not surprise the Kinges person and draw him to the effecting of their purpose, sayeth that soe many must have been acquaynted with such an action as it could not have been kept secrett.

'He confesseth that if their purpose had taken effect untill they had power enough they would not have avowed the deed to be theirs; but if their power,—for their defence and safetye,—had been sufficient they themselfes would have taken it upon them.

'They meant all soe to have sent for the Prisoners in the Tower to have come to them, of whom particularly they had some consultation.

'He confesseth that the place of Rendez-vous was in Warwickshire, and that armour was sent thither, but the particuler thereof he knowes not.

'He confesseth that they had consultation for the takinge of the Lady Marye into their possession, but knew not how to come by her.

'And confesseth that provision was made by some of the conspiracye of some armour of proofe this last Summer for this Action.

'He confesseth that the powder was bought of the common Purse of the Confederates.'

None of this appears in the final confession, but there is little of a sinister nature that can be read into its omission.

The published version ends with Fawkes' signature and a list of names of 'principall persons' involved in the plot who aren't mentioned in the body of the confession, namely Digby, Rookwood, Tresham, Grant and Robert Wintour. This last name had originally been down as Robert Keyes, then subsequently altered before publication.

When I was assembling the above outline, something occurred to me concerning one of the seemingly more trivial points. It doesn't really matter whether Fawkes went to investigate the 'rushing' noise on his own initiative or whether he was sent by the others, other than that it adds to the list of discrepancies between the two accounts. What could be significant, however, is what this scenario implies. In both versions, Fawkes was not underground with the miners – he was above acting as a 'sentinell'. This is important, and as far as I'm aware it is something no one has ever queried. Because to act as a look-out, Fawkes must surely have been loitering outside the house they had rented. It is possible that he was looking out of a window, but this assumes not only that there was one which pointed in the right direction, but that it afforded a good enough field of vision to allow him to provide an early warning should anyone be seen coming from any direction. After all, by the time someone actually passed in front of the window it would already be too late. Even if he didn't hang around outside some of the time he must have come and gone from that house numerous times.

Either way, what this means is that in this area of tightly packed buildings, and with the plotters occupying one close enough to the Lords' chamber to tunnel towards it, Fawkes must, better than any man at that time, have been very familiar with the layout of the surrounding houses and the comings and goings associated with them. It is stretching credibility to believe that he would not have attracted attention – but that is not my main point. Not only is it almost impossible to accept that he, if not the miners themselves, could not easily see that their mine was on the wrong level – that they were tunnelling not directly beneath the nearby Queen's Chamber, but a publicly accessible ground floor cellar which they could have wandered into at any time for a look around (as Fawkes ultimately did), with the Queen's

Chamber above that. More to the point, in all those months, how could Fawkes not have noticed that something as bulky as coal was being moved in and out of the premises the tunnellers were aiming for? Gerard tells us that the old House of Lords was about fifty yards from the Thames, and that the house that Percy hired as their base was 'near the Prince's Chamber, and on the side towards the river', so the house and the Lords' building can barely have been more than spitting distance from each other.

There may have been other buildings which obstructed Fawkes' view of the Lords – but logic would dictate that the tunnellers would then have to breach the foundations of whichever building or buildings was in their line of sight, yet there is no mention in any of the reports of the diggers needing to overcome such an obstacle.

In his own statement, the only other to be published (in the *King's Book*), Tom Wintour makes no mention of hearing any rushing sound of coals or the alarm it caused, nor of sending Fawkes to investigate. He was one of the excavators, yet he merely says that 'opportunity was given to hire the cellar', as if the reader already knows what he means by this – but this is actually the first mention of its existence in his lengthy account. Without Fawkes' explanation in his own confession, Wintour's mention of a cellar would be make no sense because their aim had been to dig directly beneath the Lords and excavate a hole in which to place the barrels of gunpowder. He probably hadn't been given the opportunity of reading what Fawkes said, so it is suspicious that in an otherwise detailed, step-by-step story he left out a crucial point such as that. If, however, Wintour's statement had been written (or at least dictated) by one of his interrogators who already knew what the reference to the cellar meant, then this omission would make sense.

Chapter 10

The Published Confessions: The Declaration of Thomas Wintour, 23 November 1605

There are a few peculiarities about the version of Wintour's Declaration preserved in the archives. Firstly, it is actually a copy in the hand of Cecil's secretary Levinius Munck. It was shown to King James, who demanded certain changes, which were duly made for the published version. In particular, Monteagle's name is left out of the version that was presented before the public. Also, there were no witness names at the bottom of the letter written by Munck – these were added later by Cecil. Stranger still, it has been pointed out by numerous commentators that while the supposed original declaration which *is* in Wintour's handwriting is dated 25 November, the date on the copy is the 23rd.

The declaration written by Wintour himself is in private hands. What follows is the version presented to the public in the *King's Book*:

'23 9br, 1605.

'My Most Honourable Lords.

'Not out of hope to obtain pardon for speaking - of my temporal part I may say the fault is greater than can be forgiven - nor affecting hereby the title of a good subject for I must redeem my country from as great a danger as I have hazarded the bringing her into, before I can purchase any such opinion; only at your Honours' command, I will briefly set down my own accusation, and how far I have proceeded in this business which I shall the faithfuller do since I see such courses are not pleasing to Almighty God; and that all, or the most material parts have been already confessed.'

William Waad had told Cecil that Wintour was ready to write his declaration now that he 'doth find his hand so strong'. Gerard interprets this as meaning that Wintour was tortured like Garnet and could only write once his hand had recovered. Although it wouldn't be at all surprising if Winter *was* tortured, this may not be what Waad was referring to. Gerard seems to be forgetting that when a number of the plotters, Wintour among them, were pursued to Holbeche House after Fawkes' arrest (something we will look at in more depth in a later chapter) Tom was hit in the right arm by a crossbow bolt. We have no way of knowing if he was right-handed, but statistically it is likely, and a feasible explanation as to why he might need time to recover before taking up a pen:

> 'I remained with my brother in the country for Allhollantide, in the year of our Lord 1603, the first of the King's reign, about which time, Mr Catesby sent thither, entreating me to come to London, where he and other friends would be glad to see me. I desired him to excuse me, for I found not myself very well disposed, and (which had happened never to me before) returned the messenger without my company. Shortly I received another letter, in any wise to come. At the second summons I presently came up and found him with Mr John Wright at Lambeth, where he brake with me how necessary it was not to forsake my country (for he knew I had then a resolution to go over), but to deliver her from the servitude in which she remained, or at least to assist her with our uttermost endeavours. I answered that I had often hazarded my life upon far lighter terms, and now would not refuse any good occasion wherein I might do service to the Catholic cause; but, for myself, I knew no mean probable to succeed.

Wintour doesn't seem to have been a quarrelsome rake in the mould of Catesby, Wright and one or two of the others, so when he speaks of 'hazarding his life' he may be talking about his military experience in Europe during the previous decade:

> 'He said that he had bethought him of a way at one instant to deliver us from all our bonds, and without any foreign help to replant again the Catholic religion, and withal told me in a word it was to blow up the Parliament House with gunpowder; for, said he, in that place have they done us all the mischief, and perchance God hath designed that place for their punishment. I wondered at the strangeness of the

conceit, and told him that true it was this strake at the root
and would breed a confusion fit to beget new alterations, but
if it should not take effect (as most of this nature miscarried)
the scandal would be so great which the Catholic religion
might hereby sustain, as not only our enemies, but our friends
also would with good reason condemn us. He told me the
nature of the disease required so sharp a remedy, and asked
me if I would give my consent. I told him Yes, in this or what
else soever, if he resolved upon it, I would venture my life;
but I proposed many difficulties, as want of a house, and of
one to carry the mine; noise in the working, and such like.
His answer was, let us give an attempt, and where it faileth,
pass no further. But first, quoth he, because we will leave no
peaceable and quiet way untried, you shall go over and inform
the Constable of the state of the Catholics here in England,
entreating him to solicit his Majesty at his coming hither that
the penal laws may be recalled, and we admitted into the rank
of his other subjects.

Gerard notes that 'you shall go over' is actually an insertion in the
handwriting of Sir Edward Coke, the Attorney General:

'Withal, you may bring over some confidant gentleman such
as you shall understand best able for this business, and named
unto me Mr Fawkes. Shortly after I passed the sea and found
the Constable at Bergen, near Dunkirk, where, by the help of
Mr Owen, I delivered my message, whose answer was that he
had strict command from his master to do all good offices for
the Catholics, and for his own part be thought himself bound
in conscience so to do, and that no good occasion should be
omitted, but spake to him nothing of this matter.

'Mr Owen' was Hugh Owen, a target of Cecil's for some time. Gerard
points out that his name also crops up in the *King's Book* version of Fawkes'
confession – yet it doesn't feature in the original:

'Returning to Dunkirk with Mr Owen, we had speach whether
he thought that the Constable would faithfully help us or no.
He said he believed nothing less, and that they sought only
their own ends, holding small account of Catholics. I told him,

that there were many gentlemen in England, who would not forsake their country until they had tried the uttermost, and rather venture their lives than forsake her in this misery; and to add one more to our number as a fit man, both for counsel and execution of whatsoever we should resolve, wished for Mr Fawkes whom I had heard good commendations of. He told me the gentleman deserved no less, but was at Brussels, and that if he came not, as happily he might, before my departure, he would send him shortly after into England. I went soon after to Ostend, where Sir William Stanley as then was not, but came two days after. I remained with him three or four days, in which time I asked him, if the Catholics in England should do anything to help themselves, whether he thought the Archduke would second them. He answered, No; for all those parts were so desirous of peace with England as they would endure no speach of other enterprise, neither were it fit, said he, to set any project afoot now the peace is upon concluding. I told him there. was no such resolution, and so fell to discourse of other matters until I came to speak of Mr Fawkes whose company I wished over into England. I asked of his sufficiency in the wars, and told him we should need such as he, if occasion required. He gave very good commendations of him; and as we were thus discoursing and I ready to depart for Nieuport and taking my leave of Sir William, Mr Fawkes came into our company newly returned and saluted us. This is the gentleman, said Sir William, that you wished for, and so we embraced again. I told him some good friends of his wished his company in England; and that if he pleased to come to Dunkirk, we would have further conference, whither I was then going: so taking my leave of both, I departed. About two days after came Mr Fawkes to Dunkirk, where I told him that we were upon a resolution to do somewhat in England if the peace with Spain helped us not, but had as yet resolved upon nothing. Such or the like talk we passed at Gravelines, where I lay for a wind, and when it served, came both in one passage to Greenwich, near which place we took a pair of oars, and so came up to London, and came to Mr Catesby whom we found in his lodging. He welcomed us into England, and asked me what news from the Constable. I told him Good words, but I feared the deeds would not answer. This was the beginning of Easter term and about the midst of the same term (whether sent for by Mr Catesby, or upon some business of his own) up came Mr Thomas Percy. The first word he spake (after he came into our company) was Shall we always, gentlemen, talk and never do anything? Mr Catesby took him aside and had speech about somewhat to be done, so as first we might all take an oath of secrecy, which we resolved within two or three days to do, so as there we met behind St. Clement's, Mr Catesby, Mr Percy, Mr Wright, Mr Guy Fawkes, and myself, and having, upon a primer given each other the oath of secrecy in a chamber where no other body was, we went after into the next room and heard mass, and received the blessed sacrament upon the same.'

This is the occasion when Wintour would have met Father Gerard, who took Mass on this occasion, perhaps for the first time. It was one of several meetings between Gerard and the plotters which would ultimately lead to him becoming a fugitive until he managed to slip out of the country:

'Then did Mr Catesby disclose to Mr Percy, and I together with Jack Wright tell to Mr Fawkes the business for which they took this oath which they both approved; and then Mr Percy sent to take the house, which Mr Catesby, in my absence, had learnt did belong to one Ferris, which with some difficulty in the end he obtained, and became, as Ferris before was, tenant to Whynniard. Mr Fawkes underwent the name of Mr. Percy's man, calling himself Johnson, because his face was the most unknown, and received the keys of the house, until we heard that the Parliament was adjourned to the 7 of February. At which time we all departed several ways into the country, to meet again at the beginning of Michaelmas term. Before this time also it was thought convenient to have a house that might answer to Mr. Percy's, where we might make provision of powder and wood for the mine which, being there made ready, should in a night be conveyed by boat to the house by the Parliament because we were loth to foil that with often going in and out. There was none that we could devise so fit as Lambeth where Mr Catesby often lay, and to be keeper thereof, by Mr. Catesby's choice, we received into the number Keyes, as a trusty honest man.

'Some fortnight after, towards the beginning of the term, Mr Fawkes and I came to Mr Catesby at Moorcrofts, where we agreed that now was time to begin and set things in order for the mine, so as Mr Fawkes went to London and the next day sent for me to come over to him. When I came, the cause was for that the Scottish Lords were appointed to sit in conference on the Union in Mr. Percy's house. This hindered our beginning, until a fortnight before Christmas, by which time both Mr Percy and Mr Wright were come to London, and we against their coming had provided a good part of the powder, so as we all five entered with tools fit to begin our work, having provided ourselves of baked-meats, the less to need sending abroad.'

It is interesting that Wintour slips in this brief, almost casual mention of the gunpowder bearing in mind what a controversial subject it has become. The government's monopoly on the sale of it and how hard it was supposed to be to obtain; how much the plotters really got hold of, if any at all: these are all crucial matters, and it is interesting that in so detailed and apparently open an account, Wintour says nothing of where and how he and Fawkes obtained the all-important gunpowder. Another very valid observation raised by Gerard relates to a corrected error clearly visible in the original document. The phrase 'So all we five entered with tools fit to begin our work' originally read 'So all we five entered with <u>took</u> fit to begin our work'. This isn't the kind of spelling mistake a person would naturally make in the way, say, they might write 'to' rather than 'two'. But it certainly *is* the kind of error someone *who was copying from a previously prepared draft* might make:

'We entered late in the night, and were never seen, save only Mr. Percy's man, until Christmaseve, in which time we wrought under a little entry to the wall of the Parliament House, and underpropped it as we went with wood. Whilst we were together we began to fashion our business, and discourse what we should do after this deed were done. The first question was how we might surprise the next heir; the Prince happily would be at the Parliament with the King his father: how should we then be able to seize on the Duke? This burden Mr Percy undertook;

that by his acquaintance he with another gentleman would enter the chamber without suspicion, and having some dozen others at several doors to expect his coming, and two or three on horseback at the Court gate to receive him, he would undertake (the blow being given, until which he would attend in the Duke's chamber) to carry him safe away, for he supposed most of the Court would be absent, and such as were there not suspecting, or unprovided for any such matter. For the Lady Elizabeth it were easy to surprise her in the country by drawing friends together at a hunting near the Lord Harrington's, and Ashby, Mr. Catesby's house, being not far off was a fit place for preparation.

'The next was for money and horses, which if we could provide in any reasonable measure (having the heir apparent) and the first knowledge by four or five days was odds sufficient. Then, what Lords we should save from the Parliament, which was agreed in general as many as we could that were Catholics or so disposed. Next, what foreign princes we should acquaint with this before or join with after. For this point we agreed that first we would not enjoin princes to that secrecy nor oblige them by oath so to be secure of their promise; besides, we know not whether they will approve the project or dislike it, and if they do allow thereof, to prepare before might beget suspicion and not to provide until the business were acted; the same letter that carried news of the thing done might as well entreat their help and furtherance. Spain is too slow in his preparations to hope any good from in the first extremities, and France too near and too dangerous, who with the shipping of Holland we feared of all the world might make away with us. But while we were in the middle of these discourses, we heard that the Parliament should be anew adjourned until after Michaelmas, upon which tidings we broke off both discourse and working until after Christmas. About Candlemas we brought over in a boat the powder which we had provided at Lambeth and layd it in Mr. Percy's house because we were willing to have all our danger in one place. We wrought also another fortnight in the mine against the stone wall, which was very hard to beat through, at which time we called in Kit Wright, and near to Easter as we wrought the third time, opportunity was given to hire the cellar, in which we resolved to lay the powder and leave the mine.

Although Wintour says that Kit Wright was invited to join the conspiracy at or after Candlemas (February 2), one of Fawkes' confessions seems to put it before Christmas. Is this merely a question of one man's memory lapse, or of people tinkering with the confessions and not realising they had failed to match up the accounts of the two men?

'Now by reason that the charge of maintaining us all so together, besides the number of several houses which for several uses had been hired, and buying of powder, &c., had lain heavy on Mr Catesby alone to support, it was necessary for to call in some others to ease his charge, and to that end desired leave that he with Mr Percy and a third whom they should call might acquaint whom they thought fit and willing to the business, for many, said he, may be content that I should know who would not therefore that all the Company should be acquainted with their names. To this we all agreed.

'After this Mr Fawkes laid into the cellar (which he had newly taken) a thousand of billets and five hundred of faggots, and with that covered the powder, because we might have the house free to suffer anyone to enter that would. Mr Catesby wished us to consider whether it were not now necessary to send Mr Fawkes over, both to absent himself for a time as also to acquaint Sir William Stanley and Mr Owen with this matter. We agreed that he should; provided that he gave it them with the same oath that we had taken before, viz., to keep it secret from all the world. The reason why we desired Sir William Stanley should be acquainted herewith was to have him with us so soon as he could, and, for Mr Owen, he might hold good correspondency after with foreign princes. So Mr Fawkes departed about Easter for Flanders and returned the later end of August. He told me that when he arrived at Brussels, Sir William Stanley was not returned from Spain, so as he uttered the matter only to Owen, who seemed well pleased with the business, but told him that surely Sir William would not be acquainted with any plot as having business now afoot in the Court of England, but he himself would be always ready to tell it him and send him away so soon as it were done.

'About this time did Mr Percy and Mr Catesby meet at the Bath where they agreed that the company being yet but few,

Above left: Arrest of Guy Fawkes.

Above right: Execution of Guy Fawkes.

Below: Execution of Guy Fawkes.

Above: Guy Fawkes' lantern.

Left: Robert Cecil.

Above left: King James I.

Above right: Percy.

Below: Execution of Father Garnet.

Above: Robert Catesby meets his death at Holbeche House.

Left: Monteagle.

Right: Old Lords, exterior showing garden.

Below: House of Lords

Guy Fawkes' Cellar.

A replica House of Lords is blown up.

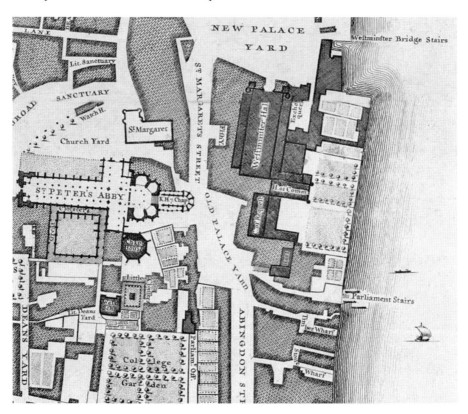

Plan of old Westminster showing House of Lords.

Percy's house at
Lambeth.

House in Dunchurch
where plotters awaited
news of plot.

Ashby St Ledgers,
home of Catesby,
where the
plotters met.

White Webbs.

Huddington Court, home of Wintours, where the plot planning occurred.

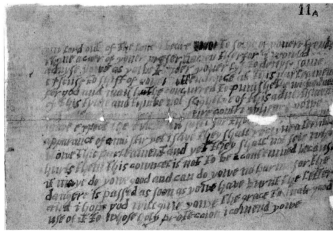

Monteagle letter.

Mr Catesby should have the others' authority to call in whom he thought best, by which authority he called in after Sir Everard Digby, though at what time I know not, and last of all Mr Francis Tresham. The first promised, as I heard Mr Catesby say, fifteen hundred pounds. Mr Percy himself promised all that he could get of the Earl of Northumberland's rent, and to provide many galloping horses, his number was ten. Meanwhile Mr Fawkes and I myself alone bought some new powder, as suspecting the first to be dank, and conveyed it into the cellar and set it in order as we resolved it should stand. Then was the Parliament anew prorogued until the 5 of November; so as we all went down until some ten days before. When Mr Catesby came up with Mr Fawkes to a house by Enfield Chase called White Webbs, whither I came to them, and Mr Catesby willed me to inquire whether the young Prince came to Parliament, I told him that his Grace thought not to be there. Then must we have our horses, said Mr Catesby, beyond the water, and provision of more company to surprise the Prince and leave the Duke alone. Two days after, being Sunday at night, in came one to my chamber and told me that a letter had been given to my Lord Monteagle to this effect, that he wished his lordship's absence from the Parliament because a blow would there be given, which letter he presently carried to my Lord of Salisbury.'

The unnamed 'one' who brought Wintour news of the Monteagle letter was, according to Tesimond, Thomas Ward, the servant who was initially given the letter to take to his master:

'On the morrow I went to White Webbs and told it to Mr Catesby, assuring him withal that the matter was disclosed and wishing him in any wise to forsake his country. He told me he would see further as yet and resolved to send Mr Fawkes to try the uttermost, protesting if the part belonged to myself he would try the same adventure. On Wednesday Mr Fawkes went and returned at night, of which we were very glad. Thursday I came to London, and Friday Mr Catesby, Mr Tresham and I met at Barnet, where we questioned how this letter should be sent to my Lord Monteagle, but could not conceive, for Mr Tresham forsware it, whom we only suspected. On Saturday night I met Mr Tresham again in Lincoln's Inn Walks, where he told such speeches that my Lord of Salisbury should use to the King, as I gave it lost the second time, and repeated the same to Mr Catesby, who hereupon was resolved to be gone, but stayed to have Mr Percy come up whose consent herein we wanted. On Sunday night came Mr Percy, and no "Nay," but would abide the uttermost trial.

'This suspicion of all hands put us into such confusion as Mr Catesby resolved to go down into the country the Monday that Mr Percy went to Sion and Mr Percy resolved to follow the same night or early the next morning. About five o'clock being Tuesday came the younger Wright to my chamber and told me that a noble man called the Lord Monteagle, saying rise and come along to Essex House, for I am going to call up my Lord of Northumberland, saying withal "the matter is discovered." "Go back Mr Wright," quoth I, "and learn what you can at Essex Gate." Shortly he returned and said, "Surely all is lost, for Leyton is got on horseback at Essex door, and as he parted, he asked if their Lordships would have any more with him, and being answered "No," is rode as fast up Fleet Street as he can ride. "Go you then," quoth I, "to Mr Percy, for sure it is for him they seek, and bid him begone: I will stay and see the uttermost." Then I went to the Court gates, and found them straitly guarded so as nobody could enter. From thence I went down towards the Parliament House, and in the middle of King's Street found the guard standing that would not let me pass, and as I returned, I heard one say, "There is a treason discovered in which the King and the Lords shall have been blown up," so then I was fully satisfied that all was known, and went to the stable where my gelding stood, and rode into the country. Mr Catesby had appointed our meeting at Dunchurch, but I could not overtake them until I came to my brother's which was Wednesday night. On Thursday we took the armour at my Lord Windsor's, and went that night to one Stephen Littleton's house, where the next day, being Friday, as I was early abroad to discover, my man came to me and said that a heavy mischance had severed all the company, for that Mr Catesby, Mr Rokewood and Mr Grant were burnt with gunpowder, upon which sight the

rest dispersed. Mr Littleton wished me to fly and so would he. I told him I would first see the body of my friend and bury him, whatsoever befel me. When I came I, found Mr Catesby reasonable well, Mr Percy, both the Wrights, Mr Rokewood and Mr Grant. I asked them what they resolved to do. They answered "We mean here to die." I said again I would take such part as they did. About eleven of the clock came the company to beset the house, and as I walked into the court was shot into the shoulder, which lost me the use of my arm. The next shot was the elder Wright struck dead; after him the younger Mr Wright, and fourthly Ambrose Rokewood. Then, said Mr Catesby to me (standing before the door they were to enter), " Stand by me, Mr Tom, and we will die together." "Sir," quoth I, "I have lost the use of my right arm and I fear that will cause me to be taken." So as we stood close together Mr Catesby, Mr Percy and myself, they two were shot (as far as I could guess, with one bullet), and then the company entered upon me, hurt me in the belly with a pike and gave me other wounds, until one came behind and caught hold of both my arms, and so I remain,
'Your humble and penintent prisoner, Thomas Winter
'Taken before us
Nottingham, Suffolk, Northampton, Salisbury, Mar, Dunbar, Popham.
EDW. COKE,
W. WAAD.'

Another thing worthy of note here is that he has spelled his name 'Winter', whereas – as a surviving letter he wrote to Grant shows – he usually went with the spelling I have used in this book: 'Wintour'. Not only that, but the confession signature looks quite unlike the one appended to the Grant letter. Various explanations have been put forward regarding these issues. The most obvious one is that spelling in general, as most people know, wasn't set in stone in quite the way it is now. But although this includes names, Gerard managed to find examples of his signature, and in all cases except this document he called himself 'Wintour'. Gardiner suggested that he changed it deliberately because it was the form the authorities used and he wanted to gain their acceptance and compassion. This reason doesn't ring true, but there is another explanation as to why – if it even is his hand – he might have deliberately misspelt his name. As I understand it, military personnel and others working in danger zones, where they might be captured and forced to make 'confessions' in front of the camera, sometimes make deliberate errors either because they are trained to do so or are using their own initiative. This sends a message to those in the know that they are acting under duress. I quite like the idea that in misspelling his name Thomas Wintour has sent a message down the centuries, telling us that he was coerced into his confession and we shouldn't believe a word of it!

Other people on the fringes of the plot were also questioned and add to the circumstantial evidence that all was not what it seemed. The wife of the recently deceased Whynniard, the landlord, informed her inquisitors that Guy Fawkes kept the rent payments up to date right up to two days before he was supposed to blow the place up. Even more notably, she said that on 4 November, he had workmen in the house doing repair work. What are we to make of this remarkable revelation? It is just about feasible that he wanted to keep the rent up to date in order to avoid being chased for it at an awkward moment – although we are only talking about a couple of days; the Whynniards knew the place was being rented by men of status so it is unlikely that a payment that was two days late would have led to a major problem. And Fawkes could easily have fobbed them off by making an excuse for the short delay. But for Fawkes to bother with repairs to a house which he was about to blow up – and to invite outsiders into the plotters' lair at this late stage – is almost beyond belief.

Another anomaly from among the several statements and confessions made by Fawkes is that when he was first examined he is supposed to have said that he took some of the gunpowder into the cellar in Christmas 1604. The initial negotiations for the hiring of the cellar were between Fawkes and a Mrs Bright – yet when she was later interviewed she said that the plotters didn't take over the use of the cellar till March of 1605. Before then it was being used to store coal and the gunpowder couldn't possibly have been taken in at that point.

Gerard's summary regarding the confessions of Fawkes and Wintour is apt:

> 'It is upon these narratives, stamped with features so incompatible with their trustworthiness, that we entirely depend for much of prime importance in the history of the conspiracy...'

Chapter 11

The Subsequent Arrests

What happened to Guy Fawkes' accomplices after his arrest is yet another aspect of the story about which there is cause for closer scrutiny.

Most of the remaining conspirators fled in the direction of the comparative safety of Catholic Midlands, where some of them hailed from and which most of them would have known well. It was here that, had Fawkes succeeded in blowing up the king and Parliament, people were to have flocked to the cause and an armed uprising would have ensued. The intention, as allegedly outlined by Fawkes under interrogation, was that King James' eldest daughter Elizabeth would be kidnapped and made a kind of puppet queen. One of her first pronouncements, prepared by the plotters, would be that she would refrain from interfering in the religion of the country.

Catesby, Jack Wright and Bates were already heading north anyway, in keeping with the original plan. The *King's Book* describes it thus:

> 'The news (I say) of this so strange and unlooked for accident, was no sooner divulged, but some of those Conspirators, namely, Winter, and the two Brothers of Wrights thought it high time for them to hasten out of the Town (for Catesby was gone the night before, and Percy at four of the clock in the morning the same day of the Discovery) and all of them held their course, with more haste than good speed, to Warwickshire…'

Although they were planning and hoping to gather support for their uprising, they were not averse, according to the official account, to taking what they felt they needed with or without the owners' permission:

> '…about the same hour that Fawkes was taken in Westminster, one Graunt, a Gentleman having associated unto him some

others of his opinion, all violent Papists, and strong Recusants, came to a Stable of one Benock, a Rider of Great Horses, and having violently broken up the same, carried along with them all the great Horses that were therein, to the number of seven or eight, belonging to divers Noblemen and Gentlemen of that Country…'

Tom Wintour kept his nerve long enough to investigate the rumours and make sure they were true, then also set off and eventually joined the others at Ashby St Ledgers in Northamptonshire. The group stopped at various places along the way, helping themselves to arms and other supplies and trying, in vain, to persuade more men to rally to their cause. Their trek took them finally to Holbeche House, a few miles north of Stourbridge.

The fleeing plotters were being pursued by Sir Richard Verney, the Sheriff of Warwickshire, and Sir Richard Walsh, Sheriff of Worcestershire. One of the stranger, yet widely accepted, stories of the gunpowder plot is that while the fugitives were at Holbeche, owned by the staunchly Catholic Stephen Littleton, they decided they needed to attend to some gunpowder (the *King's Book* says weighing two pounds) which had become wet or damp during their journey. We are told that they spread it out on a 'platter' before an open fire to dry it out, and that a coal or spark fell into the powder causing it to ignite. 'It pleased GOD,' says the *King's Book*, 'that in the mending of the fire in their chamber, one small sparkle should flie out'. The result is sometimes referred to as a fire, but often an explosion. Now, even as naughty schoolboys we discovered that if you emptied the contents of a few 'bangers' onto the ground and applied a match to it, the outcome was a very brief and rather disappointing flash, followed by a lot of smoke. (I think we called it a 'genie', and I recall finding it pretty anti-climactic.) That is the limit of my expertise in the field of explosives, but I would stick my neck out and say that applying a light to a relatively small amount of gunpowder spread thinly in the open (and which presumably had not yet dried out) would not – *could* not – cause an explosion. The official story, though, is quite unambiguous on this; Catesby and Rookwood were injured by burns, and John Grant was actually blinded. But unless all three men were standing over the pan of powder (and why would they be?) and Grant had had his face directly over it (and why would he?) I find this scenario hard to believe.

And credibility is stretched even further by the *King's Book*, which not only describes the powder as 'blowing up', but goes on to say that it 'blew up the roof of the house' in a blast powerful enough to launch a much larger linen bag full of more powder, which had been beneath the original pan of gunpowder, out through the hole in the roof caused by the explosion, and that the said bag landed in the courtyard 'whole and unfired'. This scenario is typical of the Gunpowder Plot story as a whole, in that while there might be some truthful basis to it, taken as a whole there are just too many implausibilities. Even if the uncontained powder could have caused an explosion, which I don't believe for a moment, how could the blast have sent a bag of anything, let alone powder, shooting through the roof when, according to the *King's Book* it 'was 'set *under* the Platter' (my italics). This seems to defy the laws of physics.

There is absolutely no evidence for the suggestion I'm about to make, nor have I come across it in any of the many accounts I have read – but, bearing in mind other anomalies in the story of Holbeche, is it possible that some of the plotters were captured and tortured in the hope of some quick information as to the whereabouts of others, hence the burns and blinding?

One of the arguments against people like Percy having been in some way, at some point, working for Cecil, is that he and four others were killed in a desperate gun battle once they were cornered at Holbeche House. But once again, is this quite how that particular episode went? How much do we really know for sure? The author of the almost contemporary *Politician's Catechism* said:

> 'It is very certaine that Percy and Catesby might have been taken alive, when they were killed, but Cecil knew full well that these two unfortunate Gentlemen would have related the story lesse to his owne advantage…therefore they were dispatched when they might have been made prisoners, having no other weapons, offensive or defensive, but their swords.'

The encounter at this (then) Staffordshire country house is routinely described as a 'last stand', 'battle' or 'gunfight'; 'The battle now raged… with great violence,' says Thomas Lathbury, writing in the early nineteenth century. Gerard, however, describes the 'defenders' as being defenceless; the trapped men had no firearms and 'might all have been captured without difficulty'. And oddly enough, the *King's Book* itself comes close to concurring with this picture. It says that the besieged men were not only left unable to defend themselves as a result of the 'explosion' but realised that

God was punishing them with the same stuff (the gunpowder) with which they had planned to wreak havoc. Thus they:

> 'did all fall down upon their knees, praying GOD to pardon them for their bloudy enterprize; And thereafter giving over any further debate, opened the Gate, suffered the Sheriffs people to rush in furiously among them, and desperately sought their own present destruction'.

In other words, they let the enemy in and welcomed their own deaths. There is not even a hint that they offered the slightest armed resistance.

Jardine reports that the plotters still left at Holbeche 'resolved to make a last stand', but the actual detail of events doesn't live up to that billing. Tom Wintour was put out of action after being shot through the arm by a crossbow bolt while 'crossing the court', upon which Catesby is supposed to have cried 'Stand by me, Mr Tom, and we will die together!'; the Wright brothers were the next to be shot; one musket ball went through both Catesby and Percy; Rookwood was shot in the arm, then speared by a pike. Nowhere is there a mention of a raised sword or even a suicidal charge.

There is a suspicious symmetry, a neatness to it, which is almost reminiscent of a second-rate novel or B-Movie – the Wrights killed almost as a pair, the cry of defiance, Catesby and Percy dealt with by a single bullet. The *King's Book* describes Catesby, Percy and Tom Wintour 'joyning backs together' before the onslaught, which would seem to contradict the picture of Wintour receiving his wound when crossing the courtyard – unless he is supposed to have linked up with his comrades after having been shot. Tom Wintour's confession says 'I walked into the court' in a quite matter-of-fact tone. He lost the use of his arm as a result of the wound he received, and it seems he must have retreated into the house because he then describes the brief exchange he had with Catesby, which took place while 'standing before the door they [the sheriff's men] were to enter'. His recollection was that after he was hit, the 'elder Wright' (Jack) was then shot dead, after which his younger brother Kit, then Ambrose Rookwood were struck. Finally, Catesby and Percy were pierced by one ball 'as far as I could guess'. Wintour then describes being struck by a pike in the abdomen and receiving other wounds before being grabbed from behind and detained.

Much of the detail of what happened comes from a letter dated 9 November sent to London by Sir Richard Walsh, the sheriff of Worcestershire – but like so many things in this story it raises as many questions as answers.

Walsh says that those plotters heading north from London 'armed themselves at all points in open rebellion' and 'took…by force great store of armour, artillery of the said Lord Windsor's, and passed that night into the county of Staffordshire unto the house of one Stephen Littleton, Gentleman, called Holbeche…' But 'artillery' refers to heavy, long-range weapons like cannon which are on wheels and must be pulled by horses over any distance. Is it feasible that this handful of men commandeered such heavy weaponry and hauled it through the English countryside? And then didn't bother to set it up to head off invaders?

Even Walsh doesn't claim that those holed up inside Holbeche tried to defend themselves, just that they refused to come out, and that his men set fire to part of the house (presumably unopposed) and then and 'assaulted some part of the rebellious persons left in the said house'. He reports the death of Catesby, and three others 'verily thought wounded to death': Percy, John and Christopher Wright. In this version, written fresh after the event, there is no mention of Tom Wintour being shot; only one – not both – of the Wright brothers is listed as being hit. Rookwood being both shot and stabbed is missing, as is the 'two-in-one' shot which is alleged to have taken care of Catesby and Percy.

When taken all together, this has much more of the whiff of an execution than a fight to the death. Is it any coincidence that those killed at Holbeche, particularly Catesby and Percy, were the men who had been in from the start, the ones who had started the ball rolling? Percy was the fifth man to join the group, but had had preliminary discussions with Catesby well before the latter started to gather his men about him. The MP Sir Edward Hoby, writing to an ambassador, declared 'Percy is dead: who it is thought by some particular men could have said more than any other.' The *King's Book* goes out of its way to justify the killing of men who were at that point, don't forget, no more than suspects. It speaks of 'the necessity to have Percy preserved alive, if it had been possible' but that 'the far distance of the way (which was above an hundred miles)' prevented this order from reaching the pursuers before it was too late. However, the plotters themselves covered the distance in a day, whereas anyone bearing such a proclamation had three days in which to deliver it – the time it took for the sheriff's men to launch their attack – almost certainly with the added bonus of the authority to demand fresh horses at any place along the way. We know from Tesimond that more than one messenger did arrive before Holbeche was raided, and that the news of Percy's death was conveyed to London in the space of a day without any difficulty.

Furthermore, it is known that John Streete, the man who supposedly scuppered the government's plans of bringing Percy back alive by shooting him, was subsequently granted a pension of two shillings a day for the rest of his life. We don't know what status in life this Streete had, but just by way of example, this was about twice what a skilled labourer would earn. And just to complicate the 'two men killed by one shot' legend further (the *King's Book* specifically stating that 'two with one shot, Catesby, and Percy were slain'), an official document relating to Streete's pension paints a slightly different picture because it mentions Catesby and Percy having been killed 'with two bulletts at one shott'. This might indicate that it was believed Streete had 'double-loaded' his musket. This practice was not unknown, but as far as I'm aware it was generally done for close-range combat and led to less accurate shooting – which, if so, would make the killing of two men at once even more remarkable – and perhaps even likelier to have been a point-blank range execution.

Gerard wryly observes that 'the rebels…did not succeed in killing a single one of their assailants', and that 'the attacking party were not only allowed to shoot, but selected just the wrong men as their mark, precisely those who, being chiefly implicated in the beginnings of the Plot, could have afforded the most valuable information'. Goodman, in the *Court of King James*, says, 'Some will not stick to report that the great statesman sending to apprehend these traitors gave special charge and direction for Percy and Catesby, "Let me never see them alive" who it may be would have revealed some evil counsel given.'

Chapter 12

Trial

It took a surprisingly long time to bring the prisoners to trial. The Attorney General, Sir Edward Coke, put this down to twenty-three 'several' (i.e. not necessarily consecutive) days which had then been spent in examination. However, a great deal of this time had been spent not in trying to extract confessions from the plotters about their roles, but in trying to obtain proof that the Jesuit priests were fully aware of the Plot and even provided encouragement and guidance. Yet in the face of relentless physical and psychological pressure, and despite admitting their own part in the story and that of other plotters, the conspirators continued to vehemently deny that Garnet and his fellow priests were aware of or had anything to do with the actual plan to blow up parliament and kill the king. But every chain has its weak link, and on the 13th of January, Thomas Bates, Catesby's servant, cracked.

He told his interrogators that after having been recruited into the Plot by his master and pledged his fidelity, Catesby insisted that he visit Father Tesimond to receive the sacrament. During his confession, he informed them, he had told Tesimond all about what was planned, and in response the priest advised him to obey his master because it was for a good cause, but that he should tell no one else about it – not even another priest. A royal proclamation was soon issued in the names of Garnet, Gerard, and Greenway (Bates was using Tesimond's alias, which was probably the only name he knew him by), and the trial of the plotters finally went ahead a few days later.

Gerard links the lengthy delay in bringing the plotters before the court directly with the arrest of Garnet, and a wish to avoid any troublesome contradiction of the prosecution's insistence that he and other Jesuit priests knew the full facts of the Plot and condoned the idea:

> 'The execution of Faukes and his companions following close
> upon their arraignment, all that had been elicited, or was said

to have been elicited, at their trial, became henceforth evidence which could not be contradicted, the prosecution thus having a free hand in dealing with their subsequent victim. In view of this circumstance it has been noted as remarkable that whereas the conspirators had been kept alive and untried for nearly three months, they were thus summarily dealt with at the moment when it was known that the capture of Father Garnet was imminent, and, as a matter of fact, he was taken on the very day on which the first company were executed. It would appear that nothing should have seemed more desirable than to confront the Jesuit superior with those whom he was declared to have instigated to their crime, instead of putting them out of the way at the very moment when there was a prospect of doing so.'

Early on the morning of 27 January, Tom and Robert Wintour, Guy Fawkes, John Grant, Ambrose Rookwood, Robert Keyes, and Thomas Bates were taken from the Tower by boat to Westminster Hall to face a special commission comprising Cecil, the Earls of Nottingham, Suffolk, Worcester, Devonshire and Northampton, the Lord Chief Justice Sir John Popham, Sir Thomas Fleming, Sir Thomas Walmisley and Sir Peter Warburton. It has been suggested that King James himself was also present, incognito, and it would perhaps be surprising if he *hadn't* taken steps to quietly secrete himself somewhere in the great hall so that he could observe the proceedings.

While awaiting their summons to appear before the illustrious gathering, the prisoners were placed in the Star Chamber. They would, to a man, have been perfectly aware that despite its outward appearance of sober and proper legal procedure, this would be what in modern parlance is known as a show-trial. There was never any question that they would be able to argue their way out of this situation, that anything they might say or any evidence they might provide would make the slightest difference. The only possible outcome was that in a short time every one of them would be hauled through the streets of London and subjected to one of the most terrifying and painful ordeals imaginable, from which death would be a blessed release. The plotters may or may not have been aware that a few days earlier a motion had been put before Parliament 'to stay judgment until Parliament should have time to consider some extraordinary mode of punishment, which might surpass in horror even the scenes which usually occurred at the execution of traitors'. Fortunately, this was voted down.

But this was not a secret trial; the crowd of spectators was great and some left eye-witness accounts, including Father Gerard. One MP complained that members of the public had invaded an area set aside for his fellow politicians. While they waited for proceedings to begin, herded together on what Jardine ominously calls a 'scaffold' – some sort of wooden platform built especially for the event – the prisoners ran their rosaries through their fingers as they prayed, while also smoking pipes ('taking tobacco, as if hanging were no trouble to them').[1] Digby was described by Gerard as looking like 'the goodliest man in the whole Court', but of course not all spectators were so magnanimous considering what the men had planned to do, and Sir John Harington,[2] who had at one time been a poet popular with Elizabeth, decided that the men at the bar 'bore an evil mark in their foreheads, for more terrible countenances never were looked upon'.

After the lengthy indictment had been put to them, all of the accused men pleaded not guilty, 'which excited some surprise', bearing in mind confessions they had made.

Sir Edward Philips, his Majesty's Sergeant at Law, then made the following statement, as recorded in the *King's Book*:

> 'The matter that is now to be offered to you, my Lords the Commissioners, and to the Trial of you the Knights and Gentlemen of the Jury, is matter of Treason; but of such horrour, and monstrous nature, that before now, The Tongue of Man never delivered, The Ear of Man never heard, The Heart of Man never conceited, Nor the Malice of Hellish or Earthly Devil ever practised...'

The ultimate charge against the prisoners at the bar outlined the plotters' intentions that:

> '1. The King, the Queen, the Prince, the Lords Spiritual and Temporal, the Knights and Burgesses of the Parliament, should be blown up with Powder.
> 2. That the whole Royal Issue Male should be destroyed.
> 3. That they would take into their custody Elizabeth and Mary, the Kings Daughters, and proclaim the Lady Elizabeth Queen.
> 4. That they should feign a Proclamation in the Name of Elizabeth, in which no mention should be made of alteration of Religion, nor that they were parties to the Treason, until they

had raised power to perform the same, and then to proclaim,
All grievances in the Kingdom should be reformed.'

The case for the prosecution was set out in great detail by Coke, a Norfolk man then aged around fifty-five, who had led the prosecution of Raleigh. He took his listeners right back to the inception of the Plot, and emphasising the status of most of those involved ('Gentlemen of good houses, of excellent parts, howsoever most perniciously seduced, abused, corrupted, and Jesuited, of very competent fortunes and States; Besides that Percy was of the house of Northumberland') but laying the blame for the involvement of the lowly Bates at the doors of both his employer Catesby, and the Catholic priests ('he was wound into this Treason by his Master, so was he resolved, when he doubted of the lawfulness thereof, by the Doctrine of the Jesuits'). His speech was full of anti-Catholic and anti-Jesuit invective, and Longueville describes it as a 'pompous harangue'.

Once the Attorney General had finished his speech, the confessions and statements of Fawkes and the other prisoners were read to the court, the prisoners were all duly found guilty, and asked why the sentence of death should not be passed on them. We are told that none but Rookwood had anything to say in their own defence – presumably because they knew it would be useless. Thomas Wintour made what he knew must be a vain plea that he be executed for the crimes of both himself and his brother. Robert himself simply asked the court to show mercy – as did the hapless Bates. Grant 'a good while was mute', perhaps choked with emotion, but we will now never know. Finally, he made the weak defence that he was guilty of something he intended to do but which had never been put into effect.

Rookwood put on a more spirited show. He -

> 'first excused his denial of the Indictment, for that he had rather lose his life than give it. Then did he acknowledge his offence to be so heinous, that he justly deserved the indignation of the King, and of the Lords, and the hatred of the whole Commonwealth; yet could he not despair of Mercy at the hands of a Prince, so abounding in Grace and Mercy: And the rather, because his Offence, though it were incapable of any excuse, yet not altogether incapable of some extenuation, in that he had been neither Author nor Actor, but onely perswaded and drawn in by Catesby, whom he loved above any worldly man: And that he had concealed it, not for any malice to the Person

of the King, or to the State, or for any ambitious respect of his own, but onely drawn with the tender respect, and the faithful and dear affection he bare to Mr Catesby his Friend, whom he esteemed more dear than any thing else in the world. And this mercy he desired not for any fear of the image of Death, but for grief that so shameful a Death should leave so perpetual a blemish and blot unto all Ages upon his Name and Blood. But howsoever that this was his first Offence, yet he humbly submitted himself to the Mercy of the King, and prayed, that the King would herein imitate God, who sometimes doth punish...yet not mortally.'[3]

Popham asked Fawkes how he in particular, having been caught virtually red-handed, could possibly claim not to be guilty. He had, after all, as good as openly boasted that it had been his desire and intention to blow up the Houses of Parliament. Fawkes replied that neither he nor his fellow conspirators refuted the contents of their confessions, and made the intriguing observation that he had done so in respect of 'certain conferences mentioned in the indictment, which, he said, that he knew not of'.

A conversation between Robert Wintour and Guy Fawkes a few days previously was then revealed to the court. The two men were in adjacent rooms or cells in the Tower for a time, and it was common practice to have people lurking nearby for the specific purpose of listening in on such chatter in the hope of picking up more incriminating evidence. Wintour is alleged to have said that 'he and Catesby had Sons, and that Boys would be men, and that he hoped they would revenge the cause... Also that they were sorry, that no body did set forth a Defence or Apology of their Action; but yet they would maintain the cause at their deaths'. If this gossip is true, Wintour also told Fawkes about a dream he had when he was at Holbeche, before the supposed 'explosion' of the small amount of exposed powder:

'he thought he saw Steeples stand awry, and within those Churches strange and unknown faces. And after, when the foresaid blast had, the day following, scorched divers of the Confederates, and much disfigured the faces and countenances of Grant, Rookwood, and others: Then did Winter call to mind his Dream, and to his remembrance thought, that the faces of his Associates so scorched, resembled those which he had seen in his Dream.'

Digby was charged on a separate indictment to the others and was the only one of the plotters to plead guilty. He then spoke at length, explaining that he had been drawn into the scheme not through 'ambition, nor discontentment of his estate, neither malice to any in Parliament, but the friendship and love he bare to Catesby, which prevailed so much, and was so powerful with him, as that for his sake he was ever contented and ready to hazard himself and his Estate.' There were also the religious elements – the broken promises made to Catholics, his desire to restore Catholicism to England and fear of ever stricter anti-Catholic laws. He asked that since only he was to blame for his own actions, his family should not be punished financially or otherwise after his death:

> 'Then prayed the pardon of the King…for his guilt. And lastly,
> he entreated to be beheaded, desiring all men to forgive him,
> and that his death might satisfie them for his trespass.'

His entreaties were given short shrift by Coke the Attorney General, at least partly in respect of the lateness of the day ('for it grew now dark'). His loyalty to Catesby excused nothing and was 'mere folly, and wicked conspiracy', his religious protestations amounted to 'error and heresie', and if his family were recusants before the Plot they would receive no preferential treatment in the future. Where was his sympathy and tenderness when he was plotting to kill the king and his family?

At this point Cecil hastily stepped in to defend the king (whom he must have known was listening in from the shadows) from Digby's accusations of broken promises towards the Catholics. He cleared His Majesty of having 'at any time given the least hope, much less promise of Toleration'. Just to turn the screw further, Cecil poured scorn on Digby's earlier denials of being privy to the Plot, citing the testimony of none other than Guy Fawkes (who was still present with the other accused at the bar). He was reminded of Fawkes' statement that some months ago he had visited Digby's house, where, in view of a spell of wet weather, he (Fawkes) had expressed a concern that the gunpowder in the cellar 'was grown dank', and recommended that they brought in a fresh supply. Finally, Monteagle was singled out for praise 'for his Loyal and honourable care of his Prince and Countrey, in the speedy bringing forth of the Letter sent unto him'.

Digby was also addressed by Henry Howard, the Earl of Northampton. He too defended James against charges of going back on promises of toleration, and his words are notable because Northampton was almost certainly a Catholic himself, albeit not openly so. A cynic might say that it was another opportunity for Howard to curry favour with the monarch, as he seems to have been prone to do; but it would also be reasonable to say that his revulsion at the extremes to which Digby and his fellow conspirators had been prepared to go was genuine and something which was felt by many other Catholics throughout the land.

The case for the prosecution closed, the Sergeant, Sir Edward Philips, rose and 'prayed the judgment of the court upon the verdict of the Jury against the seven first prisoners, and against Sir Everard Digby upon his own confession.' It then fell to the Lord Chief Justice to pronounce the statutory sentence for High Treason upon all of the prisoners at the bar: that they were to be hanged, drawn and quartered. Before their lordships could leave, Digby bowed and said, 'If I may but hear any of your Lordships say you forgive me, I shall go more chearfully to the Gallows'.

'God forgive you,' came the reply, 'and we do.'

The condemned men were then sent back to the Tower and shuffled through Traitor's Gate to await their fate.

Chapter 13

Consequences

Cecil certainly benefited from the Gunpowder Plot. He was made a member of the Order of the Garter in the year that the Oath of Allegiance was introduced and quickly became a feted figure. His contemporary, the writer Edmund Howes, observed that Cecil:

> 'set forward from his house in the Strand, being almost as honourably accompanied, and with as great a train of lords, knights, gentlemen, and officers of the Court, with others besides his peculiar servants, very richly attired and bravely mounted, as was the King when he rid in state through London.'

The Earl of Northumberland, whom Cecil had believed to be linked with the 'treason' of Raleigh and Cobham, and who some considered to be Cecil's rival, did not fare so well. Despite the government taking great pains to publicly absolve him of any involvement in the Plot (the *King's Book* describes him as 'one of His Majesties greatest Subjects and Counselors' [*sic*]), he soon found himself in the Star Chamber being questioned about his ties with his kinsman Thomas Percy, and pressed to reveal whether he had had any prior knowledge of the Plot. The grilling of Northumberland threw up neither evidence nor confession, but although he was cleared of the more serious accusations he was still found guilty of what were little more than technicalities and punished with a severity not far short of what he would have received had the greater charge been proven. He was removed from all official positions, heavily fined and sent to the Tower, where he was kept until 1621. Although he remained wealthy and lived there in great comfort, it was still imprisonment and his wife died before he was released. Cecil himself also passed away before Northumberland was released, but the latter never forgave the former. According to Gerard, Northumberland declared that 'the blood of Percy would refuse to mix with that of Cecil if they were poured together in the same basin'.

Regardless of the extent to which Cecil knew about the Plot or was even somehow behind it, and regardless of the extent to which the headstrong and potentially shocking actions of a few men failed to represent the Catholic population as a whole, everyone is agreed that the uncovering of what Catesby and the rest had planned became the springboard for a renewed attack on Catholicism in England.

Jardine said that:

> 'It fixed the timid and wavering mind of the king in his adherence to the Protestant party, in opposition to the Roman Catholics; and the universal horror, which was naturally excited...by so barbarous an attempt, was artfully converted into an engine for the suppression of the Roman Catholic Church: so that the ministers of James I, having procured the reluctant acquiescence of the king, and the cordial assent of public opinion, were enabled to continue in full force the severe laws previously passed against Papists, and to enact others of no less rigour and injustice.'

In his speech to Parliament a few days after the Plot had come to light, King James called for cool heads and emphasised that he didn't blame all Catholics for the devastation that had nearly been inflicted on all of them:

> 'As it may very well be possible, that the zeal of your hearts shall make some of you in your speeches, rashly to blame such as may be innocent of this attempt; but upon the other part I wish you to consider, that I would be sorry that any being innocent of this practise...should receive blame or harm, for the same.'

Privately, however, he did tell Sir John Harington (with whom Princess Elizabeth, a kidnap target for the plotters, had been residing) that the 'whole legion of Catholics' were implicated. In fact, the crackdown had already started before he gave his speech. The parliamentary session still went ahead on 5 November, and a bill was introduced 'for the better execution of penal statutes against Recusants'.[1] On 23 January, a bill for a public thanksgiving was prefaced with a reference to 'malignant and devilish papists, Jesuits, and seminary priests...' The Popish Recusancy Act came into force that same year, impinging upon the freedoms of Catholics, among other things local magistrates could enter a person's premises to look for weapons, and

Catholics couldn't practice law or medicine. The following year, acts were introduced demanding that recusants attend their Protestant parish church or face 'penalties and forfeitures', and an Oath of Allegiance was brought in which although it applied to all, was clearly aimed at Catholics. Richard Challoner said that it was 'worded on purpose in such a manner that the Catholics might be divided in their opinions about the lawfulness of it'[2]. It required acknowledgment among other things that 'princes which be excommunicated by the pope may be deposed or murdered by their subjects or by any other whatsoever. And I do believe that the pope has no power to absolve me from this oath'. Robert Drury, a Catholic priest (but not a Jesuit) was executed for refusing to take the oath within months of it becoming law.

This was a relatively rare event, but the aftershock of the Plot continued for decades, even, it could be argued, centuries. The finger of blame routinely pointed in the direction of Catholics after any kind of natural or man-made disaster, the Great Fire of London being one of the most famous. Suspicions that the country was being led back in the direction of Catholicism lingered, and was one of the contributory factors in the downfall of Charles I and the outbreak of civil war. Those fears persisted during under his son, Charles II, whose own Catholic sympathies created a constitutional crisis and during whose reign the Popish Plot of the late 1670s, which had as much basis in fact as the Great Fire being started by Catholics, led to a situation not dissimilar to the Salem Witch Trials – and in fact resulted in a similar number of executions. The same religious atmosphere continued into the reign of James II, who actually did convert to Catholicism and produced an heir who was of the same persuasion. This was one of the main factors leading to the Glorious Revolution of 1688 and his replacement by the Protestant William and Mary, but even ten years later Parliament thought it necessary to bring in the Popery Act, whose full title – An Act for the further preventing the Growth of Popery – gives a flavour of the thinking behind it. One element brought about a change in the way inheritance worked. When a Catholic died his estates would be divided up among his sons, thus potentially reducing them in size from generation to generation, whereas if the eldest son converted to Protestantism he inherited the whole estate. Conditions did gradually improve for Catholics. But it wasn't until 1829 that they were given the vote and granted similar rights to Protestants, and even then feelings ran so high that the Duke of Wellington (by then the prime minister) entered into a duel with the Earl of Winchelsea, who was against the change in law, over a perceived insult he had issued to the duke.

Chapter 14

Verdict

'We may here pause to review the extraordinary story to which we have been listening. A group of men, known for as dangerous characters as any in England, men, in Cecil's own words, "spent in their fortunes", "hunger-starved for innovations," "turbulent spirits," and "fit for all alterations," take a house within the precincts of a royal palace, and close to the Upper House of Parliament, dig a mine, hammer away for over two months at the wall, acquire and bring in four tons of gunpowder, storing it in a large and conspicuous chamber immediately beneath that of the Peers, and covering it with an amount of fuel sufficient for a royal establishment--and meanwhile those responsible for the government of the country have not even the faintest suspicion of any possible danger. "Never," it is said, "was treason more secret, or ruin more apparently inevitable," while the Secretary of State himself declared that such ruin was averted only by the direct interposition of Heaven, in a manner nothing short of miraculous.'

John Gerard, *What Was the Gunpowder Plot?*

Gerard draws attention to the words of Cecil's contemporary Sir Robert Naunton, describing the latter as 'his craft's master' in foreign intelligence and domestic affairs 'who could tell at any moment what ships there were in every port of Spain, their burdens, their equipment, and their destination'; he also draws attention to Father Richard Blount, the Jesuit priest who succeeded Father Garnet as the Superior of the English mission, who said that Cecil 'could discover the most secret business transacted in the Papal Court before it was known to the Catholics in England'; he points to letters preserved in state archives which show that 'he could intercept letters written from Paris to Brussels, or from Rome to Naples':

'What was his activity at home [sic] is sufficiently evidenced by the reports furnished by his numerous agents concerning everything done throughout the country, in particular by Recusants… That those so remarkably wide-awake in regard of all else should have been blind and deaf to what was passing at their own doors appears altogether incredible.'

Stephen Alford, in *The Watchers,* his 2012 account of the network of spies and codebreakers operating during the reign of Elizabeth, echoes one of Gerard's points when he declares that Cecil 'oversaw an intelligence system probably even more formidable than Sir Francis Walsingham's had been'.

The Mine

The supposed tunnel from the rented house to beneath the Lords' chamber is at least as problematical as the Monteagle letter, albeit not nearly as crucial to the Plot. To explore the technical side of things, I sought an opinion from Bob Bradley, a mining historian and former miner, and he believes that the digging of the tunnel was feasible. 'The strata is called the London clay and is a relatively soft rock', he informed me, pointing out that many miles of London Underground tunnels were dug by pick and shovel methods. According to Bob, it could have been started with a small shaft like a well and the dirt winched up by windlass. The tunnel would have been small, maybe less than a metre square, just sufficient for a man to crawl and be able to turn round. By pick and shovel and filling bags, boxes or buckets for example with the debris which would then be pulled to the entrance and probably taken away in a cart and thrown into the river or just spread around. A few boards and bits of wood could have supported it.

But being possible still doesn't mean it happened, and in my opinion the weight of evidence is strongly against it.

I don't believe that these 'gentlemen of blood and fortune' who had never done a day's manual work in their lives and who all had manservants to do their dirty work, their lifting and carrying for them, were capable of digging a viable tunnel. I don't even believe that they would have started one in the first place, but even if they did, there is obviously more to mining beneath tons of earth than just digging a hole – you need to know what you're doing and shore it up correctly, otherwise at some point it is going to collapse and bury you alive. Neither do I believe in the idea of them depositing the spoil in the garden, as they are said to have done – there is no account of them using the river to dispose of it, whereas the garden is specifically mentioned; there would have been just too much material. I don't believe they could have hacked away at the stone foundations for weeks without alerting someone – not just neighbours and passers-by, but someone in the coal cellar above, which we know was in use because that's supposed to be how the tunnellers were alerted to it.

Then we come back to the inconvenient problem of the spoil. Bob Bradley told me there is a basic rule of thumb that once earth has been disturbed the volume tends to double, because of the voids between lumps and so on. He calculated that even a 0.9m square tunnel just ten metres long would result in something like sixteen tonnes of earth. Not one person reported seeing either holes in the ground or large amounts freshly scattered earth in the garden where it is alleged to have been deposited (assuming it was even somehow flattened down, unlikely in itself with such a large amount).

Most of all, though, I don't believe that they could be foolish enough to not realise that they were actually tunnelling beneath what would presumably have been the substantial stone floor of a large space beneath their target. If there had been a mine, we would have accounts by people who saw it, either at the time or afterwards during excavations, but there is not a single eye-witness account to any such tunnel.

The way the 'miners' discovered the truth about the cellar was from hearing a rushing noise from above caused by a delivery of coal. Remember, though, that they hadn't actually broken through the foundation wall of the Lords' chamber, so they couldn't have been hearing noises from directly above – they were in a subterranean passage on the *outside* of the building they were aiming for.

And if they were in a position to hear bags of coal being emptied or shovelled, surely those in the cellar could hear men hacking at the foundations?

And if Guy Fawkes was employed as a lookout, how come he was completely unaware of the coming and going of the coal merchants or whoever the people were who were dealing with the coal?

As an aside, as well as there being no eye-witness record of the tunnel, there doesn't appear to be any witness to the huge stack of gunpowder barrels or the removal of them either, other than those insiders sent by Cecil when Fawkes was arrested.

My one nagging doubt is over what possible benefit there might be for Cecil to invent such a story. The only answer I can come up with is that it draws more of the thirteen deeper into the plot and makes them more obviously culpable. Without the mine, those men need not have spent much, if any, time in and around Westminster – they would just be people who had talked of doing a deed which hadn't happened yet and which they probably knew never really would happen. Working on the mine ties them physically to the attempt to blow Parliament up, puts them physically on the spot and demonstrates clear intent. Others have suggested it was a story invented by Wintour or one of the other plotters – but not only would they have even less reason to do so, they would have been aware that the story could be disproved within seconds.

The Gunpowder

Is it possible that not only the story of the mine, but the gunpowder itself was a government invention? Could it be that what was contained in the barrels was not gunpowder but sand or earth (perhaps with the addition of a layer of powder on top to fool the plotters if any inspection were made)? Is it too outrageous to even speculate that there never were barrels of any kind beneath the pile of wood in the cellar? One might think that this is taking the conspiracy theory a step too far, but numerous commentators have put forward just such scenarios. The two most obvious objections to this idea are that the there was a sensational trial supported by confessions mentioning the bringing in of the barrels themselves; and there were witnesses to the barrels when Fawkes was apprehended.

Some of the faultlines inherent in this defence are immediately obvious. The confessions were not only extracted under torture, but bear clear signs of having been 'edited' by the authorities. We do not really know how far we can believe the words contained within them. But there is more to it than that. Even though the trial of the plotters was a public occasion in front of a packed Westminster Hall, we have surprisingly little accurate and detailed information about what was actually said. Our prime source, by far, is again from government publications written in an undisguisedly partial manner. Gerard has this to say about the trial and what we know about it:

110

'On the threshold of our inquiry we are met by a most singular and startling fact. As to what passed on the trial of the conspirators, what evidence was produced against them, how it was supported,—nay, even how the tale of their enterprise was told—we have no information upon which any reliance can be placed. One version alone has come down to us of the proceedings upon this occasion—that published "by authority"—and of this we can be sure only that it is utterly untrustworthy. It was issued under the title of the True and Perfect Relation, but, as Mr Jardine has already told us, is certainly not deserving of the character which its title imports. "It is not true, because many occurrences on the trial are wilfully misrepresented; and it is not perfect, because the whole evidence, and many facts and circumstances which must have happened, are omitted, and incidents are inserted which could not by possibility have taken place on the occasion. It is obviously a false and imperfect relation of the proceedings; a tale artfully garbled and misrepresented to serve a State purpose, and intended and calculated to mislead the judgment of the world upon the facts of the case." Again the same author remarks, "that every line of the published trial was rigidly weighed and considered, not with reference to its accuracy, but its effect on the minds of those who might read it, is manifest." Moreover, the narrative thus obviously dishonest, was admittedly issued in contradiction of divers others already passing "from hand to hand", which were at variance with itself in points of importance, and which it stigmatized as "uncertain, untrue, and incoherent".'

In consequence, to quote Mr Jardine once more, there is no trial since the time of Henry VIII in regard of which we are so ignorant as to what actually occurred.

Besides which, even if Fawkes did proudly boast that he had intended to 'blow you Scotch beggars back to your native mountains' when questioned by either James or a Scottish lord, as is alleged, it is not quite the same as saying the powder was actually in place. That assertion only comes from confessions which had passed through the hands of Cecil and those around him. There are supposed to have been approximately four imperial tons of gunpowder in place by the time all the barrels had been hauled into the cellar, but even that depends on what is meant by a 'barrel' since the term is sometimes used loosely to describe barrel-like containers of varying sizes. If they were all gunpowder barrels in the true sense of the word as it was understood at that time, as Gerard has suggested, the total amount of powder would have exceeded six tons. In a statement made on 20 January, Guy Fawkes said that the first twenty barrels brought into the cellar were full-sized ('whole barrels'). Gerard concedes that some of the barrels were smaller – but that some were 'hogsheads', which in some contexts could be larger than a standard barrel. (Others have disputed these figures, insisting they were actually much lower. This includes Gerard's 'rival' Gardiner, who rushed to publish a counter-argument to Gerard's take on the whole Plot (*What the Gunpowder Plot Was*) in the same year that Gerard's book came out. He believes there to have been closer to one-and-a-half tons of gunpowder.)

Whatever the exact weight of powder involved it was a lot of barrels, and it has often been asked how, at a time when the government tightly controlled the sale and distribution of gunpowder, anyone – let alone men who were known Catholics, known associates of Jesuits priests, and known to have taken part in an armed rebellion just a few years earlier – could accumulate such a store of explosives; and if they could, how they could they do so unbeknownst to the government. The usual answer is that it came from abroad and/or the 'black market'. Spink speculates that at least some of it could have come from Flanders with the help of Fawkes' contact Hugh Owen. But such a huge amount? The ports were closely monitored by both the regular authorities and government spies, and one can safely assume that anyone touting gunpowder around in Britain during an era when invasion and uprising was a constant threat would have also been known to the authorities. But Owen himself was very well known to Cecil – who would have loved to have got his hands on him – and the idea that he could have shipped numerous barrels of powder to England without it coming to Cecil's notice is hard to believe.

Gerard calculated that the amount of powder the plotters are supposed to have amassed equated to more than a quarter of the total amount leaving the government store in 1607, and equal to the whole amount required by Dover Castle. In other words, a man with great military experience (Fawkes – but he wasn't the only one) oversaw the risky acquisition and transportation of enough gunpowder to supply an army or major fortress in order to blow up one building.

As for the transportation of so many barrels, however heavy they were, Spink provides us with a theory as to how the powder might have reached the cellar. He argues that it was not shifted in the barrels but in powder bags (such as those that are said to have caused the problems at Holbeche) which in turn could have been stored in padlocked hampers. In this scenario, the barrels were then obtained separately and taken, empty, to the cellar and filled in situ. However, although this makes sense from a logistical and practical point of view, it might be said to double the risks. Not only must there have been several consignments of the hampers – and assuming that this was a common way of transporting gunpowder, which I suspect it was – then not only might this lead to some suspicious glances, but so might the continued arrival of barrels, empty or otherwise, at a house next door to the House of Lords from which mystery men could be observed coming and going at all hours.

But who actually saw the powder, the great stack of barrels, anyway? What proof is there from anyone outside Cecil's circle or sphere of influence? For centuries some have looked upon the powder in the same way as the mine – there is no impartial witness testimony. And just as no one saw the tunnel as it was at the time of the smashing of the plot, nor afterwards even as a visibly filled in or blocked up trace, neither did anyone see all those barrels in place, or being removed from harm's way. Early writers pointed to the fact that there was also no record of the powder being safely deposited in the royal stores, but records eventually came to light showing that the powder was returned to the Ordnance stores at the Tower. The figure stated in their records is even less than the one Gardiner came up with: 1,800lb, or an eigth of an imperial ton. (There was a note added saying that the powder was 'decayed', which perhaps adds weight to the idea that it had been originally obtained from dubious sources.)

Of course, a true conspiracy theorist might say that there *were* thirty-six barrels of gunpowder beneath the House of Lords despite all the apparent difficulties in obtaining them that must have existed – because they were supplied by Cecil or his under-cover agents in order to make sure that the plotters were caught red-handed!

The Monteagle Letter

The mystery of the Monteagle letter and the idea of whether Cecil employed an agent provocateur are almost certainly not connected and should be treated as two separate issues. If there had been a mole in the plotters' camp he is highly unlikely to have been the person who wrote to Monteagle. The dramatic arrest of Fawkes on the eve of the opening of Parliament suited Cecil – it had great propaganda value. The Monteagle letter was not only unnecessary in order to achieve this but might even have spoiled everything.

Thanks to the dilatory response to the letter, Fawkes could easily have fled with the other plotters; in fact, there was even time – between the letter being delivered and any action being taken – for the barrels of gunpowder themselves to be spirited away.

The way the letter *is* connected with the notion that Cecil was aware of what Catesby and his band were up to is circumstantial but, to me, compelling. The tardy and seemingly casual reaction of Cecil to the receipt of the letter strongly indicates that he knew all along what was going on: he knew who was involved, he knew about the gunpowder in the cellar, and he knew when it was due to be ignited; hence the lack of urgency. Even the *King's Book* itself drops a hint in this direction. Regarding Cecil's reaction to Montague when he arrived with the letter, it states:

> 'Whereupon the said Earl of Salisbury having read the Letter, and heard the manner of the coming of it to his hands, did greatly encourage, and commend my Lord for his discretion, telling him plainly, that whatsoever the purpose of the Letter might prove hereafter, yet did this accident put him in mind of divers advertisements he had received from beyond the Seas, wherewith he had acquainted, as well the King himself, as divers of His Privy Counsellors, concerning some business the Papists were in, both at home and abroad, making preparations for some combination amongst them against this Parliament time.'

This 'business' in question is described as a 'petition for toleration of religion'; but that sort of thing was nothing new or sinister, and it is not clear why he should connect something as apparently legitimate and harmless as a petition with something as dark and ominous as that threatened in a letter delivered in such a melodramatic fashion. Furthermore, this doesn't seem to quite square with what the account in the *King's Book* goes on to say, namely that 'The tender care which they ever carried to the preservation of His Majesties Person, made them apprehend, that some perilous attempt did thereby appear to be intended against the same'.

There is, no doubt, an element of Cecil pandering to James' ego in allowing him to work out what it meant, but Cecil was a million miles from being casual in matters of espionage, nor inept at figuring out what his enemies were up to. If the letter really had come as a surprise to him, with the opening of Parliament just days away, there is absolutely no doubt that he would have reacted swiftly and decisively.

A professional handwriting analysis carried out in 1967, and published in the *Observer* newspaper, decided that there were strong indications of 'deliberation and over-control', and concluded that the writing was 'disguised'. The opinion of the expert, Joan Cambridge, who was accustomed to appearing as an expert witness in court cases, was that it was 'extremely unlikely' that Tresham wrote the letter, but a seventy per cent probability that Cecil was the author. She declared that 'I'm reasonably satisfied in my own mind' that he was the author.

Although I accept the weight of this professional assessment (but I wouldn't rule out the master forger we heard about earlier, Arthur Gregory, as the man who actually put pen to paper) and could easily believe that Cecil would pull off a stunt like writing the letter, I still lean towards Tresham, unaware of the extent of Cecil's knowledge of the Plot and desperate to save at least one person's life, as the sender of the warning. Cecil simply didn't need to create such a pretence – he could more easily have he obtained knowledge of the plot from informants. The letter allowed him to boost the king's standing and ego, but to me that isn't a strong enough reason on its own for risking such a charade. I don't see it as a mere coincidence that the Monteagle letter was sent just days after Tresham's late entry into the group. I also, however, strongly suspect that other members of the Lords received similar letters or oral warnings, sent to them by other plotters.

Were Any of the Plotters Traitors?

There are few historians who would be surprised if Cecil had prior knowledge of the Plot, but the idea that one or more of the plotters themselves might have been working for him in some way is far more controversial.

I rule out Guy Fawkes immediately, and no expansion on that point is even necessary. Jack Wright was a friend of Fawkes and possibly also of Father Tesimond (who was placed in grave danger because of the Plot) from their schooldays, which makes it much less likely that he would betray them in such a way.

Even before the Gunpowder Plot, Tom Wintour actively sought Spanish backing for a Catholic rebellion in England so can't easily be viewed as a prime candidate.

Robert Keyes was a very minor player and a relatively late addition to the group, so not likely to have been much value as a mole.

The same applies to Thomas Bates, with the proviso that he was Catesby's 'servant' (though, as we have seen, more of a manager than a servant in the traditional sense). If Catesby was a government plant, one would have expected that Bates, as his servant, was either in on it, or at least aware of it; however, because of his lowly status and the fact that he went to his death making no mention of anything of the sort, I cross him off too.

Robert Wintour was a somewhat reluctant plotter, roped in to provide financial support; there are no signs that he had any influence within the group.

There is also little to indicate any suspicion regarding John Grant, who sheltered Jesuit priests and had a reputation for doing his best to hinder the pursuivants who came looking for them.

Kit Wright was a 'well-built' young man who was supposedly brought in to help with digging the tunnel, so doesn't stand out as anyone who could have played the part of a double-agent.

Ambrose Rookwood was close to both Digby and Catesby, but when he learned what the ultimate goal of the Plot was, he protested against the indiscriminate bloodshed that would be involved. This could have been an act, of course, but there are no compelling reasons to suspect any treachery on his part.

Sir Everard Digby was young and one of the last men to be brought into the conspiracy, and a highly unlikely candidate as a 'plant'. That leaves us three suspects to choose from.

Robert Catesby

> 'It has been said, in excuse for the conspirators, that there are reasons for suspecting the idea of the Gunpowder Plot to have been conceived in the first instance by Cecil, who had it suggested to Catesby, through a third person – possibly Mounteagle – with the deliberate intention of bringing discredit upon the English Catholics, and thereby giving cause for the enactment of severer measures for their repression.'
>
> Longueville, *Life of a Conspirator: Being a Biography of Sir Everard Digby*

Longueville was implying that Cecil got someone to take advantage of Catesby's impulsive nature, and perhaps naivety, by inducing him to set the plot in motion. But can we go a step further than that? Might Catesby's actions have been those of an agent provocateur who knew the value of obtaining spiritual approval? Was he someone who resorted to such underhand methods (thus placing the life of at least one priest in jeopardy) in order to ensnare as many disaffected Catholic gentlemen as possible? Or even to ensnare the Jesuits themselves?

Most of his recruits would have baulked at such extreme and indiscriminate violence had not Catesby ostensibly gained priestly approval; and, as a matter of record, they wanted to try to minimise the number of deaths. If Catesby really was so passionate about the Catholic cause, would he really have deliberately deceived and endangered a senior priest?

Catesby married Catherine Leigh, a Protestant, and their son Robert was baptised at the Protestant parish church of Chastleton in Oxfordshire just a few years before the Gunpowder Plot. And then there were his money problems arising from his part in the Essex rebellion – Catesby had had to sell his estate at Chastleton to cover the fine. Is it possible that he had agreed to incriminate Catholic troublemakers on some sort of promise of the kind of helping hand that had been given to Monteagle? He was a decadent spendthrift with suspect morals and strong Protestant connections, the kind of man who might put his scruples to one side if the right kind of rewards were dangled before him. There are two possible scenarios. One is that he was an out-and-out, coldly calculating double-agent acting on Cecil's behalf, charged with roping in as many dangerous Catholics as possible and promised handsome remuneration and protection for doing so. This would have the double advantage for Cecil of greatly lessening the chance of any future uprising, as well as providing the king with ammunition to introduce anti-Catholic legislation that would receive widespread sympathy. In this scenario, Catesby was then executed to prevent Cecil's dark dealings from becoming public knowledge. The alternative picture is that, knowing Catesby's reputation for wildness and rashness, Cecil targeted him by sending a convincing intermediary (like Monteagle or Northumberland) to cajole him into action. Cecil may have dreamt the scheme up out of thin air or had perhaps already heard of the traitorous mutterings of Catesby and his friends and decided to give them a helping hand.

It seems clear that Catesby deceived those plotters who had qualms about the cost in human life, especially Catholic ones, which was bound to occur when the powder was detonated. Digby's biographer speaks of 'how grossly Sir Everard was deceived by Catesby, when he was assured that Jesuit Fathers had approved of the conspiracy in general, though they knew not the particulars'. Father Gerard says that Catesby wangled approval for his scheme from Father Garnet by 'cunning means'. He did this by leading a general conversation towards the wars in the Low Countries – playing on the fact that Garnet knew he had been thinking of travelling to fight there – and asked 'how far it might be lawful for the party that hath the just quarrel to proceed in sacking or destroying a town of the enemy's, or fortress'. Garnet said that in a just war it was lawful for those that had right on their side to wage battle against their enemies. But what, wondered Catesby, if an action such as sacking the fortifications of an enemy led to the deaths of innocent people, children and suchlike? Garnet's reply was that it 'could never be lawful in itself, to kill an innocent', by which he meant deliberately so. But what, persisted Catesby, if it happened as part of the general attack; collateral damage as we would now call it. Then, replied Garnet, since the war was a just one, the accidental deaths of innocents in the sacking of a town or fortress could not be helped and was also just. This was enough for Catesby's purposes. Garnet would later say 'And in truth I never imagined anything of the King's Majesty, nor of any particular, and thought it, as it were, an idle question…' And writing from the Tower after his arrest, 'Master Catesby did me much wrong... He did it to draw in others.'

It was also Catesby who pressed his fellow plotters not to reveal to their confessors what they really intended to do. The best slant that can be put on it is that it meant that if they were caught, the priests could honestly deny any knowledge of what was planned. A cynic might say he proposed this course of action because he knew the priests would warn Digby and the others that the Plot was spiritually unacceptable and attempt to talk them out of it.

One argument against the traitor theory is the question of why none of the captured men queried the confessions made in their names and which were read out at their trials. Similarly, if any of them were moles or suspected others of such treachery, why didn't they make some sort of outcry to that effect before being executed? To me, this again rules out the men who stood trial and appear to have gone to their deaths without querying the official version of events: Fawkes; Digby; the Wintours; Grant; Bates; Rookwood; and Keyes. However, there is an interesting passage in the *King's Book* concerning Guy Fawkes, who, when asked why he pleaded Not Guilty, replied that 'he had so done in respect of certain conferences mentioned in the Indictment, which, he said, that he knew not of'. We have looked at various suspicious discrepancies between versions of his statements, but what exactly did he mean here? We are not told. Could it be that the only plotter or plotters who knew the *full* story had been disposed of (at Holbeche) or had already died in the Tower (Tresham)?'

Catesby's servant George Bartlet is reported to have made a death-bed confession that the former made numerous surreptitious visits to Cecil under cover of darkness just before Fawkes was caught. Nevertheless, I am not persuaded by Catesby as an agent provocateur; I believe he was a genuine hot-head, perhaps even a fantasist; one who wasn't always good at thinking through the consequences of his actions, yet who had the charisma to suck others into his foolhardy schemes. The deepest and most tantalising suspicions are those surrounding Percy and Tresham.

Francis Tresham

If there was a suspect character among the plotters, Francis Tresham has to be a good candidate. He has long been many people's favourite as the sender of the Monteagle letter and even Catesby and Tom Wintour suspected him of it, which perhaps should be given more weight than it usually is. Father Tesimond reported being told by Catesby that he always harboured suspicions about Tresham, and regretted inviting him to join the conspiracy[1]. He is the only plotter who didn't eventually take to his heels when Fawkes' arrest became known. More than that, according to an account written by John Stow in 1614, *The Annales, or Generall Chronicle of England*, he not only remained at court but offered his 'special services' in bringing the culprits to justice. This could have been a monumental bluff on his part, acted out to try to show his innocence – but if he believed he still had time to escape, it would seem a very rash piece of judgement. As it was, 'within few dayes he was restrayned, examined, and then sent to the Tower, where he confest all'.

That Tresham was one of the plotters was known to the government from 7 November at the latest, yet his name didn't appear in their published proclamations for several days. Why? There was a claim made in *The Politician's Catechism* in 1662 – so within living memory of the Plot – that Tresham had privileged access to Cecil's house 'even at midnight' along with an anonymous companion, and that they were 'the secretary's instruments' in relation to the Gunpowder Plot. According to Dr Lingard[2], when Tesimond visited Tresham in the Tower, the latter recounted that, after learning about the Monteagle letter, he told Tom Wintour that 'the existence of the mine had been communicated to the ministers', though he did not know how they had found out. If this is true, it would cast further doubt on the authorised version of Guy Fawkes' arrest, since, if Cecil knew about the mine, he would have known where to look for Fawkes and any other plotters well before he finally took action, and wouldn't have needed the Monteagle letter to galvanise him into action.

Tresham's was one of at least two convenient deaths following the Plot's exposure, the other being Whynniard from whom the plotters rented the house and vault. Bishop Goodman in *The Court of King James*, says that when he heard the news 'what Percy intended' he [Whynniard] 'instantly fell into a fright and died'. Even on its own such an occurrence might seem suspicious, but in view of everything else we know it is positively sinister.

As we have already seen, Tresham is supposed to have died of 'natural causes', a long-standing condition,[3] yet one of which there is no record or mention at any time before his arrest. But does the story end there?

Why is Tresham the only one of the arrested plotters who was allowed visitors? His wife, sister and servant were all granted access to him. This has led to suspicions that he could have escaped – or more likely been allowed to escape by the authorities – disguised as one of those incomers.

Why was Tresham's mother allowed to retain ownership of his property and lands after his death? Bates' estates were confiscated, rather than going to his wife.

Dudley Carleton, who was one of Northumberland's men, sent a report to England in December 1605, saying that he had seen two Englishmen in Calais whose demeanour was that of men trying to avoid being recognised – and 'One of them looked like Francis Tresham'. Although this is before Tresham is supposed to have died in the Tower, the editor of the Folio edition of Tesimond's narrative believes that Tresham slipped away from the Tower before that date. His servant said that a confession he wrote on his 'deathbed' was kept back for over three weeks, meaning that Tresham could have left the Tower before the end of November.

The following year, a man turned up at the English embassy in Madrid. He wouldn't reveal his identity, but wished to be put in touch with Cecil, 'who, he saith, doth also know himself by some late events'. There followed a series of letters from Madrid to Cecil's secretary from two men going by the names of John Jude and Matthew Brunninge, and the handwriting of the latter, says the Folio editor, resembles that of Tresham:

> 'to a remarkable degree… One cannot say that Bruninge and
> Francis Tresham wrote identically, but one could claim that the

differences are those that a man might introduce who wished
to disguise his own hand…'

It is also interesting to note, though, that according to Bishop Goodman,
Tresham was attended to by 'Butler, the great physician at Cambridge' who
believed Tresham had been poisoned.

Not all the plotters were convinced that the cryptic Monteagle letter,
when news of it broke, necessarily meant the plan had to be abandoned.
It was Tresham who urged his fellow conspirators to abort the mission
immediately. If he had been a traitor, would he have done this? Possibly. It
could indicate that the plan had gone as far as it needed to – neither he nor
Cecil would actually want Parliament to be blown up, so it would be in his
interest to put a stop to it now they were all as good as incriminated. Cecil
almost certainly already knew of Guy Fawkes' whereabouts in my opinion,
so he could be picked up at any time, and from there things would proceed
just as they did when he actually was arrested on 4 November.

Piecing together the stories of Father Tesimond and Tresham himself after his
arrest, it seems clear that if Tresham was innocent of treachery, this late entrant
to the scheme who had perhaps ignored his better judgement and committed
himself in haste only to repent at leisure, got cold feet when the full horror of
what they were about to do hit him. He had advocated postponing the attack till
the end of the parliamentary session. This was hardly realistic, since it would
have entailed either trying to keep dozens of barrels of gunpowder hidden for
many further months in the bowels of the parliament buildings themselves, or
taking the equally risky step of hauling them all back the way they had come and
the inherent chances of discovery that came with such a move. Not to mention
the need to go through the whole process once again when they *did* finally
decide to launch their attack. It is hard to believe that Tresham ever thought his
postponement proposal would be seriously considered by the other plotters, and
he specifically said in his confession that he raised it as a way of getting the plot
called off altogether – although of course the possibility exists that he told his
captors this in an attempt to save his own skin.

Although it would make sense that if Tresham were a government mole
or agitator he might attempt to prevent the explosion from taking place once
there was enough evidence to ensnare everyone, what doesn't really add
up is that having seen it through this far, he wouldn't want to let it run till
the government could gain the publicity coup of arresting Fawkes virtually
in the act. That, together with the facts that Tresham supposedly put up
£2,000 of his own money and especially that he didn't get involved early

enough to affect the course of the conspiracy in any major way, make him a good candidate for the author of the Monteagle Letter and even a possible escapee, but an unlikely agent provocateur.

Thomas Percy

This is the man who conveniently had one house where powder could be stored and was able to openly acquire the lease of another where the mine could be started, and for me the strongest possibility for the role of a secret tool of Cecil's. He was described by the editor of the Folio edition of *The Narrative of Oswald Tesimond* as 'the least plausible of all the plotters… His function was, most probably, that of *agent-provocateur*'. Gerard calls him 'unusually wild and dissolute' and describes the part he played in the plot as 'very singular'. He was also apparently a bigamist, with a wife in London and another in Warwickshire – and both were arrested and questioned once the plot fell apart.[4]

The Folio editor points to the fact that as a young man, Percy had a reputation for being someone who was inclined to reach for his sword at the slightest provocation, adding with a hint of cynicism that he changed his ways 'in a remarkable fashion' upon converting to Catholicism, giving 'considerable cause for wonder to those who had known him previously'. There is no doubt that the Jesuit missionaries had great success in both bringing lapsed Catholics back into the fold and converting new ones, but it is also well known that some of those who appeared to embrace the old religion were in fact government spies and informers.

As with Tresham, there were some who had their suspicions about Percy even at the time. Gerard cites a man called Cary, examined in the aftermath of the Plot, as declaring that he was 'no Papist, but a Puritan'. He also highlights Percy's surprisingly insouciant manner in not only hiring the house and cellar in his own name, but in enlisting 'sundry Protestant gentleman' to help in this cause, including Dudley Carleton – another who, far from suffering from his assisting of, however unwittingly, a leading plotter, 'subsequently rose rapidly in favour'.

Goodman, a contemporary of the plotters who became the Anglican bishop of Gloucester, was told by the lawyer Sir Francis Moore that in the run-up to the plot 'several times he met Mr Percy coming out of the great 'statesman's [i.e. Cecil's] house, and wondered what his business should be there'. This would be a strange thing to make up. What is equally suspicious is that Percy dined with his relative the Earl of Northumberland on 4 November, literally hours before Fawkes was caught. The earl said they discussed the running of his estate, and although he was charged with involvement in the plot, there was not sufficient proof to condemn him. Northumberland was a Catholic sympathiser, so while this meeting may suggest that Percy told him what was afoot, it is less likely to imply that Percy himself was some sort of government mole. It is, however, interesting to note that it was Northumberland who was responsible for Percy's appointment to the Honourable Corps of Gentlemen at Arms just weeks after he had joined the conspiracy and five months before the planned day of destruction. It was a role, as we have seen, that gave him a valid reason to openly seek accommodation in Westminster.

Another anomaly involving Percy concerns a letter Cecil wrote to his government's ambassadors in the second week of October 1605. Percy had travelled north in the run-up to the opening of parliament, returning to London on 2 November. Cecil claimed that Percy's whereabouts had been a mystery and that he had only learned about them from the interrogation of Fawkes. However, on 25 October Percy had been issued with on official pass declaring that he was travelling on 'the king's especial service' (presumably in his capacity as a captain of the Pensioners-in-Ordinary). It required that 'all mayors, sheriffs, and postmasters…provide him with three good horses all along the road'. Thus, there was nothing at all surreptitious about either his whereabouts or travels at this time – so why would Cecil imply as much? We have already heard that early in his reign, James I was asked why had he included so many Catholics in his court and mentioned using tame ducks in order to catch wild ones; it has been suggested that Percy was just such a decoy. It is also worth noting the meeting at the Duck and Drake inn (perhaps appropriately!) on the Strand on 20 May 1604 when Percy was first introduced to the group as it stood then (Catesby, Tom Wintour, Jack Wright and Fawkes). It was Percy, the newcomer, rather than the leader Catesby to whom the others always deferred, who cried, 'Shall we always, gentlemen, talk and never do anything?'. It is purely conjecture, of course, but if one were looking for a candidate for someone sent to infiltrate the group and provoke a bunch of dreamers into men of action, this incident would certainly put him in the frame.

The hiring of the cellar perhaps bears one last examination, because in addition to the fact that Percy hired it in his own name (at a time when I feel certain his movements would have been of interest to Cecil's spies) there is a detail about the transaction which is often overlooked. The tenancy of the cellar was a somewhat complicated matter. Ultimately the Whynniards (who also rented out the house next to the Lords' chamber to the plotters) were the lessors of the cellar; Fawkes went to enquire of Ellen, wife of Andrew Bright, who appeared to be the current tenant, as to whether it might be rented out. Gerard reports Mrs Whynniard as claiming, when questioned, that the cellar wasn't Mrs Bright's to let out because the lease was held by 'one Skinner'; Gardiner, in his riposte to Gerard's book, says that Mrs Bright *was* Skinner, or rather his widow, having subsequently married Andrew Bright. It is not clear where he got this from, but the state papers refer to 'Mr Skynner *alias* Bright', which could simply refer to confusion regarding the present and previous names of Mrs Bright – but could also be taken literally to mean that Skinner went under an alias.

The reason this rather convoluted story is interesting is that an Anthony Skinner active at this period is believed to have been a government spy. He had been servant to a Cardinal Allen and was arrested on returning to England in 1592 for plotting against Elizabeth. He was tortured and sentenced to be executed, but reprieved under slightly mysterious circumstances and rumoured to have become an informant.[5] In one account, he is said to have been 'well acquainted' with the government's code-breaker and secret letter-opener Thomas Phelippes.[6] Anthony Skinner is also linked to White Webbs, the plotters' sometime hideout; his description agrees with that of Skinner of White Webbs.[7] A final interesting fact is that he is reported to have been rejected by the Jesuits – could it be that, in league with Cecil and with a grudge against the Society of Jesus, he somehow played a part in luring, or at least allowing, the plotters into a trap?

For us to believe that any of the plotters were infiltrators or agents provocateurs, we have to also accept that they in turn were double-crossed by the government (with the possible exception of Tresham – see above). Most of them were executed and all of them died in one way or another (again, if Tresham really did die); and although they might have done it for money, position or even secret anti-Catholic sentiment, it would be beyond belief that they would knowingly and willingly sacrifice themselves in such a way.

The only way the 'inside job' theory can hold water is if the guilty party or parties were assured that they would be spared the fate of their accomplices. This would *seem* to rule out Percy and Catesby, since they were both shot dead in the raid on Holbeche House. If there was, or they believed there was, some assurance that they would be protected once the plot was exposed, they are unlikely to have holed up with the others when the raid was imminent. They would surely have slipped away and deserted their fellow plotters – there must have been ample opportunity to do so. *Unless*, that is, they had been promised that although they would be rounded up along with everyone else just to keep up appearances, they would eventually either be cleared of the charges or allowed to escape into exile. Could there even be some sort of dark humour at work on the part of Cecil in the way that Holbeche played out? Percy and Catesby were said to have been killed by the same ball passing through their bodies. If there is any truth in the Percy/Catesby theory, might there be some sort of deliberate symbolism at play here, a fabrication that would only mean something to those in the know?

My gut instinct tells me that Percy and Catesby, at least, were executed at Holbeche, not killed in any kind of battle or last stand, and that there was a reason for it that which Cecil took with him to his grave. And my suspicion is also that Tresham didn't die in the Tower but was helped to escape to Europe by Cecil himself. But in neither case would it necessarily be proof of duplicity. Catesby and Percy could have been murdered to protect the part played by Monteagle or others, and Tresham could have been spared for a well-intentioned collusion with Monteagle over the letter. I'm absolutely sure that he was appalled when he discovered the full extent of what was intended, when it sank in, and that he could well have visited Cecil (and we have heard that he did on more than one occasion) and said something along the lines of, 'Look, I've discovered that something truly horrific is being planned, something that can't be allowed happen – but if I tell you everything, can we devise a way of bringing it to light that won't put my life at risk from either the plotters or subsequent criminal proceedings?'

Ultimately, then, I have grave doubts about Percy but not quite enough to fully persuade me that he or any of the plotters were out-and-out traitors. I do, though, believe that the official and still widely-believed account of the Gunpowder Plot was cooked up by Cecil, who tampered with confessions and other evidence, who knew about the Plot at least weeks and probably months before Guy Fawkes was arrested, and who was content to let it run till the last minute for propaganda purposes. A year before Fawkes was discovered, in a letter to Britain's ambassador in France, Cecil stated that the doings of priests were 'always known to him'. And we can be sure that if he knew what the priests were doing, he would also have known what those they were ministering to, people like Catesby and the others, were doing in the run-up to 5 November.

He allowed it to play out for as long as he dared partly to give the plotters enough rope to hang themselves, but mainly, I believe, to engender an atmosphere where stronger measures against Catholics in general, and Jesuits especially, would seem perfectly justified and attract popular support. It was a conspiracy within a conspiracy.

Appendix A

King James' Speech To Parliament Regarding the Plot

MY Lords Spiritual and Temporal, and you the Knights and Burgesses of this Parliament; It was far from my thoughts, till very lately, before my coming to this place, that this Subject should have been ministered unto me, whereupon I am now to speak. But now it so falleth out, That whereas in the preceding Session of this Parliament, the principal occasion of my Speech was, to thank and congratulate all you of this House, and in you, all the whole Common-wealth (as being the representative Body of the State) for your so willing, and loving receiving, and embracing of me in that place, which God and Nature by descent of Bloud, had in his own time provided for me: So now my subject is, to speak of a far greater Thanksgiving than before I gave to you, being to a far greater person, which is to GOD, for the great and miraculous Delivery he hath at this time granted to me, and to you all, and consequently to the whole Body of this Estate, I must therefore begin with this old and most approved Sentence of Divinity, Misericordia Dei supra omnia opera ejus. For Almighty GOD did not furnish so great matter to his Glory, by the Creation of this great World, as he did by the Redemption of the same. Neither did his Generation of the little World, in our old and first ADAM, so much set forth the praises of GOD in his Justice and Mercy, as did our Regeneration in the last and second ADAM.

And now I must crave a little pardon of you, That since Kings are in the word of GOD it self called Gods, as being his Lieutenants and Vicegerents on earth, and so adorned and furnished with some sparkles of the Divinity; to compare some of the Works of GOD the Great King, towards the whole and general World, to some of his Works towards Me, and this little world of my Dominions, compassed and severed by the Sea from the rest of the Earth. For as GOD for the just punishment of the first great Sinner in the original world, when the Sons of GOD went in to the Daughters of Men, and the cup of their iniquities of all sorts

126

was filled, and heaped up to the full, did by a general deluge and overflowing of waters, baptize the World to a general destruction, and not to general purgation (only excepted Noah and his family, who did repent and believe the threatenings of God's judgement:) So now, when the World shall wax old as a Garment, and that all the impieties and sins that can be devised against both the first and second Table, have, and shall be committed to the full measure; GOD is to punish the World the second time by Fire, to the general destruction and not purgation thereof. Although as it was done in the former to Noah and his Family by the waters; So shall all we that believe be likewise purged, and not destroyed by the Fire. In the like sort, I say, I may justly compare these two great and fearful Dooms-days, wherewith GOD threatened to destroy me, and all you of this little World that have interest in me. For although I confess, as all mankind, so chiefly Kings, as being in the higher places like the high Trees, or stayest Mountains, and steepest Rocks, are most subject to the daily tempests of innumerable dangers; and I amongst all other Kings, have ever been subject unto them, not only ever since my birth, but even as I may justly say, before my birth, and while I was yet in my Mothers belly: yet have I been exposed to two more special and greater dangers than all the rest.

The first of them, in the Kingdom where I was born, and passed the first part of my life: And the last of them here, which is the greatest. In the former, I should have been baptized in bloud, and in my destruction, not only the Kingdom, wherein I then was, but ye also by your future interest, should have tasted of my ruine. Yet it pleased GOD to deliver me, as it were, from the very brink of death, from the point of the dagger, and so to purge me by my thankful acknowledgement of so great a benefit. But in this which did so lately fall out, and which was a destruction prepared not for me alone, but for you all that are here present, and wherein no rank, age, or sex should have been spared; This was not a crying sin of bloud as the former, but it may well be called a roaring, nay, a thundering sin of Fire and Brimstone, from the which, God hath so miraculously delivered us all. What I can speak of this, I know not: Nay rather, what can I not speak of it? And therefore I must for horror say with the Poet. Vox faucibus haeret.

In this great and horrible attempt, whereof the like was never either heard or read, I observe three wonderful, or rather miraculous events.

First, in the cruelty of the Plot it self, wherein cannot be enough admired the horrible and fearful cruelty of their Device, which was not only for the destruction of my Person, nor of my Wife and Posterity only, but of the whole Body of the State in general; wherein should neither have been spared, or distinction made of young nor of old, of great nor of small, of man nor of woman: The whole Nobility, the whole Reverend Clergy, Bishops, and most part of the good Preachers, the most part of the Knights and Gentry; yea, and if that any in this Society were favourers of their Profession, they should all have gone one way: The whole Judges of the Land, with the most of the Lawyers and the whole Clerks: And as the wretch himself that is in the Tower, doth confess, it was purposely devised by them, and concluded to be done in this house; That where the cruel Laws (as they say) were made against their Religion, both place and persons should all be destroyed and blown up at once. And then consider therewithal the cruel form of that practice: for by three different sorts in general may mankind be put to death.

The First, by other men, and reasonable creatures, which is least cruel: for then both defence of men against men may be expected, and likewise who knoweth what pity GOD may stirr up in the hearts of the Actors at the very instant? besides the many ways and means, whereby men may escape in such a present fury.

And the Second way more cruel than that, is by Animal and unreasonable creatures: for as they have less pity then men, so is it a greater horror, and more unnatural for men to deal with them: But yet with them both resistance may avail, and also some pity maybe had, as was in the Lyons, in whose Den Daxiel was thrown; or that thankful Lyon, that had the Roman slave in his mercy.

But the Third, which is most cruel and unmerciful of all, is the destruction by insensible and inanimate things; and amongst them all, the most cruel are the two Elements of Water and Fire; and of those two the Fire most raging and merciless.

Secondly, How wonderful it is when you shall think upon the small, or rather no ground, whereupon the Practisers were enticed to invent this Tragedy. For if these Conspirators had only been bankrupt persons, or discontented upon occasion of any disgraces done unto them; this might have seemed to have been but a work of revenge. But for my own part, as I scarcely ever knew any of them, So cannot they alledge so much as a pretended cause of grief: And the wretch himself in hands doth confess, That there was no cause moving him or them, but meerly, and only Religion. And specially, that Christian men, at least so called, Englishmen, born within the Countrey, and one of the specials of them, my sworn Servant, in an Honorable place, should Practise the destruction of their King, his Posterity, their Countrey and all: wherein their following obstinacy is so joyned to their former malice, as the fellow himself that is in hand, cannot be moved to discover any signes or notes of repentance, except only, that he doth not yet stand to avow, that he repents for not being able to perform his intent.

Thirdly, The discovery hereof is not a little wonderful, which would be thought the more miraculous by you all, if you were as well acquainted with my natural disposition, as those are who be near about me. For as I ever did hold suspition to be the sickness of a Tyrant, so was I so far upon the other extremity, as I rather contemned all advertisements, or apprehensions of practises. And yet now at this time was I so far contrary to my self, as when the Letter was shewed to me by my Secretary, wherein a general obscure advertisement was given of some dangerous blow at this time, I did upon the instant interpret and apprehend some dark phrases therein, contrary to the ordinary Grammer construction of them, (and in another sort then I am sure any Divine, or Lawyer in any University would have taken them) to be meant by this horrible form of blowing us up all by Powder; and thereupon ordered, that search to be made, whereby the matter was discovered, and the man apprehended: whereas if I had apprehended or interpreted it to any other sort of danger, no worldly provision or prevention could have made us escape our utter destruction. And in that also, was there a wonderful providence of God, that when the party himself was taken, he was but new come out of his house from working, having his Firework for kindling ready in his pocket, wherewith as he confesseth, if he had been taken but immediately before, when he was in the House, he was resolved to have blown up himself with his Takers.

One thing for my own part have I cause to thank GOD in, That if GOD for our sins had suffered their wicked intents to have prevailed, it should never have been spoken nor written in ages succeeding, that I had died ingloriously in an Ale-house, a Stews, or such vile place, but mine end should have been with the most Honourable and best company, and in that most Honourable and fittest place for a King to be in, for doing the turns most proper to his Office; And the more have We all cause to thank and magnifie GOD for this his merciful Delivery. And specially I for my part, that he hath given me yet once leave, whatsoever should come of me hereafter, to assemble you in this Honourable place; And here in this place, where our general destruction should have been, to magnifie and praise him for Our general delivery; That I may justly now say of mine enemies and yours, as David doth often say in the Psalm, Inciderunt in foveam, quam fecerunt. And since Scipio an Ethnick, led only by the light of Nature, That day when he was accused by the Tribunes of the people of Rome, for mispending and wasting in his Punick wars the Cities Treasure, even upon the sudden brake out with that diversion of them from that matter, calling them to remembrance how that day, was the day of the year, wherein GOD hath given them so great a victory against Hannibal, and therefore it was fitter for them all, leaving other matters, to run to the Temple to praise GOD for that so great delivery, which the people did all follow with one applause: How much more cause have we that are Christians to bestow this time in this place for Thanksgiving to GOD for his great Mercy, tho we had had no other errand of assembling here at this time; wherein if I have spoken more like a Divine, than would seem to belong to this place, the matter it self must plead for mine excuse: for being here come to thank God for a Divine work of his Mercy, how can I speak of this deliverance of us from so hellish a practise, so well, as in language of Divinity, which is the direct opposite to so damnable an intention? And therefore may I justly end this purpose, as I did begin it with this Sentence, The mercy of God is above all his works.

It resteth now, that I should shortly inform you what is to be done hereafter upon the occasion of this horrible and strange accident. As for your part that are my faithful and loving Subjects of all degrees, I know that your hearts are so burnt up with zeal in this errand, and your tongues so ready to utter your dutiful affections, and your hands and feet so bent to concurr in the execution thereof, (for which as I need not to spurr you, so can I not but praise you for the same:) As it may very well be possible, that the zeal of your hearts shall make some of you in your speeches, rashly to blame such as may be innocent of this attempt; But upon the other part I wish you to consider, That I would be sorry that any being innocent of this practise, either domestical or forrain, should receive blame or harm, for the same. For although it cannot be denied, That it was the only blind superstition of their errors in Religion, that led them to this desperate device; yet doth it not follow, That all professing that Romish Religion were guilty of the same. For as it is true, That no other sect of Heretiques, not excepting Turk Jew, nor Pagan, no not even those of Calicute who adore the Devil, did ever maintain by the grounds of their Religion, That it was lawful, or rather meritorious (as the Romish Catholicks call it) to murther Princes or people for quarrel of Religion. And although particular men of all professions of Religion have been some Thieves, some Murtherers, some Traitors, yet ever when they came to their end and just punishment, they confessed their fault to be in their nature, and not in their profession, (These Romish Catholicks only excepted:) Yet it is true on the other side, That many honest men blinded peradventure with some opinions of Popery, as if they be not found in the questions of the Real presence, or in the number of the Sacraments, or some such School-question: yet do they either not know, or at least, not believe all the true grounds of Popery, which is indeed, The mistery of iniquity. And therefore do we justly confess, that many Papists, especially our forefathers, laying their only trust upon Christ and his Merits at their last breath, may be, and oftentimes are saved; detesting in that point, and thinking the cruelty of Puritans worthy of Fire, that will admit no salvation to any Papist. I therefore thus do conclude this point, That as upon the one part many honest men, seduced with some errors of Popery, may yet remain good and faithful Subjects: So upon the other part, none of those that truly know and believe the whole grounds, and School-conclusions of their Doctrine, can ever prove either good Christians, or faithful Subjects. And for the part of forrain Princes and States, I may so much the more acquite them, and their Ministers, of their knowledge and consent to any such villany, as I may justly say, that in that point I better know all Christian Kings by my self, that no King nor Prince of Honor will ever abase himself so much, as to think a good thought of so base and dishonourable a Treachery: wishing you therefore, that as GOD hath given me an happy peace and amity, with all other Christian Princes my neighbors (as was even now very gravely told you by my L. Chancellor) that so you will reverently judge and speak of them in this case. And for my part I would wish with those antient Philosophers, that there were a Christal window in my breast, wherein all my people might see the secretest thoughts of my heart, for then might you all see no alteration in my mind for this accident, further than in those two points. The first, caution and wariness in government: to discover and search out the mysteries of this wickedness as far as may be: The other, after due trial, Severity of punishment upon those that shall be found guilty of so detestable and unheard of villany. And now in this matter, if I have troubled your ears with an abrupt Speech, undigested in any good method or order; you have to consider that an abrupt, and unadvised Speech doth best become in the relation of so abrupt and unorderly an accident.

And although I have ordained the Proroguing of this Parliament until after Christmass upon two necessary respects: whereof the first is, that neither I nor my Council can have leasure at this time both to take order for the apprehension and trial of these Conspirators, and also to wait upon the daily affairs of the Parliament, as the Council must do. And the other reason is, the necessity at this time of divers of your presences in your Shires that have Charges and Commandements there. For as these wretches thought to have blown up in a manner the whole world of this Island, every man being now come up here, either for publick causes of Parliament, or else

131

for their own private causes in Law, or otherwise: So these Rebels that now wander through the Countrey, could never have gotten so fit a time of safety in their passage, or whatsoever unlawful Actions, as now when the countrey by the foresaid occasions is in a manner left desolate, and waste unto them. Besides that, It may be that I shall desire you at your next Session, to take upon you the Judgment of this Crime: for as so extraordinary a Fact deserves extraordinary Judgment, So can there not I think (following even their own Rule) be a fitter Judgement for them, then that they should be measured with the same measure wherewith they thought to measure us: and that the same place and persons, whom they thought to destroy, should be the just avengers of their so unnatural a Parricide: Yet not knowing that I will have occasion to meet with you my self in this place at the beginning of the next Session of this Parliament (because if it had not been for delivering of the Articles agreed upon by the Commissioners of the Union, which was thought most convenient to be done in my presence, where both Head and Members of the Parliament were met together, my presence had not otherwise been requisite here at this time:) I have therefore thought good for conclusion of this Meeting, to discourse to you somewhat anent the true nature and definition of a Parliament, which I will remit to your memories, till your next sitting down; that you may then make use of it as occasion shall be ministred.

For albeit it be true, that at the first Session of my first Parliament, which was not long after mine Entry into this Kingdome, It could not become me to informe you of any thing belonging to Law or State here: (for all knowledge must either be infused, or acquired, and seeing the former sort thereof is now with Prophesie, ceased in the World, it could not be possible for me, at my first Entry here, before Experience had taught it me, to be able to understand the particular Mysteries of this State:) yet now that I have reigned almost three years amongst you, and have been careful to observe those things that belong to the Office of a King, albeit that Time be but a short time for experience in others, yet in a King may it be thought a reasonable long time, especially in me, who, although I be but in a manner a new King here, yet have been long acquainted with the office of a King in such another Kingdom, as doth nearest of all others agree with the Lawes and Customes of this State. Remitting to your consideration to judge of that which hath been concluded by the Commissioners of the Union, wherein I am at this time to signifie unto you, That as I can bear witness to the foresaid Commissioners, that they have not agreed nor concluded therein any thing, wherein they have not foreseen as well the Weale and Commodity of the one Countrey, as of the other; So can they all bear me record, that I was so far from pressing them to agree to any thing, which might bring with it any prejudice to this People; as by the contrary I did ever admonish them, never to conclude upon any such Union, as might carry hurt or grudge with it to either of the said Nations: for the leaving of any such thing, could not but be the greatest hinderance that might be to such an Action, which GOD by the Laws of nature had provided to be in his own time, and hath now in effect perfected in my Person; to which purpose my Lord Chancellor hath better spoken, then I am able to relate.

And as to the nature of this high Court of Parliament, It is nothing else but the Kings great Council, which the King doth assemble, either upon occasion of interpreting, or abrogating old Lawes, or making of new, according as ill manners shall deserve, or for the publick punishment of notorious evil doers, or the praise and reward of the vertuous and well deservers; wherein these four things are to be considered.

First, Whereof this Court is composed.
Secondly, What Matters are proper for it.
Thirdly, To what end it is ordained.
And Fourthly, What are the meanes and wayes whereby this end should be brought to pass.

As for the thing it self, It is composed of a Head and a Body: The Head is the King, the Body are the members of the Parliament. This Body again is subdivided into two parts; The Upper and Lower House: The Upper compounded partly of Nobility, Temporal men, who are heritable Councellors toto the high Court of Parliament by the honor of their Creation and Lands: And partly of Bishops, Spiritual men, who are likewise by the vertue of their place and dignity Counsellors, Life-Renters, or Ad vitam of this Court. The other House is composed of Knights for the Shire; and Gentry, and Burgesses for the Towns. But because the number would be infinite for all the Gentlemen and Burgesses to be present at every Parliament, Therefore a certain number is selected and chosen out of that great Body, serving onely for that Parliament, where their persons are the representation of that Body.

Now the Matters whereof they are to treat ought therefore to be general, and rather of such matters as cannot well be performed without the assembling of that general Body, and no more of these generals neither, then necessity shall require: for as in Corruptissima Republica sunt plurimae leges: So doth the life and strength of the Law consist not in heaping up infinite and confused numbers of Lawes, but in the right interpretation and good execution of good and wholsome Laws. If this be so then, neither is this a place on the one side for every rash and harebrain fellow to propone new Laws of his own invention: nay rather I could wish these busie heads to remember that Law of the Lacedemonians, That whosoever came to propone a new Law to the People, behoved publickly to present himself with a Rope about his neck, that in case the Law were not allowed, he should be hanged therewith. So wary should men be of proponing Novelties, but most of all, not to propone any bitter or seditious Laws, which can produce nothing but grudges and discontentment between the Prince and his people: nor yet is it on the other side a convenient place for private men under the colour of general Laws, to propone nothing but their own particular gain, either to the hurt of their private neighbours, or to the hurt of the whole State in general, which many times under fair and pleasing Titles, are smoothly passed over, and so by stealth procure without consideration, that the private meaning of them tendeth to nothing but either to the wreck of a particular party, or else under colour of publique benefit to pill the poor people, and serve as it were for a general Impost upon them for filling the purses of some private persons.

And as to the end for which the Parliament is ordained, being only for the advancement of Gods glory, and the establishment and wealth of the King and his people: It is no place then for particular men to utter there their private conceipts, nor for satisfaction of their curiosities, and least of all to make shew of their eloquence, by tyning the time with long studyed and eloquent Orations. No, the reverence of GOD, their King, and their Countrey being well setled in their hearts, will make them ashamed of such toyes, and remember that they are there as sworn Councellors to their King, to give their best advice for the furtherance of his Service, and the flourishing Weale of his Estate.

And lastly, if you will rightly consider the means and wayes how to bring all your labors to a good end, you must remember, That you are here assembled by your lawful King to give him your best advices, in the matters proposed by by him unto you, being of that nature, which I have already told, wherein you are gravely to deliberate, and upon your consciences plainly to determine how far those things propounded do agree with the Weale, both of your King, and of your Country, whose weales cannot be separated. And as for my self, the world shall ever bear me witness, That I never shall propone any thing unto you, which shall not as well tend to the Weale publick, as to any benefit for me: So shall I never oppone my self to that, which may tend to the good of the Common-wealth, for the which I am ordained, as I have often said. And as you are to give your advice in such things, as shall by your King be proposed: So is it on your part your duties to propone any thing that you can, after mature deliberation judge to be needful, either for these ends already spoken of, or otherwise for the discovery of any latent evil in the Kingdom, which peradventure may not have come to the Kings eare....

In conclusion then, since you are to break up, for the Reasons I have already told you, I wish such of you as have any charges in your Countreys, to hasten you home for the repressing of the insolencies of these Rebels, and apprehension of their persons, wherein, as I heartily pray to the Almighty for your prosperous success: So do I not doubt, but we shall shortly hear the good newes of the same; And that you shall have an happy return, and meeting here to all our comforts.

Appendix B

Extracts from the King's Book

Author's notes:

1. The actual *King's Book* is an exceedingly lengthy tome. Although this is an abridged version it is still quite long, but it is more interesting than it might at first appear, and towards the end there is a fascinating partial transcript of the trial of Father Garnet. Among other material I have cut some of the legal and religious polemic and most of the passages in Latin, along with any parts which have already been quoted or summarised in the main narrative.

2. There was never anything officially called 'the King's Book' at the time we are dealing with. To some, the speech in Appendix A above constitutes the said document, while to others, including Gerard whose lead I'm following, it is the publication given below. I have also broken up some of the lengthier paragraphs in order to make the whole thing a little more readable.

A DISCOURSE Of the Manner of the Discovery of the Gunpowder-Plot, together with the Examinations and Confessions of some of the most notorious Conspirators 'concern'd in it.

There is a time when no man ought to keep silence. For it hath ever been held as a general rule, and undoubted Maxime, in all well governed Commonwealths, (whether Christian, and so guided by the Divine Light of GOD'S Word; or Ethnick, and so led by the glimmering twilight of Nature) yet howsoever their profession was, upon this ground have they all agreed, That when either their Religion, their King, or their Countrey was in any extreme hazard; no good Countreyman ought then to withhold either his tongue or his hand, according to his calling and faculty, from aiding to repel the Injury, repress the Violence, and avenge the Guilt upon the Authors thereof…

EXTRACTS FROM THE KING'S BOOK

...The King being upon his return from his Hunting exercise at Royston, upon occasion of the drawing near of the Parliament time, which had been twice Prorogued already, partly in regard of the season of the year, and partly of the Term; As the winds are ever stillest immediately before a storm; and as the Sun blenks often hottest to foretell a following shower: So at that time of greatest calm, did this secretly hatched thunder begin to cast forth the first flashes, and flaming lightnings of the approaching tempest. For the Saturday of the week, immediately preceding the King's return, which was upon a Thursday (being but ten days before the Parliament) The Lord Mountegle, Son and Heir to the Lord Morley, being in his own Lodging, ready to goe to supper, at seven of the clock at night, one of his Footmen (whom he had sent of an errand over the street) was met by an unknown man, of a reasonable tall personage, who delivered him a Letter, charging him to put it in my Lord his Masters hands: which my Lord no sooner received, but that having broken it up, and perceiving the same to be of an unknown, and somewhat unlegible hand, and without either Date or Subscription; did call one of his men unto him for helping him to read it. But no sooner did he conceive the strange contents thereof, although he was somewhat perplexed what construction to make of it (as whether of a matter of consequence, as indeed it was, or whether some foolish devised Pasquil, by some of his enemies to scare him from his attendance at the Parliament) yet did he, as a most dutiful and loyal Subject, conclude not to conceal it, whatever might come of it.

[There follows an account of the discussions over the Monteagle letter, which are covered extensively in the relevant chapter. We resume with the arrest of Fawkes.]

At what time it was determined; that the said Lord Chamberlain should, according to his custom and Office, view all the Parliament Houses, both above and below, and consider what likelyhood or appearance of any such danger might possibly be gathered by the sight of them: but yet, as well for staying of idle rumours, as for being the more able to discern any mystery, the nearer that things were in readiness, his journey thither was ordained to be deferred till the afternoon, before the sitting down of the Parliament, which was upon the Munday following. At what time he (according to this conclusion) went to the Parliament house, accompanied with my Lord Mountegle, being in zeal to the Kings service, earnest and curious to see the event of that accident, whereof he had the fortune to be the first discoverer: where having viewed all the lower rooms, he found in the Vault, under the Upper House, great store and Provisions of Billets, Faggots and Coals: And enquiring of Whyneard, Keeper of the Wardrobe, to what use he had put those lower Rooms and Cellars: he told him, That Thomas Percy had hired both the House, and part of the Cellar or Vault under the same, and that the Wood and Coal therein was the said Gentlemans own provision. Whereupon the Lord Chamberlain, casting his eye aside, perceived a fellow standing in a corner there, calling himself the said Percy's man, and keeper of that house for him, but indeed was Guido Fawkes, the owner of that hand, which should have acted that monstrous Tragedy.

The Lord Chamberlain looking upon all things with a heedful indeed, yet in outward appearance with but a careless and rackless eye (as became so wise and diligent a minister) he presently addressed himself to the King in the said Privy Gallery, where in the presence of the Lord Treasurer, the Lord Admiral, the Earls of Worcester, Northampton, and Salisbury, he made his report, what he had seen and observed there: noting, that Mountegle had told him; That he no sooner heard Thomas Percy named to be the possessor of that house, but considering both his backwardness in Religion, and the old dearness in friendship, between himself, and the said Percy, he did greatly suspect the matter, and that the Letter should come from him. The said Lord Chamberlain also told, That he did not wonder a little at the extraordinary great provision of Wood and Coal in that house, where Thomas Percy had so seldom occasion to remain: As likewise it gave him in his mind, that his man looked like a very tall and desperate fellow.

This could not but increase the Kings former apprehension and jealousie: whereupon he insisted (as before) that the House was narrowly to be searched, and that those Billets and Coals should be searched to the bottom, it being most suspitious that they were laid there only for covering of the Powder. Of the same mind also, were all the Counselors then present. But upon the fashion of making of the search, was it long debated: for upon the one side they were all so jealous of the Kings safety, that they all agreed, that there could not be too much caution used for preventing his danger. And yet upon the other part, they were all extream loth and dainty, that in case this Letter should prove to be nothing but the evapouration of an idle brain; then a curious search being made, and nothing found, should not only turn to the general scandal of the King and the State, as being so suspicious of every light and frivilous toy, but likewise lay an ill savoured imputation upon the Earl of Northumberland, one of His Majesties greatest Subjects and Counselors; this Thomas Percy being his kinsman, and most confident familiar. And the rather were they curious upon this point, knowing how far the King detested to be thought suspicious or jealous of any of His good Subjects, though of the meanest degree. And therefore, though they all agreed upon the main ground, which was to provide for the security of the Kings Person, yet did they much differ in the circumstances, by which this action might be best carried with least dinne and occasion of slander. But the King himself still persisting that there were divers shrewd appearances, and that a narrow search of those places could pre-judge no man that was innocent, he at last plainly resolved them, That either must all the parts of those rooms be narrowly searched, and no possibility of danger left unexamined, or else he and they all must resolve not to meddle in it at all, but plainly to go the next day to the Parliament, and leave the success to Fortune, which he believed they would be loth to take upon their consciences: for in such a case as this, an half doing was worse than no doing at all. Whereupon it was at last concluded, That nothing should be left unsearched in those Houses: And yet for the better colour and stay of rumour, in case nothing were found, it was thought meet, that upon a pretence of Whyneards missing some of the Kings stuff or Hangings which he had in keeping, all those rooms should be narrowly ripped for them.

And to this purpose was Sir Thomas Knevet, (a Gentleman of His Majesties Privy Chamber) employed, being a Justice of Peace in Westminster, and one, of whose antient fidelity, both the late Queen, and our now Sovereign have had large proof: who according to the trust committed unto him, went about the midnight next after to the Parliament house, accompanied with such a small number, as was fit for that errand. But before his entry into the house, finding Thomas Percy's alledged man standing without the doors, his Cloaths and Boots on, at so dead a time of the night, he resolved to apprehend him, as he did, and thereafter went forward to the searching of the house, where after he had caused to be overturned some of the Billets and Coals, he first found one of the small Barrels of Powder, and after all the rest, to the number of thirty six Barrels, great and small: And thereafter searching the fellow, whom he had taken, found three Matches, and all other instruments fit for blowing up the Powder, ready upon him, which made him instantly confess his own guiltiness, declaring also unto him, That if he had happened to be within the house when he took him, as he was immediately before (at the ending of his work) he would not have failed to have blown him up, house and all.

Thus after Sir Thomas had caused the wretch to be surely bound, and well guarded, by the company he had brought with him, he himself returned back to the Kings Palace, and gave warning of his succese to the Lord Chamberlain, and Earl of Salisbury, who immediately warning the rest of the Council that lay in the house, as soon as they could get themselves ready, came, with their fellow-Counselors, to the Kings Bed-chamber, being at that time near four of the clock in the morning. And at the first entry of the Kings Chamber door, the Lord Chamberlain; being not any longer able to conceal his joy, for the preventing of so great a danger, told the King in a confused haste, that all was found and discovered, and the Traitor in hands, and fast bound.

Then, Order being first taken for sending for the rest of the Counsel, that lay in the Town, The prisoner himself was brought into the House, where in respect of the strangeness of the accident, no man was stayed from the [...] ight, or speaking with him. And within a while after, the Council did examine him; Who seeming to put on a Roman resolution, did both to the Council, and to every other person that spake with him that day, appear so constant and setled upon his grounds, as we all thought we had found some new Mutius Scaevola, born in England. For notwithstanding the horror of the Fact, the guilt of his conscience, his suddain surprising, the terror which should have been strucken in him, by coming into the presence of so grave a Council, and the restless, and confused questions that every man all that day did vex him with, yet was his countenance so far from being dejected, at he often smiled in scornful manner, not only avowing the Fact, but repenting only, with the said Scaevola, his failing in the execution thereof, whereof (he said) the Devil and not GOD was the Discoverer: answering quickly to every mans objection, scoffing at any idle questions, which were propounded unto him, and jesting with such as he thought had no authority to examine him- All that day could the Counsel get nothing out of him touching his Complices, refusing to answer to any such questions which he thought might discover the Plot, and laying all the blame upon himself; Whereunto he said, he was moved only for Religion and conscience sake, denying the King to be his lawful Sovereign, or the Anointed of GOD in respect he was an Heretick, and giving himself no other name than John Johnson, servant to Thomas Percy.

But the next morning being carried to the Tower he did not there remain above two or three days, being twice or thrice in that space re-examined, and the Rack only offered and shewed unto him, when the masque of his Roman fortitude did visibly begin to wear and slide off his face; And then did he begin to confess part of the truth, and thereafter to open the whole matter, as doth appear by his depositions immediately following.

[There follows the Declaration of Guido Fawkes and Thomas Wintour's Confession, both of which have already been reproduced. The *King's Book* then resumes]:

But here let us leave Fawks in a Lodging fit for such a Guest, and taking time to advise upon his conscience; and turn our selves to that part of History, which concerns the fortune of the rest of his partakers in that abominable Treason...

[The flight into Warwickshire]:

This company, and hellish society thus convened, finding their purpose discovered, and their treachery prevented, did resolve to run a desperate course, and since they could not prevail by so private a Blow, to practise by a publick Rebellion, either to attain to their Intents, or at least to save themselves in the throng of others. And therefore gathering all the company they could unto them and pretending the quarrel of Religion, having intercepted such provision of Armour, Horses, and Powder, as the time could permit, thought by running up and down the Countrey both to augment peece and peece their number (dreaming to themselves that they had the vertue of a Snow-ball, which being little at the first, and tumbling down from a great hill groweth to a great quantity, by encreasing it self with the Snow that it meeteth by the way) and also that they beginning first this brave shew in one part of the Countrey, should by their Sympathy and example stir up and incourage the rest of their Religion in other parts of England to rise, as they had done there. But when they had gathered their Force to the greatest, they came not to the number of Fourscore, and yet were they troubled all the hours of the day to keep and contain their own servants from stealing from them; who (notwithstanding of all their care) dayly left them, being far inferior to Gedeons Hoste in number, but far more in faith, or justness of Quarrel.

And so after that this Gatholique [sic] Troop had wandered a while through Warwick-shire to Worcester-shire, and from thence to the edge and borders of Stafford-shire, this gallantly armed Band had not the honor at the last, to be beaten with a Kings Lieutenant, or extraordinary Commissioner sent down for the purpose, but only by the ordinary Sheriff of Worcester-shire, were they all beaten, killed, taken and dispersed. Wherein ye have to note this following circumstance so admirable, and so vively displaying the greatness of Gods justice, as it could not be concealed without betraying in a manner the glory due to the Almighty for the same.

Although divers of the Kings Proclamations were posted down after these Traitors, with all the speed possible, declaring the odiousness of that bloudy attempt, the necessity to have Percy preserved alive, if it had been possible, and the assembly together of that rightly damned crew, now no more darned Conspirators, but open and avowed Rebels: yet the far distance of the way (which was above an hundred miles) together with the extreme deepness thereof, joyned also with the shortness of the day, was the cause that the hearty and loving affections of the Kings good Subjects in those parts prevented the speed of His Proclamations. For upon the third day after the flying down of these Rebels, which was upon the Friday next after the discovery of their Plot, they were most of them all surprized by the Sheriff of Worcester-shire at Holbeach, about the noon of the day, and that in manner following.

Graunt, of whom I have made mention before for taking the great Horses, who had not all the preceding time stirred from his own house till the next morning after the attempt should have been put in execution, he then laying his account without his Host (as the proverb is) that their Plot had, without failing, received the day before, their hoped for success; took, or rather stole out those horses (as I said before) for enabling him, and so many of that soulless society that had still remained in the Countrey near about him, to make a suddain surprize upon the Kings elder Daughter, the Lady ELIZABETH, having her residence near by that place, whom they thought to have used for the colour of their treacherous designe (His Majesty her Father, her Mother, and male Children being all destroyed above) And to this purpose also [...]ad that Nimrod Digby, provided his hunting match against that same time, that numbers of people being flocked together upon the pretence thereof, they might the easilier have brought to pass the suddain surprize of her Person.

Now the violent taking away of those horses long before day, did seem to be so great a riot in the eyes of the Common people, that knew of no greater Mystery: And the bold attempting thereof, did ingender such a suspition of some following Rebellion in the hearts of the wiser sort, as both great and small began to stirr and arm themselves, upon this unlooked for accident. Among whom, Sir Fulke Grevil the elder, Knight, as became one both so antient in years, and good reputation, and by his Office being Deputy-Lieutenant of Warwick-shire tho unable in his Body, yet by the zeal and true fervency of his mind, did first apprehend this foresaid Riot, to be nothing but the sparkles and sure indices of a following Rebellion; whereupon both stoutly and honestly he took order to get into his own hands, the Munition and Armor of all such Gentlemen about him, as were either absent from their own houses, or in doubtful guard; And also sent such direction to the Towns about him, as thereupon did follow the striking of Winter by a poor Smith, who had likewise been taken by those vulgar people, but that he was rescued by the rest of his company, who perceiving that the Countrey before them, had notice of them, hastened away with the loss in their own sight, Sixteen of their followers being taken by the Townsmen, and sent presently to the Sheriff at Warwick, and from thence to London.

But before Twelve or Sixteen hours past, Catesby, Percy the Winters, Wrights, Rookwood, and the rest, bringing then the assurance, that their main Plot was failed and betrayed, whereupon they had builded the golden Mountains of their glorious hopes: They then took their last desperate resolution to flock together in a Troop and wander, as they did, for the reasons aforetold. But as upon the one part, the zealous duty to their God and their Sovereigne was so deeply imprinted in the hearts of all the meanest and poorest sort of the people (although then knowing of no further mystery than such publick misbehaviours, as their own eyes taught them) as notwithstanding of their fair shews and pretence of their Catholick cause, no creature, Man or Woman through all the Countrey, would once so much as give them willingly a cup of drink, or any sort of comfort or support, but with execrations detested them: So on the other part, the Sheriffs of the Shires, where through they wandred, convening their people with all speed possible, hunted as hotly after them, as the evilness of the way, and the unprovidedness of their people upon that sudden could permit them.

Sir Richard Walsh, Sheriff of Worcester... [did] dutifully and hotly pursue them thorow his Shire; and having gotten sure trial of their taking harbor at the house above named, he did send Trumpeters and Messengers to them, commanding them in the Kings name to render unto him, His Majesties Minister; and knowing no more at that time of their guilt, than was publickly visible, did promise, upon their dutiful and obedient rendring unto him to intercede at the Kings hands, for the sparing of their lives: Who received only from them this scornful answer (they being better witnesses to themselves of their inward evil consciences) That he had need of better assistance, than of those few numbers that were with him, before he could be able to command or controul them.

But here fell the wondrous work of Gods Justice, That while this message passed between the Sheriff and them, The Sheriff's and his people's zeal being justly kindled and augmented by their arrogant answer, and so they preparing themselves to give a furious assault; and the other party making themselves ready within the house to perform their promise by a defence as resolute; It pleased GOD, that in the mending of the fire in their chamber, one small sparkle should flie out, and light among less than two pound weight of Powder, which was drying a little from the chimney; which being thereby blown up, so maimed the faces of some of the principal Rebels, and the hands and sides of others of them (blowing up with it also a great bag full of Powder, which notwithstanding never took fire) as they were not only disabled, and discouraged hereby from any further resistance, in respect

143

Catesby himself, Rookwood, Grant, and divers others of greatest account, among them were thereby made unable for defence: but also wonderfully strucken with amazement in their guilty consciences, calling to memory, how GOD had justly punished them with that same Instrument, which they should have used for the effectuating of so great a sin…as they presently (see the wonderful power of Gods Justice upon guilty consciences) did all fall down upon their knees, praying GOD to pardon them for their bloudy enterprize; And thereafter giving over any further debate, opened the Gate, suffered the Sheriffs people to rush in furiously among them, and desperately sought their own present destruction; The three specials of them joyning backs together, Catesby, Percy, and Winter, whereof two with one shot, Catesby, and Percy were slain, and the third, Winter, taken and saved alive.

And thus these resolute and high aspiring Catholicks, who dreamed of no less than the destruction of Kings and Kingdomes, and promised to themselves no lower estate than the Government of great and antient Monarchies; were miserably defeated, and quite overthrown in an instant, falling in the pit which they had prepared for others; and so fulfilling that sentence which his Majesty did in a manner prophesie of them, In his Oration to the Parliament: some presently slain, others deadly wounded, stripped of their Clothes, left lying miserably naked, and so dying rather of cold, then of the danger of their wounds; and the rest that either were whole, or but lightly hurt, taken and led prisoners by the Sheriff, the ordinary Minister of Justice, to the Gaole, the ordinary place even of the basest Malefactors, where they remained till their sending up to London, being met with a huge confluence of people of all sorts, desirous to see them, as the rarest sort of Monsters; fools to laugh at them, women and children to wonder, all the common people to gaze, the wiser sort to satisfie their curiosity, in seeing the outward cases of so unheard of a villany: and generally all sorts of people, to satiate and fill their eyes with the sight of them, whom in their hearts they so far admired and detested: Serving so for a fearful and publick spectacle of Gods fierce wrath and just indignation.

What hereafter will be done with them, is to be left to the Justice of His Majesty and the State. Which as no good Subject needs to doubt will be performed in the own due time by a publick and an exemplary punishment…

And thus, whereas they thought to have effaced our memories, the memory of them shall remain (but to their Perpetual Infamy) and we (as I said in the beginning) shall, with all thankfulness, eternally preserve the memory of so great a benefit. To which let every good Subject say, AMEN…

That whereas our Sovereign Lord the King had, by the advise and assent of his Council...appointed a Parliament to be holden at his City of Westminister: That Henry Garnet, Superior of the Jesuits within the Realm of England, (called also by the several names of Wally, Darcy, Roberts, Farmer, and Henry Philips) Oswald Tesmond Jesuit, otherwise called Oswald Greenwel; John Gerrard Jesuit, (called also by the several names of Lee and Brook) Robert Winter, Thomas Winter, Gentlemen, Guy Fawkes, Gent. otherwise called Guy Johnson; Robert Keyes Gent. and Thomas Bates Yeoman, late Servant to Robert Catesby Esq. together with the said Robert Catesby and Thomas Piercy, Esquires; John Wright and Christopher Wright, Gent. in open Rebellion and Insurrection against his Majesty, lately slain, and Francis Tresham Esq. lately dead, as false Traitors against our said Sovereign Lord the King, did Traiterously meet and assemble themselves together; and being so met, the said Henry Garnet, Oswald Tesmond, John Gerrard, and other Jesuits, did maliciously, falsly, and traiterously move and perswade as well the said Thomas Winter, Guy Fawkes, Robert Keyes, and Thomas Bates; as the said Robert Catesby, Thomas Percy, John Wright, Christopher Wright, and Francis Tresham; That our said Sovereign Lord the King, the Nobility, Clergy, and the whole Commonalty of the Reof England [sic] (Papists excepted) were Hereticks, and that all Hereticks were accursed and Excommunicate; and that no Heretick could be a King, but that it was lawful and meritorious to kill our said Sovereign Lord the King, and all other Hereticks within this Realm of England, for the advancing and enlargement of the pretended and usurped Authority and Jurisdiction of the Bishop of Rome, and for the restoring of the Superstitious Romish Religion within this Realm of England.

To which Traiterous perswasions, the said Thomas Winter, Guy Fawkes, Robert Keyes, Thomas Bates, Robert Catesby, Thomas Percy, John Wright, Christopher Wright, and Francis Tresham, traiterously did yield their assents: And that thereupon the said Henry Garnet, Oswald Tesmond, John Gerrard, and divers other Jesuits; Thomas Winter, Guy Fawkes, Robert Keys, and Thomas Bates; as also the said Robert Catesby, Thomas Percy, John Wright, Christopher Wright, and Francis Tresham, traiterously among themselves did conclude and agree, with Gun-powder, as it were with one blast, suddenly, traiterously, and barbarously to blow up and tear in pieces our said Sovereign Lord the King, the Excellent, Virtuous, and Gracious Queen Anne his dearest Wife, the most Noble Prince Henry their Eldest Son, the future Hope and Joy of England, and the Lords Spiritual and Temporal...and divers other faithful Subjects and Servants of the King...to be assembled in the House of Parliament...

And further did most traiterously conspire and conclude among themselves, That not onely the whole Royal Issue Male of our said Sovereign Lord the King should be destroyed and rooted out, but that the Persons aforesaid...should surprise [...] Persons of the Noble Ladies, Elizabeth and Mary, Daughters of our said Sovereign Lord the King, and falsly and traiterously should Proclaim said Lady Elizabeth to be the Queen of this Realm of England; and thereupon should publish a certain traiterous Proclamation in the Name of the said Lady Elizabeth, wherein it was especially agreed, by and between the said Conspirators, That no mention should be made at the first of the alteration of Religion established within this Realm of England...

And that the said Thomas Winter [et al] ...by the like traiterous advise and counsel of the said Henry Garnet, John Gerrard, Oswald Tesmond, and other Jesuits...did traiterously amongst them selves conclude and agree, to dig a certain Mine under the said House of Parliament, and there secretly under the said House to bestow and place a great quantity of Gun-powder; and that according to the said traiterous conclusion, the said Thomas Winter [et al] ...afterwards secretly...did dig and make the said Mine unto the midst of the foundation of the wall of the said house of Parliament, the said foundation being of the thickness of three yards, with a traiterous intent to bestow and place a great quantity of Gunpowder in the Mine... and that the said Thomas Winter [et al] ...finding and perceiving the said work to be of great difficulty by reason of the hardness and thickness of the said wall, and understanding a certain Cellar under the said house of Parliament, and adjoyning to a certain house of the said Thomas Percy then to be letten to farm for a yearly Rent, the said Thomas Percy, by the traiterous procurement as well of the said Henry Garnet [et al] traiterously did hire the Cellar aforesaid for a certain yeerly Rent and term; & then those Traitors did remove twenty barrels full of gunpowder out of the said house of the said Thomas Percy, and secretly and traiterously did bestow and place them in the Cellar aforesaid under the said House of Parliament, for the traiterous effecting of the Treason, and traiterous purposes aforesaid.

And that afterwards the said Henry Garnet [et al] traiterously did meet with Robert Winter [et al], ...and did require the said Robert Winter, John Grant, Ambrose Rookwood and Francis Tresham, to joyn themselves as well with the said Henry Garnet, Oswald Tesmond, John Gerrard, Thomas Winter, Guy Fawkes, Robert Keys and Thomas Bates, as with the said Robert Catesby, Thomas Percy, John Wright and Christopher Wright...and traiterously to provide horse, armour, and other necessaries, for the better accomplishment and effecting of the said Treasons; To which traiterous motion and request, the said Robert Winter, John Grant, Ambrose Rookwood and Francis Tresham, did traiterously yield their Assents...

And thereupon several corporal Oathes in form abovesaid Traiterously did take, and the Sacrament of the Eucharist by the hand of the said Jesuits did receive, to such intent and purpose as is aforesaid; And horses, armour, and other necessaries, for the better effecting of the said Treasons, according to their traiterous assents aforesaid traiterously did provide; And that afterwards all the said false Traitors did traiterously provide and bring into the Cellar aforesaid, ten other barrels full of Gunpowder newly bought, fearing least the former Gunpowder so as aforesaid bestowed and placed there, was become Dankish, and the said several quantities of Gunpowder aforesaid, with Billets and Fagots, least they should be spied, secretly and traiterosly did cover;

And that afterwards the said Traitors traiterously provided and brought into the Cellar aforesaid, four Hogsheads full of Gunpowder, and layed divers great Iron Bars, and stones upon the said four Hogsheads, and the [...] other quantities of Gunpowder; And...lest they should be espied, secretly and traiterously did likewise cover; And that the said Guy Fawkes... had prepared, and had upon his person Touchwood and Match, therewith traiterously to give fire to the several Barrels, Hogsheads and quantities of Gunpowder aforesaid, at the time appointed for the execution of the said horrible Treasons; And further, that after the said horrible Treasons were by the great favour and mercy of God in a wonderful manner discovered, not many hours before it should have been executed, as well the said Henry Garnet [et al] did flie and withdraw themselves...to stir up, and procure such Popish persons as they could, to joyn with them in actual, publick and open Rebellion, against our said Sovereign Lord the King, and to that end did publish divers fained and false rumors, that the Papists throats should have been cut: And that thereupon divers Papists were in Arms, and in open publick and Actual Rebellion against our said Sovereign Lord the King, in divers parts of this Realm of England.

To this Indictment, they all pleaded, Not Guilty; and put themselves upon God and the Countrey...

The Proceeding wherein is properly to be divided into three general Heads.
1. First, Matter of Declaration.
2. Secondly, Matter of Aggravation.
3. Thirdly, Matter of Probation.

THE GUNPOWDER PLOT DECEIT

My self am limited to deal onely with the matter of Declaration, and that is
contained within the compass of the Indictment onely.

For the other two, I am to leave to him to whose place it belongeth.

The Substance of which Declaration consisteth in four parts.
1. First, in the Persons and Qualities of the Conspirators.
2. Secondly, in the Matter conspired.
3. Thirdly, in the mean and manner of the proceeding and execution of
   the Conspiracy.
4. And Fourthly, of the end and purpose why it was so conspired.

As concerning the first, being the Persons They were
Garnet,
Jesuits not then taken.
Gerrard, Tesmond,
Thomas Winter

At the Bar.
Guy Fawkes, Robert Keyes, Thomas Bates, Everard Digby, Ambrose
Rookewood, John Graunt, Robert Winter.

Robert Catesby, Slain in Rebellion.
Thomas Piercy, John Wright, Christopher Wright.

Francis Tresham, Lately dead.

All grounded Romanists, and corrupted Scholars of so Irreligious and
Traiterous a School.

As concerning the second, which is the Matter Conspired, it was,
1. First, to deprive the King of his Crown.
2. Secondly, to murder the King, the Queen, and the Prince.
3. Thirdly, to stir Rebellion and Sedition in the Kingdom.
4. Fourthly, to bring a miserable destruction among the Subjects.
5. Fifthly, to change, alter, and subvert the Religion here established.
6. Sixthly, to ruinate the state of the Commonwealth, and to bring in
   Strangers to invade it.

As concerning the third, which is the mean and manner how to compass and
execute the same. They did all conclude,

1. First, that the King and his People (the Papists excepted) were Hereticks.
2. Secondly, that they were all cursed, and Excommunicate by the Pope.
3. Thirdly, that no Heretick could be King.
4. Fourthly, that it was lawful and meritorious to kill and destroy the King, and all the said Hereticks...

That the Parliament being Prorogued till the 7th. of February, they in December made a Mine under the House of Parliament, purposing to place their Powder there: but the Parliament being then further Adjourned till the 3d. of October, they in Lent following hired the Vault, and placed therein twenty barrels of powder. That they took to them Robert Winter, Graunt, and Rookwood, giving them the Oathes and Sacrament as aforesaid, as to provide Munition.

20 July they laid in more ten Barrels of Powder, laying upon them divers great Bars of Iron, and pieces of Timber, and great massie Stones, and covered the same with Fagots, &c.

20 Septemb. they laid in more four Hogsheads of Powder, with other Stones and Bars of Iron thereupon.

4 Novemb. (the Parliament being Prorogued to the 5th.) at eleven a clock at night, Fawkes had prepared (by the procurement of the rest) Touch-wood and Match, to give fire to the Powder the next day...

First, in December, Anno Dom. 1601 do Henry Garnet, Superior of the Jesuits in England; Robert Tesmond, Jesuit; Robert Catesby, who was together with Francis Tresham, and others...employ Thomas Winter into Spain, as for the general good of the Romish Catholick cause: And by him doth Garnet write his Letters to Father Creswel, Jesuit, residing in Spain, in that behalf. With Thomas Winter doth Tesmond, alias Greeneway the Jesuit go, as an Associate and Confederate in that Conspiracy. The Message (which was principally committed unto the said Winter) was, that he should make a proposition and request to the King of Spain, in the behalf and names of the English Catholicks, that the King would send an Army hither into England, and that the Forces of the Catholicks in England should be prepared to joyn with him, and do him service...

And because that in all attempts upon England, the greatest difficulty was ever found to be the transportation of Horses; the Catholicks in England would assure the King of Spain, to have always in readiness for his use and service 1500 or 2000 Horses, against any occasion or enterprise. Now Thomas Winter undertaking this Negotiation, and with Tesmond the Jesuit coming into Spain, by means of Father Creswel the Legier Jesuit there, as hath been said, had readily speech with Don Pedro Francesa, second Secretary of State, to whom he imparted his Message, as also to the Duke of Lerma; who assured him, that it would be an office very grateful to his Master, and that it should not want his best furtherance.

Now there being at that time Hostility betwixt both Kingdoms, the King of Spain willingly embraced the motion, saying, That he took the message from the Catholicks very kindly, and that in all things he would respect them with as great care as his proper Castilians. But for his further Answer, and full dispatch, Thomas Winter was appointed to attend the Progress. In the end whereof, being in Summer-time, Count Miranda gave him this Answer in the behalf of his Master, That the King would bestow a hundred thousand Crowns to that use, half to be paid that year, and the rest the next Spring following. And withall required, that we should be as good as our promise; for the next Spring he meant to be with us, and set foot in England. And lastly, he desired on the Kings behalf of Winter, that he might have certain advertisement and intelligence, if so it should in the mean time happen that the Queen did die. Thomas Winter, laden with these hopes, returns into England about a month before Christmas, and delivered answer of all that had passed to Henry Garnet, Robert Catesby, and Francis Tresham. But soon after Set that Glorious Light, her Majesty died.

Presently after whose death was Christopher Wright, another Messenger, sent over into Spain by Garnet…Catesby and Tresham, in the name and behalf of all the Romish Catholicks in England, as well to carry news of her Majesties death, as also to continue the aforesaid Negotiation for an Invasion and Pensions… And in the Spanish Court, about two moneths after his arrival there, doth Christopher Wright meet with Guy Fawkes, who upon the two and twentieth of June was employed out of Flanders from Bruxels, by Sir William Stanley, Hugh Owen, (whose finger had been in every Treason which hath been of late years detected) and Baldwyn the Leger Jesuit in Flanders; from whom likewise the said Fawkes carried Letters to Creswel in Spain, for the countenancing and furtherance of his affairs.

Now the end of Fawkes his employment […] to give advertisement to the King of how the King of England was like to proceed rigorously with the Catholicks, and to run the same course which the late Queen did; and withall to entreat that it would please him to send an Army into England to Milford Haven where the Romish Catholicks would be ready to assist him, and then the Forces that should be transported in Spinola's Gallies, should be landed where they could most conveniently. And these their several messages did Christopher Wright and Guy Fawkes in the end intimate and propound to the King of Spain. But the King as then very honorably answered them both, that he would not in any wise further listen to any such motion, as having before dispatched an Ambassage into England to Treat concerning peace; Therefore this course by forreign forces fayling, they fell to the Powder plot, Catesby and Tresham being in at all, in the Treason of the Earl of Essex, in the Treason of Watson and Clarke, Seminary Priests, and also in this of the Jesuits, Such a greedy appetite had they to practise against the State...

...true it is they were Gentlemen of good houses, of excellent parts, howsoever most perniciously seduced, abused, corrupted, and Jesuited, of very competent fortunes and States; Besides that Percy was of the house of Northumberland, Sir William Stanley, who principally imployed Fawkes into Spain, and Iohn Talbot of Grafton, who at the least is in case of misprision of High Treason, both of great and honorable families...

Concerning Thomas Bates, who was Catesby's man, as he was wound into this Treason by his Master, so was he resolved, when he doubted of the lawfulness thereof, by the Doctrine of the Jesuits. For the manner, it was after this sort; Catesby noting that his man observed him extraordinarily, as suspecting somewhat of that which he the said Catesby went about, called him to him at his Lodging in Puddle-Wharf, and in the presence of Thomas Winter, asked him what he thought the business was they went about, for that he of late had so suspiciously and strangely mark'd them. Then did they make the said Bates take an Oath... Then they also told him that he was to receive the Sacrament for the more assurance, and thereupon he went to Confession to the said Tesmond the Jesuit; and in his Confession told him, that he was to conceal a very dangerous piece of work, that his Master Catesby and Thomas Winter had imparted unto him, and said he much feared the matter to be utterly unlawful, and therefore therein desired the counsel of the Jesuit, and revealed unto him the whole intent and purpose of blowing up the Parliament-House upon the first day of the Assembly... But the Jesuit being a Confederate therein before, resolved and encouraged him in the Action, and said that he should be secret in that which his Master had imparted unto him, for that it was for a good cause. Adding moreover, that it was not dangerous unto him, nor any offence to conceal it: And thereupon the Jesuit gave him Absolution, and Bates received the Sacrament of him, in the company of his Master Robert Catesby, and Thomas Winter...

The last Consideration is, concerning the admirable discovery of this Treason, which was by one of themselves, who had taken the Oath and Sacrament, as hath been said, against his own will: The means was, by a dark and doubtful Letter sent to my Lord Mountegle. And thus much as touching the Considerations; the Observations follow, to be considered in this Powder-Treason, and are briefly thus.

1. If the Cellar had not been hired, the Mine-work could hardly or not at all have been discovered; for the Mine was neither found, nor suspected, until the danger was past, and the Capital Offenders apprehended, and by themselves, upon Examination, confessed.

2. How the King was Divinely illuminated by Almighty God, the only Ruler of Princes, like an Angel of God, to direct and point as it were to the very place, to cause a search to be made there, out of those dark words of the Letter concerning a terrible Blow.

3. Observe a miraculous accident which befel in Stephen Littleton's house, called Holbach in Staffordshire, after they had been two days in open Rebellion, immediately before the apprehension of these Traitors: For some of them standing by the fire-side, and having set 2l. and di. of Powder to drie in a Platter before the fire, and under-set the said Platter with a great linen bag, full of other Powder, containing some fifteen or sixteen pounds; it so fell out, that one coming to put more wood into the fire, and casting it on, there flew a coal into the Platter, by reason whereof, the Powder taking fire and blowing up, scorched those who were nearest, as Catesby, Graunt, and Rookewood, blew up the roof of the house, and the linnen bag which was set under the Platter being therewith suddenly carried out through the Breach, fell down in the Court-yard whole and unfired; which if it had took fire in the room, would have slain them all there, so that they never should have come to this Trial…

Then was Sir Everard Digby Arraigned… being advertised, that he must first plead to the Indictment directly, either Guilty, or Not Guilty, and that afterwards he should be licensed to speak his pleasure, he forthwith confessed the Treason contained in the Indictment, and so fell into a Speech, whereof there were two parts, viz. Motives and Petitions. The first Motive which drew him into this action, was not ambition, nor discontentment of his estate, neither malice to any in Parliament, but the friendship and love he bare to Catesby, which prevailed so much, and was so powerful with him, as that for his sake he was ever contented and ready to hazard himself and his Estate.

His Petitions were, That sithens his offence was confined and contained within himself, that the punishment also of the same might extend onely to himself, and not be transferred either to his Wife, Children, Sisters, or others: and therefore for his Wife he humbly craved, that she might enjoy her Joynture, his Son the benefit of an Entail made long before any thought of this action; his Sisters, their just and due Portions which were in his hands; his Creditors, their rightful Debts; which that he might more justly set down under his hand, he requested, that before his death, his Man (who was better acquainted both with the men, and the particulars, than himself) might be licensed to come unto him...

To this Speech forthwith answered Sir Edw. Coke, Attorney General, but in respect of the time (for it grew now dark) very briefly. 1. For his friendship with Catesby, that it was mere folly, and wicked Conspiracy. 2. His Religion, Error, and Heresie. 3. His promises, idle and vain presumptions: As also his fears, false alarms. Concerning Wives that were Recusants, if they were known so to be before their Husbands (though they were good Protestants) took them, and yet for outward and worldly respects whatsoever, any would match with such, great reason there is, that he or they should pay for it, as knowing the penalty and burthen before... No man receives injury in that, to which he willingly and knowingly agreeth and consenteth. But if she were no Recusant at the time of Marriage, and yet afterwards he suffer her to be corrupted and seduced, by admitting Priests and Romanists into his house, good reason likewise that he, be he Papist or Protestant, should pay for his negligence and misgovernment.

4. Concerning the Petitions for Wife, for Children, for Sisters, &c. O how he doth now put on the bowels of Nature and Compassion in the peril of his private and domestical estate! But before, when the publick state of his Countrey, when the King, the Queen, the tender Princes, the Nobles, the whole Kingdom, were designed to a perpetual destruction, Where was then this piety, this Religious affection, this care? All Nature, all Humanity, all respect of Laws both Divine and Humane, were quite abandoned; then was there no conscience made to extirpate the whole Nation, and all for a pretended zeal to the Catholick Religion, and the justification of so detestable and damnable a Fact.

Here did Sir Everard Digby interrupt Mr. Attorney, and said, that he did not justifie the fact, but confessed, that he deserved the vilest death, and most severe punishment that might be; but he was an humble Petitioner for mercy, and some moderation of Justice. Whereupon Mr. Attorney repli'd, that he should not look by the King to be honoured in the manner of his death, having so far abandoned all Religion and Humanity in his Action; but that he was rather to admire the great moderation and mercy of the King, in that, for so exorbitant a crime, no new torture answerable thereunto was devised to be inflicted upon him. And for his Wife and Children, whereas he said, that for the Catholik Cause he was content to neglect the ruine of himself, his Wife, his Estate, and all; he should have his desire as 'tis in the Psalm, Let his Wife be a widow, and his Children vagabonds; let his posterity be destroyed, and in the next generation let his name be quite put out. For the paying of your Creditors, it is equal and just, but yet fit the King be first satisfied and paid, to whom you owe so much, as that all you have is too little: yet these things must be left to the pleasure of his Majesty, and the course of Justice and Law…

Then spake the Earl of Salisbury, especially to that point of his Majesties breaking of promise with Recusants, which was used and urged by Sir Everard Digby, as a motive to draw him to participate in this so hideous a Treason: Wherein his Lordship, after acknowledgment, that Sir Everard Digby was his Ally; And having made a zealous and Religious protestation, concerning the sincerity and truth of that which he would deliver; shortly and clearly defended the honour of the King herein, and freed his Majesty from all imputation and scandal of Irresolution in Religion, and in the constant and perpetual maintaining thereof; as also from having at any time given the least hope, much less promise of Toleration. To which purpose he declared, how his Majesty, as well before his coming to this Crown, as at that very time, and always since, was so far from making of promise, or giving hope of Toleration, that he ever professed he should not endure the very motion thereof from any.

And here his Lordship shewed what was done at Hampton-Court at the time of Watson's Treason, where some of the greater Recusants were convented; and being found then not to have their fingers in Treason, were sent away again with encouragement to persist in their dutiful carriage, and with promise onely of thus much favour, That those mean profits which had occurred since the Kings time to his Majesty for their Recusancy, should be forgiven to the principal Gentlemen, who had both at his Entry shewed so much Loyalty, and had kept themselves so free since from all Conspiracies.

Then did his Lordship also (the rather to shew how little truth Sir Everard Digby's words did carry in any thing which he had spoken) plainly prove, That all his protestations, wherein he denied so constantly to be privy to the Plot of Powder, were utterly false, by the testimony of Fawkes (there present at the Bar) who had confessed, That certain moneths before that Session, the said Fawkes being with Digby at his house in the Countrey, about what time there had fallen much wet; Digby taking Fawkes aside after Supper, told him, That he was much afraid that the Powder in the Cellar was grown dank, and that some new must be provided, lest that should not take fire.

Next, the said Earl did justly and greatly commend the Lord Mounteagle, for his Loyal and honourable care of his Prince and Countrey, in the speedy bringing forth of the Letter sent unto him, wherein he said, That he had shewed both his discretion and fidelity. Which Speech being ended, Digby then acknowledged, That he spake not that of the breach of promise out of his own knowledge, but from their Relation whom he trusted, and namely from Sir Tho. Tresham.

Now were the Jury returned, who having returned their Verdict, whereby they joyntly found those seven Prisoners, Arraigned upon the former Indictment, Guilty, Serjeant Philips craved Judgment against those Seven upon their Conviction; and against Sir Everard Digby upon his own Confusion...

Then the Lord Chief Justice of England, after a grave and prudent Relation and Defence of the Laws made by Queen Elizabeth against Recusants, Priests, and Receivers of Priests, together with the several occasions, progresses, and reasons of the same; and having plainly demonstrated and proved, that they were all necessary, mild, equal, moderate, and to be justified to all the world, pronounced Judgment...

And so according to the Sentence, on Thursday following, execution was done upon Sir Everard Digby, Robert Winter, John Graunt, and Thomas Bates, at the West end of Pauls Church; and on the Friday following, upon Thomas Winter, Ambrose Rookwood, Robert Keyes, and Guy Fawkes, within the old Palace-yard at Westminst. not far from the Parliament-house.

THE ARRAIGNMENT OF HENRY GARNET, Superiour of the Jesuits in England, on Friday the 28th day of March, 1606. at Guild-hall in the City of London, before the Lords Commissioners there present:
Sir Leonard Holiday, Lord Mayor.
The Earl of Nottingham.
The Earl of Suffolk.
The Earl of Worcester.
The Earl of Northampton.
The Earl of Salisbury.
The Lord Chief Justice of England.
The Lord Chief Baron of the Exchequer.

Sir Christopher Yelverton, Knight, one of His Majesties Justices of the Kings Bench...

by Sir John Croke Knight, his Majesties Serjant at Law...shewed that Henry Garnet of the profession of the Jesuits, otherwise Walley, otherwise Darcy, otherwise Roberts, otherwise Farmer, otherwise Philips (for by all those names he called himself) stood indicted of the most barbarous and damnable Treasons, the like whereof were never heard of, that he was a man... of many names, as appeared by the Indictment, but of no good Name; adorned by God and nature with many gifts and graces, if the Grace of God had been joyned with them; But that wanting...

That this Garnet...together with Catesby, lately slain in open Rebellion, and with Oswald Tesmond a Jesuit, otherwise Oswald Greenwell... traiterously did conspire and compass, To depose the King, and to deprive him of his Government.

To destroy and kill the King, and the noble Prince Henry his eldest Son: Such a King, and such a Prince, Such a Son of Such a Father, whose vertues are rather with amazed silence to be wondred at, than able by any speech to be expressed.

To stir sedition and slaughter throughout the Kingdom.

To subvert the true Religion of God, and whole Government of the Kingdom.

To overthrow the whole State of the Common wealth.

The manner how to perform these horrible treasons, the Serjeant said... his lips did tremble to speak it, but his heart praised God for his mighty deliverance. The practise so inhumane, so barbarous, so damnable, so detestable, as the like was never read nor heard of, or ever entred into the heart of the most wicked man to imagine....

This Garnet, together with Catesby and Tesmond, had speech and conference together of these treasons, and concluded most traiterously, and devilishly...

Catesby, Winter, Fawkes, with many other Traitors lately attainted of high treason, would blow up with Gun-powder in the Parliament house...And for that purpose great quantity of Gun-powder was traiterously and secretly placed, and hid by these Conspirators under the Parliament house.

This being the substance and the effect of the Indictment, Garnet did plead Not guilty to it: and a very discreet and substantial Jury, with allowance of challenges unto the prisoner, were sworn at the Bar for the trial of him. To whom the Serjeant shewed that they should have evidences to prove him guilty...They should have...Witnesses and Testimonies of the things themselves... That every one may say unto him...thou wicked subject, thou wicked servant... Of thine own mouth I judge thee, of thine own mouth I condemn thee....

The effect of that which Sir Edward Coke, Knight, His Majesties Attorney General, said at the Arraignment of Henry Garnet, Superiour of the Jesuits in England, as near to his own words as the same could be taken.

Your Lordships may perceive by the parts of the Indictment...that this is but a latter Act of that heavy and woful Tragedy, which is commonly called the Powder-treason, wherein some have already played their parts, and, according to their demerits, suffered condign punishment and pains of death. We are now to proceed against this Prisoner for the same Treason...

...there was a particular Apology spread abroad for this man, and another general for all Jesuits and Priests, together with this imputation, That King-killing, and Queen-killing was not indeed a Doctrine of theirs, but onely a Fiction and Policy of our State, thereby to make the Popish Religion to be despised, and in disgrace. Now for these men, pity it were, that the eye of their understanding should not be enlightned and cleared, that so being by demonstrative and luculent proofs convinced, they may be to their Prince and Countrey truly converted...

Concerning their Apologies, and the Fictions of State (as they term them) answer shall be made, by Gods grace, in the proper place, when I come to lay open the plots and practises of the Jesuits, to the satisfaction of all this Honourable and Great Assembly...

The coming of this Garnet into England, (which very act was a Treason) was about twenty years past, viz. in July, 1586 in the 28th. year of the Reign of the late Queen of famous and blessed memory; whereas the year before, namely the 27th. year of Eliz. there was a Statute made, whereby it was Treason for any, who was made a Romish Priest by any Authority from the Sea of Rome, sithens the first year of her Reign, to come into her Dominions. Which Statute the Romanists calumniate as a bloody, cruel, unjust, and a new upstart Law... But indeed it is both mild, merciful, and just, and grounded upon the ancient fundamental Laws of England. For...before the Bull of Impious Pius Quintus, in the 11th. year of the Queen, wherein her Majesty was Excommunicated and Deposed, and all they accursed who should yield any obedience unto her, &c. there were no Recusants in England, all came to Church, (howsoever Popishly inclined, or persuaded in most points) to the same Divine Service we now use: but thereupon presently they refused to assemble in our Churches, or joyn with us in publick Service, not for conscience of any thing there done, against which they might justly except out of the Word of God, but because the Pope had Excommunicated and Deposed her Majesty, and cursed those who should obey her: and so upon this Bull ensued open Rebellion in the North... But see the event: Now most miserable in respect of this Bull was the state of Romish Recusants, for either they must be hanged for Treason, in resisting their lawful Sovereign, or cursed for yielding the due obedience unto her Majesty... And therefore of this Pope it was said by some of his own favourits, that he was...A holy and a learned man, but over credulous; for that he was informed and believed, that the strength of the Catholicks in England was such, as was able to have resisted the Queen. But when the Bull was found to take such an effect, then was there a Dispensation given, both by Pius Quintus himself, and Gregory the 13th. That all Catholicks here might shew their outward obedience to the Queen... that is to say, They might grow into strength, until they were able to give the Queen a Mate, that the publick execution of the said Bull might take place. And all this was confessed by Garnet under his own hand, and now again openly confessed at the Bar....

But to proceed. In the 28th. year of Queen Elizabeth...came Garnet into England, breaking through the Wall of Treason... And this was at that time, when the great Armado of Spain, which the Pope blessed and Christened by the name of, The Invincible Navy... The Purveyors and Fore-runners of this Navy and Invasion, were the Jesuits, and Garnet among them, being a Traitor even in his very entrance and footing in the Land. But the Queen, with her own Ships, and her own Subjects, did beat this Armado, God himself (whose cause indeed it was) fighting for us against them, by Fire, and Seas, and Winds, and Rocks, and Tempests, scattering all, and destroying most of them...

Note here, that sithence the Jesuits set foot in this Land, there never passed four years without a most pestilent and pernicious Treason, tending to the subversion of the whole State. After that hostile Invasion in 88. the Jesuits fell again to secret and treasonable practises; for then, in the year 92, came Patrick Cullen, who was incited by Sir William Stanley, Hugh Owen, Jaques Fraunces, and Holt the Jesuit, and resolved by the said Holt to kill the Queen; to which purpose he received Absolution, and then the Sacrament at the hands of the said Jesuit, together with this ghostly counsel, That it was both lawful and meritorious to kill her...

[Cecil now runs through a list of further alleged Jesuit plots to assassinate Elizabeth]

All these Treasons were freely and voluntarily confessed by the parties themselves, under their own hands, and yet remain extant to be seen.

In the year 1601 when practises failed, then was Force again attempted; For then...was Thomas Winter imployed to the King of Spain, together with Tesmond the Jesuit, by this Garnet, who wrote his Letters to Arthur alias Joseph Creswell, (the only man whom I have heard of to change his Christian name) the legier Jesuit in Spain, for the furtherance of that negotiation...to offer the services of the English Catholicks to the King, and to deal further concerning an Invasion, with promise from the Catholicks here, of forces, both of men and horses, to be in a readiness to joyn with him. This negotiation by the means of Creswel, to whom Garnet wrote, took such effect, that the two kingdoms standing then in hostlity, the proposition of the English Romish Catholicks was accepted and entertained, an army to Invade...promised, and 100000 Crowns to be distributed amongst Romanists and discontented persons, making of a party in England, and for the furtherance of the said service granted...

Now for the time observe, that these Bulls or Briefs came upon the aforesaid Negociation of Thomas Winter into Spain, at what time an Army should shortly after have been sent to invade the Land: and this was to be put in execution... Whensoever it should happen, that that miserable Woman (for so it pleased the High Priest of Rome to call Great Queen Elizabeth) should depart this life.

And now sithence the coming of great King Iames, there have not passed, I will not say four years, but not four, nay, not two months, without some Treason. First, in March 1603. upon the death of her Majesty, and before they had seen his Majesties face, was Christopher Wright employed into Spain by Garnet, Catesby, and Tresham, to give advertisement of the Queens death, and to continue the former Negotiation of Thomas Winter. And by him also doth this Garnet write to Creswel the Jesuit in commendation, and for assistance and furtherance of his business.

As also in the 22d. of June following, was Guy Fawkes sent out of Flanders, by Baldwin the Jesuit, by Sir William Stanley, and Hugh Owen, about the same Treason... In the same June doth Garnet the Superiour, together with Gerrard and other Jesuits, and Jesuited Catholicks, labour, not onely in providing of Horses, which, by Thomas Winter and Christopher Wright... had promised the King of Spain to assist and do him service withall, at such time as the said King should send Forces to invade...

In March, 1603, Garnet and Catesby (a pestilent Traitor) confer together, and Catesby...telleth him, (though most falsly) that the King had broken promise with the Catholicks, and therefore assuredly there would be stirs in England before it were long. In September following meets Catesby and Thomas Piercy, and after an unjust, but a grievous complaint made by Catesby of the Kings proceedings... Piercy presently breaks forth into this devilish speech, That there was no way but to kill the King, which he the said Piercy would undertake to do. But Catesby, as being...a cunning, a wily, and a deep Traitor, intending to use this so furious and fiery a Spirit to a further purpose, doth, as it were, stroke him for his great forwardness; yet with sage and stayed counsel tells him, No, Tom, thou shalt not adventure thy self to so small purpose; If thou wilt be a Traitor, there is a Plot to greater advantage, and such a one as can never be discovered, viz. the Powder-Treason.

In January, in the first year of his Majesty, Garnet took out a General Pardon under the Great Seal of England, of all Treasons, which Pardon, his Majesty, of his Grace, granted to all men at his first entrance into his Kingdom... But Catesby fearing lest any of those whom he had or should take into Confederacy, being touched in Conscience with the horrour of so damnable a fact, might give it over, and endanger the discovery of the Plot, seeks to Garnet (as being the Superiour of the Jesuits, and therefore of high estimation and authority amongst all those of the Romish Religion) to have his judgment and resolution in Conscience, concerning the lawfulness of the fact, that thereby he might be able to give satisfaction to any who should in that behalf make doubt or scruple to go forward in that Treason. And therefore Catesby coming to Garnet, propoundeth unto him the Case, and asketh whether for the good and promotion of the Catholick cause against Hereticks... it be lawful or not, amongst many Nocents, to destroy and take away some Innocents also. To this question Garnet advisedly and resolvedly answered, That if the advantage were greater to the Catholick part by taking away some Innocents together with many Nocents, then doubtless it should be lawful to kill and destroy them all: And to this purpose he alledged a comparison of a Town or City which was possessed by an Enemy, If at the time of taking thereof there happen to be some few friends within the place, they must undergo the fortune of the Wars in the general and common destruction of the Enemy.

And this resolution of Garnet the Superior of the Jesuits, was the strongest, and the onely bond, whereby Catesby afterwards kept and retained all the Traitors in that so abominable and detestable a Confederacy. For in March following, Catesby, Thomas Winter, and others, resolve upon the

Powder-plot, and Fawkes, as being a man unknown, and withall a desperate person, and a Soldier, was resolved upon, as fit for the executing thereof; to which purpose he was, in April following, by Thomas Winter sought and fetched out of Flanders into England. In May, in the second year of his Majesty, Catesby, Percy, Iohn Wright, Thomas Winter, and Fawkes meet, and having upon the holy Evangelists taken an Oath of secresie and constancy to this effect;

You shall swear by the blessed Trinity, and by the Sacrament you now purpose to receive, never to disclose, directly or indirectly, by word or circumstance, the matter that shall be proposed to you to keep secret, nor desist from the execution thereof, until the rest shall give you leave.

They all were Confessed, had Absolution, and received thereupon the Sacrament, by the hands of Gerrard the Jesuit then present.

In June following Catesby and Greenwel the Jesuit confer about the Powder-treason. And at Midsummer Catesby having speach with Garnet of the Powder-treason; they said that it was so secret, as that it must prevail, before it could be discovered...

Upon the 7th. of July 1604, was the Parliament Prorogued untill the 7th. of February; and in November following, Thomas Bates, being... fetched in by Catesby his master, to participate in the Powder-treason, for better assurance of his secrecy, and prosecution thereof, is by Greenwel the Jesuit confessed, encouraged and told, that being for a good cause, he might and ought not onely conceal it, as committed unto him in secret by his master, but further said, that it was no offence at all, but justifiable and good. About this time was Robert Keyes taken into the Confederacy, and by Catesby resolved of the lawfulness thereof from the Jesuits.

In the 11th. of December they entred the Mine: and in March following, which was in 1605, was Guy Fawks sent over to Sir William Stanley with letters from Garnet, to Baldwine the Legier Jesuit there, to take order that against the time of the Blow, the forces might be brought near to the Sea side, to the end that they might suddenly be transported into England. And there doth Fawkes by consent of the confederates, give Owen the Oath of secrecy and perseverance, and then acquaints him with the whole Treason: Who having been a most malicious and inveterate Traitor, greatly applauded it, and gave his consent and counsel for the furtherance thereof...

In June following doth Greenwel the Jesuit consult with Garnet his Superior, of the whole course of the Powder-treason at large. Wherein observe the politique and subtil dealing of this Garnet. First he would not... confer of it with a lay man (other than Catesby whom he so much trusted) why so? because that might derogate from the reverence of his Place, That a Jesuit, and a Superior of them, should openly joyn with Laymen in cause of so much bloud; And therefore secondly, as he would consult of it with a Priest, and a Jesuit, one of his own order and his subject; so for his further security, he would consult thereof with Greenwel the Jesuit, as in a disguised confession. And…he at large discoursed with him of the whole Plot of the Powder-treason; And that a Protector (after the Blow given) should be chosen out of such of the Nobility as should be warned and reserved.

In this Moneth likewise was there a great conference and consultation betwixt Garnet; Catesby, and Francis Tresham, concerning the strength of the Catholicks in England, to the end that Garnet might by Letters send direct Advertisement thereof to the Pope; for that his Holiness would not be brought to shew his inclination concerning any Commotion or rising of the Catholick part, until such time as he should be certainly informed that they had sufficient and able Force to prevail.

In this Moneth also [August] doth Garnet write to Baldwine the Legier Jesuit in the Low-Countreys, in the behalf of Catesby, that Owen should move the Marquess for a Regiment of horses for him the said Catesby, not with any intent, as it was agreed, that Catesby should undertake any such charge, but that under colour of it, horses and other necessaries might be provided without suspition to furnish the Traitors.

In September following doth Parsons the Jesuit write to Garnet, to know the particulars of the Project in hand, for the journey to Saint Winifrides Well in this Moneth. It was but a Jergon, to have better opportunity by colour thereof, to confer and retire themselves to those parts.

In October doth Garnet meet the other Traytors at Coughton in Warwickshire, which was the place of Rendevouz, whither they resorted out of all Countreys.

Upon the [...]st of November, Garnet openly prayeth for the good success of the great Action, concerning the Catholick cause in the beginning of the Parliament; and prayer is more than consent...

Now was the Letter with the Lord Mountegle, whose memory shall be blessed, on the fourth of November, by the providence of the Almighty, not many hours before the Treason should have been executed, was it fully discovered.

On the 5th of November, being the time when the Traitors expected that their devilish practise should have taken effect, they convented at Dunchurch under colour of a great hunting match, appointed by Sir Everard Digby, as being a man of quality and accompt thereabout, purposing by this means to furnish themselves with company for their intended Insurrection and Rebellion; for that men being gathered together, and a tumult suddenly raised, the Traitors thought, that every or most of them would follow the present fortune, and be easily persuaded to take part with them, and that they might easily surprise the person of the Lady Elisabeth, then being in those parts, in the Lord Harringtons house.

Upon the 6th of November, early in the Morning, Catesby and the said Confederates dispatched Thomas Bates with a Letter to Garnet...earnestly intreating his help and assistance, for the raising of Wales, and putting so many as he could into open Rebellion. At what time Garnet, and Greenwell (who then of purpose was there with Garnet,) then certainly perceiving that the Plot was indeed discovered, and knowing themselves to be the chiefest Authors thereof, prophesied the overthrow of the whole order of the Jesuits, saying... But Greenwel the Jesuit being carried with a more violent and firy spirit, posteth up and down, to incite such as he could to rise up in open Rebellion. And meeting in Master Abingtons house with Hall another Jesuit, adviseth him the said Hall likewise to loose no time, but forthwith to seek to raise and stir up so many as he could...

Observe here a double consequent of this Powder-treason: 1. Open Rebellion... Garnet...for he having liberty in the Tower to write, and sending a Letter (which Letter was openly shewed in the Court before him) to an acquaintance of his in the Gatehouse, there was nothing therein to be seen but ordinary matter, and for certain necessaries: but in the Margent, which he made very great and spacious, and underneath where there remained clean paper, he wrote cunningly with the Juice of an Orange, or of a Lemmon, to publish his Innocency, and concerning his usage, and there denieth those things which before he had freely and voluntarily confessed, and said, that for the Spanish Treason, he was freed by his Majesties Pardon, and as for the Powder-treason, he hoped for want of proof against him, to avoid that well enough...

The Circumstances concurring, are concerning the Persons offending and offended. For the principal Person offending here at the Bar, he is, as you have heard, a man of many names, Garnet, Wallye, Darcy, Roberts, Farmer, Phillips: and surely I have not commonly known or observed a true man, that hath had so many false Appellations. He is by Countrey an Englishman, by Birth a Gentleman, by Education a Scholar, afterwards a Corrector of the Common Law Print, with Mr Tottle the Printer, and now is to be corrected by the Law. He hath many Gifts and Endowments of Nature, by Art Learned, a good Linguist, and by Profession a Jesuit, and a Superior, as indeed he is Superior to all his Predecessors in devillish Treason; a Doctor of Jesuits, that is, a Doctor of five Dd. as, Dissimulation, Deposing of Princes, Disposing of Kingdoms, Daunting and deterring of Subjects, and Destruction…

But note the heavy and wofull fruit of this Doctrine of Equivocation. Francis Tresham being near his natural death in the Tower, had of charity his wife permitted…to come unto him: who understanding that her husband had before directly and truly accused Garnet of the Spanish Treason, least belike her husband should depart this life, with a conscience that he had revealed any thing concerning the Superior of the Jesuits, a very little before he died, drew him to this, that his own hand being so feeble as that he could not write himself, yet he caused his servant then attending on him, to write that which he did dictate, and therein protested upon his salvation, that he had not seen the said Garnet of 16 years before, and thereupon prayed that his former confession to the contrary might in no wise take place. And that this paper of his Retractation which he had weakly, and dyingly subscribed, might after his death be delivered to the Earl of Salisbury: Whereas Master Garnet himself hath clearly confessed the Spanish Treason, and now acknowledged the same at the Bar; and he and Mistress Vaux and others directly confess and say, that Garnet and Tresham had within two years space been very often together, and also many times before… And Garnet himself being at the Bar afterwards, urged to say what he thought of such the departure of Francis Tresham out of this life, answered only this, I think he meant to Equivocate. Thus were they stayned with their own works, and went a whoring with their own Inventions…

Then were repeated the proofs for every of the particular accusations aforesaid, by the express and voluntary confessions of Garnet, and of his Complices themselves, and of two credible witnesses sworn at the Bar, and openly heard viva voce, and acknowledged by Garnet himself to be men without exception.

Then Mr Garnet having licence of the Court to answer what he could for himself, spake…

Concerning Equivocation, whereunto he answered, that their Church condemned all lying, but especially if it be in cause of Religion and faith, that being the most pernicious lye of all others… For the second point, which was the Power of the Pope in deposing of Princes, his Answer was three-fold. 1. That therein he onely propounded and followed the general Doctrine of the Church. 2. That this Doctrine of the Power of the Pope, was by all other Catholick Princes tolerated without grievance. 3. That yet for his own part, he always made a difference in the matter of Excommunicating and Deposing of Princes, betwixt the condition and state of our King, and of others, who having sometimes been Catholicks, did, or shall afterwards fall back…

Concerning the Jesuits, he saith, That if any were privy to such horrible Treasons, it was impious, especially in men of their profession: But said, That he talked with some of them about it, and that they denied it.

Touching my self, The Negociation into Spain was indeed propounded unto me, and I was also acquainted with the Negociation for Money, but ever intending it should be bestowed for the relief of poor Catholicks: But when they were there, they moved for an Army; which when they afterwards acquainted me withall, I misliked it, and said, It would be much disliked at Rome… So that I am verily perswaded, if they yielded to me, it had been good. But what their intent and meaning was in desiring an Army, I knew not; and I was charged not to meddle therein, no not with the money which was to be sent for Pensions, though it was to maintain the Title of the King.

The Earl of Salisbury then demanded, To maintain whose Title?

Garnet answered, The Title of the King of Spain.

The Earl of Northampton asked him, Why he did not oppose himself against it, and forbid it, as he might have done?...

Whereupon Garnet answered, That he might not do it; and for sending of Letters, and commending some Persons thereby, he confessed he did it often, as they were commended to him, without knowing either their Purposes, or some of their Persons: for he never knew Mr Wright for whom he writ.

The Earl of Salisbury then replied to Garnet, I must now remember you, how little any of your Answers can make for your purpose, when you would seek to colour your dealing with Baynham, by professing to write to Rome to procure a countermand of Conspiracies. And yet you know, when he took his journey towards Rome, the blow must needs have been passed before the time he could have arrived to the Popes presence, (such being your zeal and his haste for any such prevention) as it was about the 20th. of our October when he passed by Florence towards Rome.

To which Garnet made no great answer, but let it pass. And then went on with his defence of sending· Letters in commendation of many of those with which he had been formerly charged; and so confessed, that he had written in commendation of Fawkes, thinking that he went to serve as a Soldier, not knowing then of any other purpose he had in hand. And as for Sir Edmond Baynham, what he or Mr Catesby intended, he knew not in particular; only

Mr Catesby asked him in general the question, of the lawfulness to destroy Innocents with Nocents... which at first, I thought, said Garnet, had been an idle question, though afterwards I did verily think, he intended something that was not good. Whereupon having shortly after this received Letters from Rome, to prohibit all Insurrections intended by Catholicks, which might perturb this State, Garnet informed Catesby thereof, and told him That if he proceeded against the Pope's will, he could not prevail. But Catesby refused, and said, He would not take notice of the Pope's pleasure by him. Notwithstanding he shewed to Catesby the general Letter which he had received from Rome; but said, he would inform the Pope, and tell Garnet also in particular what attempt he had in hand, if he would hear it which afterwards he offered to do, but Garnet refused to hear him, and at two several times requested him to certifie the Pope what he intended to do.

Then were the two Witnesses called for, both of them Persons of good estimation, that overheard the Interlocution betwixt Garnet and Hall the Jesuit, viz. Mr Fauset, a man learned, and a Justice of Peace; and Mr Lockerson. But Mr Fauset being not present, was sent for to appear; and in the mean time Mr Lockerson, who being deposed before Garnet, delivered upon his Oath, that they heard Garnet say to Hall,

They will charge me with my Prayer for the good success of the great Action, in the beginning of the Parliament, and with the Verses which I added in the end of my Prayer

It is true indeed (said Garnet) that I prayed for the good success of that great Action; but I will tell them, that I meant it in respect of some sharper Laws, which I feared they would then make against Catholicks: And that Answer shall serve well enough.

Here Garnet replied, That for the two Gentlemen that heard the Interlocution, he would not charge them with Perjury, because he knew them to be honest men; yet he thought they did mistake some things, though in the substantial parts he confessed, he could not deny their relation. And for the main Plot, he confessed, that he was therewithall acquainted by Greenwell particularly, and that Greenwell came perplexed unto him to open something, which Mr Catesby with divers others intended: To whom he said, He was contented to hear by him what it was, so as he would not be a[...]known to Mr Catesby, or to any other, that he was made privy to it. Whereupon Father Greenwell told him the whole Plot, and all the particulars thereof, with which he protested that he was very much distempered, and could never sleep quietly afterwards, but sometimes prayed to God that it should not take effect.

To that the Earl of Salisbury replied, That he should do well to speak clearly of his devotion in that point; for otherwise he must put him in remembrance, that he had confessed to the Lords, That he had offered Sacrifice to God for stay of that Plot, unless it were for the good of the Catholick Cause; and in no other fashion (said his Lordship) was this State beholding to you for your Masses and Oblations. Adding thus much further, That he wondred why he would not write to his Superiour Aquaviva, as well of this particular Powder-Treason, as to procure prohibition for other smaller matters.

Garnet faintly answered, He might not disclose it to any, because it was matter of secret Confession, and would endanger the life of divers men.

Whereunto the Earl of Northampton replied, That that matter of Confession, which before he refused to confess, because he would save lives, he confessed it now to endanger his own life; and therefore his former Answer was idle and frivolous.

Then Garnet told the Lords, That he commanded Greenwell to disswade Catesby, which he thought he did; and if Catesby had come to him upon Allhallow-day, he thought he could so far have ruled him, as he would have been perswaded to desist.

Then said the Earl of Salisbury, Why did you refuse to hear Catesby tell you all the particulars, when he would have told you, if you had been desirous to prevent it?

Garnet replied, That after Greenwell had told him what it was which Catesby intended, and that he called to mind what Catesby said to him, at his first breaking with him in general terms, his Soul was so troubled with mislike of that particular, as he was loath to hear any more of it.

Well then (said the Earl of Salisbury) you see his heart....

To you therefore, Mr Garnet, (said the Earl of Salisbury) must I address my self, as the man in whom it appeareth best what horrible Treasons have been covered under the Mantle of Religion... as you do best know (Mr Garnet) that since your apprehension even till this day, you have been as Christianly, as courteously, and as carefully used, as ever man could be, of any quality, or any profession: Yea, it may truly be said, that you have been as well attended for health or otherwise, as a Nurse-child. Is it true or no, said the Earl?

It is most true, my Lord (said Garnet) I confess it.

...Then speaking to Garnet, he said, I pray you, Mr Garnet, what encouraged Catesby that he might proceed, but your resolving him in the first Proposition? What warranted Fawks, but Catesby's Explication of Garnet's Arguments? as appears infallibly by Winter's Confession, and by

Fawkes, that they knew the point had been resolved to Mr Catesby, by the best Authority.

Then Garnet answered, That Mr Catesby was to blame to make such application.

To that the Earl replied, That he must needs be bold with him, to drive him from the trust he had, to satisfie the world by his denials, by putting him in mind, how after the Interlocution betwixt him and Hall, when he was called before all the Lords, and was asked, not what he said, but whether Hall and he had conference together, desiring him not to equivocate; how stifly he denied it upon his Soul, reiterating it with so many detestable execrations, as the Earl said, it wounded their hearts to hear him; and yet as soon as Hall had confessed it, he grew ashamed, crying the Lords mercy, and said, he had offended, if Equivocation did not help him.

To this Garnet answered, That when one is asked a question before a Magistrate, he was not bound to answer before some Witnesses he produced against him… Then Garnet falling into some professions of his well-wishing to his Majesty, and being put in mind of the answer he had made concerning the Excommunication of Kings, wherein he referred himself to the Canon of Nos Sanctorum, he answered, That his Majesty was not yet Excommunicated.

Then the Earl of Salisbury bad him deal plainly, for now was the time, Whether in case the Pope…should Excommunicate the Kings Majesty of Great Britain, his Subjects were bound to continue their obedience?

To this he denied to answer, by which the hearers might see his mind.

From that matter he began to make request, that where he had confessed the receiving of two Brieves or Bulls from the Pope, in the Queens time, by which all Catholicks were forbidden to adhere to any Successor that was not obedient to the Church of Rome; his Majesty would be pleased to make a favourable interpretation, because he had shewed them to very few Catholicks in England, in the Queens time; and when he understood that the Pope had changed his mind, then he burnt the Bulls.

To that it was said, That belike the Pope changed his mind, when the King was so safely possessed of his Estate, and Garnet with his Accomplices began to feel their own impiety; and so, as Catesby said to Percy, did resolve roundly of that Treason, which would speed all at once.

Then Garnet began to use some speeches, that he was not consenting to the Powder-treason.

Whereupon the Earl of Salisbury said, Mr Garnet, give me but one Argument that you were not consenting to it, that can hold in any indifferent mans ear or sense, besides your bare Negative. But Garnet replied not.

Then Mr Attorney General spake in Answer of Garnet more particularly to this effect...

Concerning Garnet himself: First, for that answer of his, that he knew of the Powder-Treason by Confession; it is true which before was spoken, that such Acts as this is... are then onely commended when they are performed; but otherwise, first, Greenwel's was no Sacramental Confession, for that the Confitent was not Penitent: nay, himself hath clearly delivered under his hand, That the Powder-Treason was told him, not as a fault, but by way of consultation and advice. 2. It was a future thing to be done, and not already then executed. 3. Greenwel told it not of himself that he should do it, but of Fawkes, Percy, Catesby, Winter, and others; and therefore he ought to have discovered them, for that they were no Confitents. 4. He might and ought to have discovered the mischief, for preservation of the State, though he had concealed the persons. 5. Catesby told it unto him... out of Confession, saying, They might as well turn him out, as have kept him out. Lastly, by the Common Law, howsoever it were... he ought to have disclosed it. Now for that Garnet denied, that he was a principal Author and Procurer of this Treason, but onely that he had received knowledge thereof; the contrary is clear and manifest, both out of his own Confessions, by himself acknowledged, and apparently proved, in that he resolved Catesby concerning the lawfulness and merit thereof, and that he prayed for the good success of the Powder-Treason, which is more than either consultation or consent... Garnet might have commanded Greenwell that told him of the Powder-Treason, to have desisted, but did not: but Greenwell went still on with the Treason, and when it was disclosed, went into the Countrey to move Rebellion, which doubtless he would never have done, if Garnet had forbidden him... Moreover Mr Attorney added, how Garnet writ first for Thomas Winter, then for Kit Wright, after that for Guy Fawkes, then for Sir Edward Bainham, and afterwards for Catesby for a Regiment of Horse; and that Garnet was for the Infanta, and by his Breeves intended to keep out the King, except he should tolerate and swear to maintain the Romish Religion.

Then Mr Attorney spake of the Interlocution betwixt Garnet and Hall, and said, That in all their speeches they never named God, nor confessed their innocency; but as soon as they spake together, Hall spake first, and then Garnet said, He suspected one, whose name, they that were set to over-hear them, could not hear, to have disclosed something against them. But it may be otherwise, for he said he was much subject to that frailty of suspicion. He said, He received a Note from Rookwood, that Greenwell was gone over-Seas; and another, that Gerard was gone to father Parsons, and that Mistress Anne was in Town (meaning Mrs. Anne Vaux) and many other things were by them uttered in that conference.

By this time came in Mr Forset, who being deposed, affirmed likewise, that their examination, and the matter therein contained were true; saying further, that both of them took notes of that which they heard of Garnet and Hall, as near as possibly they could, and set down nothing in their examinations, but those things, wherein both their notes, and perfect memories agreed and assented, and that many things that were very material; and of great moment, were left out of their examinations, because both their notes and memories did not perfectly agree therein.

And now one of the Letters, which were written with sack, was shewed to the Court, by which appeared that Hall and Garnet had interlocution together. Mr Atturney... urged the examination of Garnet, wherein he confessed that when Tesmond alias Greenwell, made relation to him of the great blow by the Powder-treason, who should have the protection, Greenwell said, the Lords that should be left alive should choose a Protector. And further Mr Atturney urged the writing of another Letter written with sack to Sayer, alias Rockwood, a Priest in the Gate-house; But of this point much is formerly mentioned.

Here Mr Attorney ending, my Lord of Northampt. spake to the Prisoner this speech following.

Though no man alive can be less apt or willing than my self, to add the least grain or scruple of improvement to the weight of any mans calamity, that groans under the heavy burthen of a distressed state... whereof I have as many witnesses as the world hath eyes: yet as the case stands now in this trial, Mr Garnet... you that were so well content to let the course of conspiracy run forward to the stopping of this breath before the time, which God by nature doth prescribe between his honour, and your error, his just proceedings and your painted shews, his sincerity and your hypocricy; I could wish it possible that in a person of some other quality, you might hear the Ecchoes of your unperfect and weak answers, and thereupon judge more indifferently and evenly of the true state of your cause than you have done hitherto, being distracted with fear, or forestalled by prejudice, or, to borrow your own phrase, which is more proper to the point than any I can use, oppressed tanta nube testium, with so thick a cloud of witnesses, as concur with one voice, heart and spirit, for the conviction of your audacity.

I confess that never any man in your state gave less hold or advantage to examiners, than you have done in the whole course of proceeding, to us that were in Commission: sometime by forswearing, as upon the confession of Hall your fellow: sometime by dissembling, as about the places of your Rendezvous, which was the lapwings neast: sometimes by earnest expostulation: sometime by artificial Equivocation: sometime by Sophisticating true substances: sometime by adding false qualities: yet sat superest, as may appear, to the defeat of your inventions, and the defence of the Kings Majesty...

Your parts by nature simply considered, and in another person, would rather move compassion, than exasperate humanity: for whom would not the ruine of such a person touch, as is in apparance temperate, and in understanding ripe? But our end at this time is the same... that we may quench that fire by prevention, which you have only raked up in ashes... that it might cause a new combustion so soon as it might hit upon matter that were fit and sutable. Wherefore I must rather draw your answers to the true touch for discharge of rumors, than...beat the air: For the substance of all your evasions and slie shifts, is as the Inn-keepers of Chalcis confessed of his dishes to his guests, admiring... that they were only compounded of pork, howsoever your fine cookery may vary them.

The two Buls that in the late Queens time entred the land (with a purpose by their lowd lowing to call all their calves together, for the making of a stong party, at the shutting up of the evening against our dead Soveraign) were grased in your pastures, Mr Garnet, or to speak more properly (because they durst neither endure the light, nor admit the air) they were staul-fed at your crib, as your self confess... And what answer make you to this? merely that the purpose was imparted to very few: so much the worse: For out of publication grows discovery; and yet experience hath justified, that those very few were the very souls and spirits of that pack of Conspirators, and such as for want of patience and temperance to tary the time, when the game had been brought to bearing, should have played the chiefest parts in the late smoking Tragedy.

You say the Buls were after sacrificed in the fire by your self. But not before the Kings good Angel had cut their throats, and the best part of their proof were past, and your hopes dead of that good which in likelihood they should have brought with them. For to what use could these dumb beasts serve in seeking to prevent that lawful and undoubted right, which heaven had now proclaimed, and earth acknowledged? But let the proof be what it will, I look into the root. I wonder Mr Garnet, what Apostle warrants you in undertaking wicked Plots, in hope that good may follow; neglecting what all Laws (and the Laws of England above all) what all States and Nations conclude of men, that slily practise, and combine for anticipation of the future rights of lawfull Successors.

In excuse of Letters written with your own hand by Thomas Winter to father Creswell, when he was employed about the procurement of an Army to Invade, with supplies of Treasure proportionable for the quicker execution of so desperat an Enterprise, you answer, that the Persons were commended in your Letters, not the Plot... as though the minister had any other errand or instruction, than the main Plot it self... Or as though in this very point other mens confession in particular, beside your own in generality, had not left us marks and traces evident and plain enough to descry doubleness with diversity. You confess privity to a practice, but not for an Army: foreknowledge of a course for getting Treasure, but with a purpose, as you conceived, to employ it wholly for the relief of Catholicks. So as the reason of the reservedness of Catesby, Winter and the rest toward you, must be undoubtedly their suspicion of your over great affection and duty to the Queen; For otherwise it is certain they would have trusted you as well with their intention, as with their means: with their hopes, as with their instruments: especially considering how hard it was for them to compass their own vast desires, without help both of your credit, and of your industry.

Wright was in like manner, and with like expedition commended by you afterward for the quickening of Winters project, if any life were in it, upon the slacking of the passions of Spain, with the propositions of peace, that no time might be lost, no stone left unremoved, that might give a knock to the peace of our policy: your head wrought upon all offers, your hand walked in all Regions, your spirit steered all attempts and undertakings: and yet if protestations, qualified and protected by Equivocations, may cary weight; all this while your mind was, as good pastors to be, patient, your thoughts were obedient, and your counsels innocent.

But now to search your cunning somewhat nearer to the quick, we must observe, that when your hopes of Invasion began to cool by likelyhood of peace, your desires of supplies by the cold answers that came from Spain, your expectation of new mischief to be wrought at home without Complots abroad: when malice it self was cast into so desperate a swoun... when you for your own part, Mr Garnet, having bin once washed and regenerated in the fountain of the Kings free Pardon, from the leprous spots of former Treasons, were determined to begin upon another stock... for secretly Catesby resorts to you...to enquire whether it were lawful, considering the necessiity of the time, to undertake an enterprise, for the advancement of the Catholick Religion, though it were likely that among many that were

172

nocent, some should perish that were innocent. A man that is Religious in any kind, or but morally honest in his own kind, would expect that a Priest, a jesuit, (which title doth imply salvation, and not destruction, nay, the Superior of English jesuits) upon this rash demand, should have resorted for a safe resolution to Gods own Book, where he should have found, that God was pleased to withdraw his wrathful hand from Sodom, so as there had been only…ten justmen within that Town, and for their sakes; that the wise housholder in St. Matthew, marking how hard it would be, when the corn was ripe, to make separation, gave order to his servants to abstain from plucking up the tares…least withall they plucked up the wheat by the Roots… But far beside the Holy writ, or holy presedents, your answer, Mr Garnet, was such, as I both abhor to think, and quake to utter, that if any great advantage were to grow to the Church this way, they might destroy them all…

But that which ought most to torture and afflict the spirit (if you be the child of him, whose Name and Badge you bear) is, that your Doctrine was confidently delivered, and so speedily digested, and converted to nutriment from such a mouth as yours, considering that (according to the Prophet) knowledge should depend upon the lips of the Priest, as Rookwood, Bates and others, that did shrink at the horror of the Project when it was first laid down, received satisfaction upon the very sound of your assent, though masked with the title of a man as grave and learned, as any in the land.

And Catesby doubting of the fickleness of mens affections, in cases that concern the soul, used your admittance as a charm or spell, to keep quick spirits within the circle of combined faith, which otherwise perhaps when Hell brake loose, would have sought liberty. Your Charter only (whereupon I beseech you for your own souls health, to meditate for the time you tarry in this world) was the Base whereon some grounded their bad conscience in proceeding with this Plot, not only to the destruction of their bodies, but to the perill of their souls, without sound and true repentance… For though Christ were joyfull that he had not lost one of those whom his father gave him in charge, and came to save, and not to destroy; yet your advise was to destroy them all: Such was your burning charity...

It seems the heart of Catesby was a fertile soil for sprowting of stinking weeds hastily, into which the seed of your securing confidence was cast. For the Powder-plot which in January was barly embryo, became formatus foetus in the March next following, it quickened the next December, when the Pioneers began to dig in the thick wall: Catesby not long after imparted his conceipt secretly to you, of the great likelihood he foresaw of a lucky time of birth, and thereupon was Guy Fawks sent over by your knowledge and encouragement, to deal with Sir William Stanley, about the drawing down of Forces somewhat nearer to the Sea side for speedy transport, which if need were, might carry torches at the solemnity. But what is your answer to this employment of Guy Fawks? Forsooth that your purpose was only, to commend him as a Souldier, but not as a Conspirator. O unlucky Treason, that comes to be excused by so poor an Advocate! when Fawks himself meant nothing else than to be a Souldier, having so strange a part to play soon after in the Powder-train, but used this retreat as a colour to disguise the secret purpose that did onely tarry time, and to eschew those watchful eyes, that nearer hand would have observed both his inlets and his outlets in that place more narrowly. The point is clear, the confessions are direct, the purpose is palpable. All the lines of your level are drawn to the centre of the Powder-mine... and yet under pain of censure we must believe, that all this while you were in charity, because all this while (which it grieves me to remember) you were not afraid to communicate.

But now to weigh your Answers that concern the Powder-plot it self, which is paramount in respect of the Longitude and Latitude to all that have been, or shall ever be: Your self cannot deny, Mr Garnet, that Greenwel's overture, as you say in Confession, coming after the notice which you took of Catesbies question about Innocents, was but a fruit of your own Doctrine, an effect of your own instruction, and a conclusion drawn wholly out of your own propositions and principles. Now when we press to know what reason drew you to the concealment of a Project so pernicious both to Prince and State, without revealing it either to the King himself... or to his Ministers subordinate; you start to the shift of Confession for a formal help, which comes too short in respect of Catesby's first discovery, which your own words aver plainly to have wrought with you. I will not argue in this place what course a Confessor should take, or how far he ought to strain for the securing of a Princes life, that otherwise is sure to perish by the rage and ignorance invincible of a base Villain, (whose life answers not in value the least hair of a Princes head) because time suffers not: But I am sure, that for a matter of less weight than this, and a crime of less importance than the life both of Prince and State, Confession received a deep wound for a long time, more than a thousand years past, in the Church of Constantinople... For God forbid that matters of such weight should hang by such feeble threeds. But to this excuse of tenderness in the point of Confession, I would answer by making a great doubt, Whether this course of conference were a Confession or not: for against your bare words, which Equivocation supports, I object some likelihood, That since you kneeled sometimes, and sometimes walked up and down; since matter of conspiracy were interlaced with matter of Confession, not for ease of conscience, as should appear, but for advice in execution; since Greenwel was absolved instantly, which excludes the shift of reference; and Greenwel should be found to lie to the holy Ghost, in case this were a true Confession, in promising (Mr Garnet) as you say, to disswade the project, which he prosecuted even to the last point, as is evident: and after the Powder Camp brake up, I conclude, that though this discovery were by confession, yet it was no Supersedeas to your former knowledge from Catesby, your trusty friend: and if it were none, then it can be no protection for faith putrified. What need we seek light through cobweb-lawns, when the drift of your whole device in seeking to conclude from one what you learned of another, and from all what you affected and abetted in your heart, doth evidently prove your counsels to have been carried along with such a temper of reservedness, as whensoever mischief should be brought to light, the world might rather wonder at your caution, than commend your fidelity...

For though you pretend to have received a deep wound in Conscience at the first revealing of the plot, to have lost your sleep with vexation of spirit, to have offered and prayed to God for his preventing grace, to have required Greenwel's help and furtherance in crossing and diverting the design; yet all this while you suffered the project to proceed, you helped and assisted their endeavours that were labourers, you wrote earnestly Letters both to Baldwin and to Creswel for their furtherance of ordinary means, you gave order for a prayer to be said by Catholicks for their prosperous success...

But your tenderness herein was suitable with another dutiful desire of yours to disswade Catesby from the Plot, at his coming into Warwickshire, who never meant to come thither, but as to the Rendezvous when the Parliament had been blown up, and the storm had been blown over. It may be that your mind was perplexed and disquieted upon the meditation of strange events...the reason is very pregnant in the Word of God it self, that...since wickedness is cowardly and timorous, it gives evidence of condemnation against it self...

I will conclude with you, Mr Garnet, as Constantius did with Ascesius... set up a Ladder for your self, and climb up to Heaven alone, for Loyal minds will not sute themselves with such bad company. The worst I wish to your person standing now to be convicted at the Bar, is remorse and repentance, for the safeguard of your Soul...

Hereunto Garnet said, That he had done more than he could excuse, and he had dealt plainly with them; but he was bound to keep the secrets of Confessions, and to disclose nothing that he heard in Sacramental Confession.

Whereupon the Earl of Nottingham asked him, if one confessed this day to him, that to morrow morning he meant to kill the King with a dagger, if he must conceal it?

Whereunto Garnet answered, That he must conceal it.

Then the Earl of Salisbury desired liberty of him to ask him some questions of the nature of Confessions.

Garnet said, His Lordship might, and he would answer him as well as he could…

Then he demanded, Whether Greenwel were absolved by him or no?

Garnet said, He was.

The Earl then asked him, What Greenwel had done, to shew that he was sorry for it, and whether he did promise to desist?

Garnet answered, that Greenwel said, He would do his best.

To that the Earl replied, That it could not be so; for as soon as Catesby and Percy were in Arms, Greenwel came to them from Garnet, and so went from them to Hall at Mr. Abington's house, inviting them most earnestly to come and assist those Gentlemen in that action. Hereby (saith he) it appears, that either Greenwel told you out of Confession, and then there needs no secrecie; or if it were in Confession, he professed no penitency, and therefore you could not absolve him. To which the Earl added, That this one circumstance must still be remembred, and cannot be cleared, That when Greenwel told you what Catesby meant in particular, and you then called to mind also what Catesby had spoken to you in the general before, if you had not been so desirous to have the Plot take effect, you might have disclosed it out of your general knowledge from Catesby: but when Catesby offered to deliver you the particulars himself, as he had done to Greenwel, you refused to hear him, lest your tongue should have betrayed your heart.

To this Garnet weakly replied, That he did what he could to disswade it, and went into Warwickshire with a purpose to disswade Mr Catesby, when he should have come down. And for Mr. Greenwel's going to Father Hall, to perswade him to joyn, Garnet said, he did very ill in so doing.

To that the Earl of Salisbury replied, That his first answer was most absurd, seeing he knew Catesby would not come down till the 6th. of November, which was the day after the blow should have been given; and Garnet went into the Countrey ten days before. And for the second, he said, That he was onely glad, that the world might now see, that Jesuits were condemned by Jesuits; and Treason and Traitors laid naked by the Traitors themselves; yea, Jesuits by that Jesuit, that governs all Jesuits here, and without whom, no Jesuit in England can do any thing.

Garnet (as it should seem) being here mightily touched with remorse of his offence, prayed God and the King, that other Catholicks might not fare the worse for his sake.

Then the Earl of Salisbury said, Mr Garnet, is it not a lamentable thing, that if the Pope, or Claudius Aquaviva, or your self, command poor Catholicks any thing, that they must obey you, though it be to endanger both body and soul? And if you maintain such Doctrine amongst you, how can the King be safe? Is it not time therefore the King and the State should look to you, that spend your time thus in his Kingdom?

Garnet said very passionately, My Lord, I would to God I had never known of the Powder-Treason.

Hereupon the Lord Chief Justice of England said, Garnet, you are Superior of the Jesuits; and if you forbid, must not the rest obey? Was not Greenwel with you half an hour at Sir Everard Digby's house, when you heard of the discovery of your Treason? and did you not there confer and debate the matter together? Did you not send him to Hall, to Mr. Abington's house, to stir him up to go to the Rebels, and encourage them? Yet you seek to colour all this, but that's but a meer shift in you; and notwithstanding all this you said, No man living but one did know that you were privy to it; then belike some that are dead did know it. Catesby was never from you, (as the Gentlewoman that kept your house with you confessed) and by many apparent proofs, and evident presumptions, you were in every particular of this action, and directed and commanded the Actors; nay, I think verily, you were the chief that moved it.

Garnet said, No, my Lord, I did not.

Then it was exceedingly well urged by my Lord Chief Justice, how he writ his Letters for Winter, Wright, Fawkes, Baynham, and Catesby, principal Actors in this matchless Treason. Besides, his Lordship told him of his keeping the two Bulls to prejudice the King, and to do other mischief in the Realm; which, when he saw the King peaceably to come in, then being out of hope to do any good, he burnt them.

Here Mr Attorney caused to be read the Confession of Hall, alias Oldcorn the Jesuit, under his own hand... wherein he confessed, That Humfrey Littleton told him, That Catesby and others were sore hurt with Powder, and said that he was exceeding sory that things took no better effect; whereat Hall wished him not to be discouraged, nor to measure the cause by the event... And this he confessed, and applied to the fact of Catesby and others for the Powder-treason, and said, It would have been commendable when it had been done, though not before.

After this Mr Attorney opened, how Francis Tresham, a dilinquent Romanist, even in articulo mortis (a fearful thing) took it upon his salvation, That he had not seen Garnet in sixteen years before, when Garnet himself had confessed he had seen him often within that time: and likewise, that Garnet knew not of the Spanish Invasion, which Garnet himself confessed also, and which two things Tresham himself had formerly confessed to the Lords; yet for a recantation of these two things upon his death bed, he commanded Vavasor his man, (whom I think (said Mr Attorney) deeply guilty in this Treason) to write a Letter to the Earl of Salisbury: And to shew this his desperate recantation, Mr Treshams Letter was offered to be read.

But before the reading thereof, my Lord of Salisbury said, Because there was matter incident to him, and to that which should be read, he thought fit to say something. To which purpose he said his desire was, truly to lay open what cause there was for any faith to be given to these mens protestations, when they, to colour their own impieties, and to slander the Kings Justice, would go about to excuse all Jesuits, how foul soever, out of an opinion that it is meritorious so to do, at such time as they had no hope of themselves. Such is it to be doubted that Sir Everard Digbies protestations might be at the Bar, who sought to clear all Jesuits of those practices, which they themselves have now confessed... That such was also Treshams labour, who being visited with sickness, and his wife in charity suffered to come to him, this Letter was hatched by them, and signed by himself some few hours before his death, wherein he taketh that upon his salvation, which shall now by Garnet be disproved.

Then the Letter was read, being to this effect, That whereas since the Kings time he had had his pardon, and that to satisfie the Lords who heretofore examined him, he had accused Garnet; that now, he being weak, desired that his former examinations might be called in, because they were not true: and set down upon his salvation, that he had not seen Garnet in sixteen years before.

Then my Lord of Salisbury shewed and said, It was a lamentable thing: for within three hours after he had done this, he died; and asked Garnet what interpretation he made of this testamental protestation?

Garnet answered, It may be, my Lord, he meant to Equivocate. Here was the examination and confession of Mrs Anne Vaux offered to be read also, to confirm Treshams perjury, who confessed that she had seen Mr Tresham with Garnet at her house, three or four times since the Kings coming in, and divers times before; and that he had dined with him, and that Garnet always gave him good counsel, and would say sometimes to him, and others, Good Gentlemen, be quiet: for we must obtain that which you desire by prayer. She confessed also, that they were at Erith together the last Sommer.

After all this, Garnet being demanded, if these examinations were true, he affirmed they were. And then were his own examinations likewise read to the same effect, wherein he both confessed the seeing of Mr Tresham, and his sending into Spain about an Invasion.

Here my Lord of Salisbury concluded, That that which was said of Mr Tresham, and others, was not done against charity to the dead, but upon inevitable necessity, to avoid all their slanderous reports and practises: for he said, That even now there was currant throughout the Town, a report of a Retractation under Bates his hand, of his accusation of Greenwel; which are strange and grievous practises to think upon. But this day shall witness to the world, that all is false, and your self condemned not by any but by your self, your own confessions and actions. Alass, Mr Garnet, why should we be troubled all this day with you, poor man, were it not to make the cause appear as it deserveth? wherein, God send you may be such an example, as you may be the last Actor in this kind.

Hereupon my Lord Admiral said to Garnet, that he had done more good this day in that Pulpit which he stood in (for it was made like unto a Pulpit wherein he stood) than he had done all the days of his life time in any other Pulpit.

Then was another examination of Mrs Anne Vaux read, wherein she confessed that Mr Garnet and she were not long since with Mr Tresham, at his house in Northamptonshire, and stayed there.

After this, my Lord of Salisbury said, Mr Garnet, if you have not yet done, I would have you to understand that the King hath commanded, that whatsoever made for you, or against you, all should be read, and so it is, and we take of you what you will. This Gentlewoman that seems to speak for you in her confessions, I think would sacrifice her self for you to do you good, and you likewise for her: Therefore, good Mr Garnet, whatsoever you have to say, say on a Gods name, and you shall be heard.

Then Garnet desired the Jury, that they would allow of, and believe those things he had denied, and affirmed, and not to give credit unto those things, whereof there was no direct proof against him, not to condemn him by circumstances or presumptions.

The Earl of Salisbury demanded of him, saying, Mr Garnet, is this all you have to say?

if it be not, take your time, no man shall interrupt you.

To whom Garnet answered, Yea, my Lord.

Mr Attorney humbly desired all the Lords Commissioners, that if he had forgotten to speak of any thing material, that their Lordships would be pleased to put him in mind of it: Who was assured by my Lord of Salisbury, that he had done very well, painfully, and learnedly.

Then Mr Attorney desired the Jury might go together, who upon his motion going together forth of the Court, within less than a quarter of an hour returned, and found Henry Garnet guilty.

Whereupon Mr Sergeant Crook prayed judgment.

Then Mr Waterhouse the Clerk of the Crown demanding what he could say for himself, why judgment should not be given against him?

Garnet made answer, that he could say nothing, but referred himself to the mercy of the King, and God Almighty.

After this, the Earl of Northampton made a Learned Speech, which in it self was very copious; and the intention being to contract this Volume as much as might be, and to keep onely to matter of Fact, it was thought convenient to omit the same.

Then the Lord Chief Justice making a pithy preamble of all the apparent proofs and presumptions of his guiltiness, gave Judgment, that he should be drawn, hanged, and quartered.

And my Lord of Salisbury demanded, if Garnet would say any thing else?

Garnet answered, No, my Lord. But I humbly desire your Lordships all, to commend my life to the Kings Majesty, saying, That at his pleasure he was ready either to die or live, and do him service.

And so the Court arose.

A true Relation of all such things as passed at the Execution of Mr Garnet, the Third of May, Anno 1606.

ON the Third of May, Garnet, according to his Judgment, was executed upon a Scaffold, set up for that purpose, at the West end of St. Paul's Church. At his arise up the Scaffold, he stood much amazed, (fear and guiltiness appearing in his face.) The Deans of Pauls and Winchester being present, very gravely and Christianly exhorted him to a true and lively faith to Godward, a free and plain acknowledgment to the World of his offence; and if any further Treason lay in his knowledge, to unburthen his Conscience, and shew a sorrow and detestation of it. But Garnet impatient of perswasions, and ill pleased to be exhorted by them, desired them not to trouble him; he came prepared, and was resolved. Then the Recorder of London (who was by his Majesty appointed to be there) asked Garnet if he had any thing to say unto the people before he died; it was no time to dissemble, and now his Treasons were too manifest to be dissembled: therefore if he would, the world should witness, what at last he censured of himself, and of his fact; it should be free to him to speak what he listed. But Garnet unwilling to take the offer, said, His voice was low, his strength gone, the people could not hear him, though he spake to them; but to those about him on the Scaffold, he said, The intention was wicked, and the fact would have been cruel, and from his Soul he should have abhorred it, had it effected. But he said, He onely had a general knowledge of it by Mr Catesby, which in that he disclosed not, nor used means to prevent it, herein he had offended; what he knew in particulars was in Confession, as he said. But the Recorder wished him to be remembred, That the Kings Majesty had under his hand-writing these four points amongst others:

1. That Greenway told him of this, not as a fault, but as a thing which he had intelligence of, and told it him by way of consultation.
2. That Catesby and Greenway came together to him to be resolved.
3. That Mr Tesmond and he had conference of the particulars of the Powder-Treason in Essex long after.
4. Greenway had asked him, who should be the Protector? But Garnet said, That was to be referred till the blow was past.

These prove your privity besides Confession, and these are extant under your hand. Garnet answered, Whatsoever was under his hand was true. And for that he disclosed not to his Majesty the things he knew, he confessed himself justly condemned, and for this did ask forgivness of his Majesty. Hereupon the Recorder led him to the Scaffold to make his Confession publick.

Then Garnet said, Good Countrey-men, I am come hither this blessed day of The Invention of the holy Cross, to end all my crosses in this life: The cause of my suffering is not unknown to you; I confess I have offended the King, and am sorry for it, so far as I was guilty, which was in concealing it, and for that I ask pardon of his Majesty. The Treason intended against the King and State was bloody, my self should have detested it had it taken effect; and I am heartily sorry, that any Catholicks ever had so cruel a design. Then turning himself from the people to them about him, he made an Apology for Mrs Ann Vaux, saying, There is such an honourable Gentlewoman, who hath been much wronged in report; for it is suspected and said, that I should be married to her, or worse; but I protest the contrary, she is a vertuous Gentlewoman, and for me a perfect pure Virgin. For the Popes Breeves, Sir Edmond Baynams going over Seas, and the matter of the Powdertreason, he referred himself to his Arraignment, and his Confessions; for whatsoever is under my hand in any of my Confessions, said he, is true.

Then addressing himself to Execution, he kneeled at the Ladder foot, and asked if he might have time to pray, and how long? It was answered, he should limit himself, none should interrupt him. It appeared, he could not constantly or devoutly pray, fear of death, or hope of pardon, even then so distracted him; for oft in those Prayers he would break off, turn and look about him, and answer to what he over-heard, while he seemed to be praying. When he stood up, the Recorder finding in his behaviour as it were an expectation of a Pardon, wished him not to deceive himself, nor beguile his own Soul; he was come to die, and must die; requiring him not to equivocate with his last breath, if he knew any thing that might be danger to the King or State, he should now utter it. Garnet said, It is now no time to equivocate; how it was lawful, and when, he had shewed his mind else-where. But, saith he, I do not now equivocate, and more than I have confessed, I do not know. At his ascending up the Ladder, he desired to have warning before he was turned off. But it was told him, He must look for no other turn but death. Being upon the Gibbet, he used these words, I commend me to all good Catholicks, and I pray God preserve his Majesty, the Queen, and all their Posterity, and my Lords of the Privy Council, to whom I remember my humble duty, and I am sorry that I did dissemble with them; but I did not think they had had such proof against me, till it was shewed me: but when that was proved, I held it more honour for me at that time to confess, than before to have accused. And for my Brother Greenway, I would the truth were known; for the false reports that are, make him more faulty than he is. I should not have charged him, but that I thought he had been safe. I pray God the Catholicks may not fare the worse for my sake; and I exhort them all to take heed they enter not into any Treasons, Rebellions, or Insurrections against the King. And with this, ended speaking, and fell to praying: and crossing himself, said, In nomine Patris, & Filii, & Spiritus sancti; and prayed, Maria mater Gratiae, Maria mater misericordiae, T[...] me à malo protege, & hora mortis suscipe. Then, In manus tuas, Domine, commendo spiritum meum. Then, Per crucis hoc signum, (crossing himself) fugiat procul omne malignum. Infige crucem tuam in corde meo Domine. Let me always remember the Cross. And so returned again to Maria mater Gratiae, and then was turned off, and hung till he was dead.

Bibliography

Print Books

ALFORD, Stephen *The Watchers: Secret History of the Reign of Elizabeth I*, Allen Lane 2012

BENGTSEN, Fiona *Sir William Waad – Lieutenant of the Tower & the Gunpowder Plot*, Trafford Publishing, Oxford 2005

DAVIS, John Paul *Pity for the Guy*, Peter Owen, London 2010

EDWARDS, Francis (ed.) *The Gunpowder Plot – The Narrative of Oswald Tesimond alias Greenaway*, The Folio Society, London 1973

FRASER, Antonia *The Gunpowder Plot: Terror & Faith in 1605,* Orion Books, London 2002

HAYNES, Alan *The Gunpowder Plot*, Sutton Publishing, Stroud 2005

HOGGE, Alice *Gods' Secret Agents*, HarperCollins, London (2006)

LEE, Christopher *1603: A Turning Point in British History*, Headline Review 2004

MARTIN, Patrick H *Elizabethan Espionage*, McFarland & Co, Jefferson, NC, USA 2016

REYNOLDS, Tony *St Nicholas Owen, Priest-Hole Maker*, Gracewing, Leominster 2014

SHARPE, James *Remember, Remember the 5th of November*, Profile, London 2006

Digitised Online Books

ANON ('By a Person of Honour') *The Catholique Apology* 1776 (Google Books)

BURNET, Bishop Gilbert *Bishop Burnet's History of His Own Time* (Vol IV), Clarendon Press, Oxford 1823 (Google Books)

DICKINS, Margaret *Chastleton House*, Walker, Stratford-upon-Avon 1900 (Archive.org)

GARDINER, Samuel Rawson *What Gunpowder Plot Was*, Longmans, Green & Co, London 1897 (Project Gutenburg)

GERARD, John, SJ *What Was the Gunpowder Plot?* Osgood, McIlvaine & Co, London 1897 (Project Gutenburg)

GERARD, John SJ *Thomas Winter's Confession & the Gunpowder Plot*, London 1898 (Project Gutenburg)

GOODMAN, Dr Godfrey *The Court of King James the First* (Vol I. Ed. John Sherren Brewer), Richard Bentley, London 1839 (Archive.org)

HIGGONS, B *A Short View of the English History with Reflections* 1727 (Google books)

JANEWAY, Richard *The History of Popish Sham Plots,* London, 1682 (Google books)

JARDINE, David *A Narrative of the Gunpowder Plot,* John Murray 1857 (Archive.org)

LATHBURY, Thomas *Guy Fawkes, or A Complete History Of The Gunpowder Treason*, John W Parker, London 1839 (Project Gutenberg)

LONGUEVILLE, Thomas *The Life of a Conspirator: Being a Biography of Sir Everard Digby*, Kegan, Paul, Trench, Trübner, London (1895) (Project Gutenberg)

MARTYNDALE, Rev Hugh F *A Familiar Analysis of the Calendar of the Church of England*, London, 1831 (Google books)

MORRIS, John (ed.) *The Condition of Catholics Under James I*, Longman's, Green & Co, London 1871 (Project Gutenburg)

NAUNTON, Sir Robert *Fragmenta Regalia: Memoirs of Elizabeth and her Courtiers* (1824 edition. Originally 1641) (Project Gutenburg)

NICHOLS JB & JG *The Fawkes of York in the Sixteenth Century*, Westminster 1850 (Google books)

SPINK, Henry Hawkes Jnr *The Gunpowder Plot & Lord Mounteagle's Letter*, London 1902 (Google Books)

TAUNTON, Ethelred L *The History of Jesuits in England*, Methuen, London 1901 (Archive.org)

'VINDICATOR' (pseudonym) *A True Account of the Gunpowder Plot Extracted from Dr Lingard's History of England and Dodd's Church History*, London, 1851

WELWOOD, JAMES *Memoirs of the Most Material Transactions in England*, Robert Urie & Co, Glasgow 1744 (Archive.org)

BIBLIOGRAPHY

Primary Website Sources:

British History Online: *british-history.ac.uk*
Gunpowder Plot Society: *gunpowder-plot.org*
History of Parliament: *historyofparliamentonline.org*
National Archives: *nationalarchives.gov.uk*
Oxford Dictionary of National Biography: *oxforddnb.com*
UK Parliamentary historical records: *www.parliament.uk*
Wikipedia: *wikipedia.com*

Notes

Chapter 1

1 According to Dr Geraint Thomas, Centre for Explosion Studies, University of Aberystwyth, who carried out a study in 2003.
2 *The Gunpowder Plot – The Narrative of Oswald Tesimond alias Greenaway*.

Chapter 2

1 The then crime of not attending Protestant church services.
2 They certainly attended the same school, but Tesimond was five years older than Wright.
3 The *King's Book*.
4 In this context, a minor offical whose role was to track down Catholic priests.
5 Spink, *The Gunpowder Plot & Lord Mounteagle's Letter*, 1902.
6 The *King's Book*.

Chapter 3

1 He was cousin to Stephen Littleton of Holbeche House. His treachery did him no good – he was executed along with Oldcorne.

Chapter 4

1 *What Was the Gunpowder Plot?* Father John Gerard, 1897.
2 The *King's Book*.

Chapter 5

1 Percy did not become a Gentleman Pensioner till the month following the negotiations, but it might reasonably be assumed that his imminent appointment was known of.

Chapter 6

1 *The Court of King James the First* vol. I 1839 (ed. JS Brewer).
2 Available at British History Online.
3 Dictionary of National Biography.
4 Fiona Bengtsen, *Sir William Waad* 2005
5 *1603: A Turning Point in British History* 2004.

Chapter 7

1 *The Gunpowder Plot & Lord Mounteagle's Letter* London 1902.
2 *The Court of King James 1* (Vol II) 1839.
3 *Thomas Winter's Confession & the Gunpowder Plot* 1898.
4 Speaker of the Long Parliament under Charles 1.
5 Poet and politician, and a friend of Donne and Milton.
6 I believe I have identified this as Edmund Church, a Catholic landowner listed as a recusant of Wakes Colne, Essex.
7 One of the plotters.
8 His son.
9 Salisbury's nephew.
10 An Islington schoolmaster, hanged in1654 for his supposed part in a plot against Cromwell.
11 *What the Gunpowder Plot Was,* Longman's 1897.
12 *King's Book.*
13 *Guy Fawkes, or A Complete History Of The Gunpowder Treason* 1839.
14 *The Gunpowder Plot & Lord Mounteagle's Letter* 1902.

Chapter 12

1 Longueville.
2 Sometimes spelt 'Harrington'.
3 The *King's Book.*

Chapter 13

1 Gerard.
2 *Memoirs of Missionary Priests,* 1842.

Chapter 14

1 *A Narrative of the Gunpowder Plot,* 1857.
2 *A True Account of the Gunpowder Plot: Extracted from Dr Lingard's History of England,* 1851.
3 Recorded as 'stranguary': experiencing great pain in passing urine, which can be a symptom of more serious underlying conditions.
4 This is disputed, with a suggestion being that the same woman was questioned twice, but the bigamy story comes from more than one source.
5 *Elizabethan Espionage,* Patrick H Martin.
6 Cambridge University Press, Cambridge.org.
7 Cecil Papers, british-history.ac.uk.

Index

Alford, Stephen, 108
Ashby St Ledgers
  (Northamptonshire), 92
Ashley, Ralph, 22

Babington, Anthony, 19, 39-40
Babington, Plot, 20, 39-40
Bartlet, George, 53, 67, 119
Bates, Thomas, 16, 20, 17, 97,
  arrest, 67
  biography 12-13
  Garnet, cited in trial of, 179
  Holbeche, flight to, 91
  Plot, enlisted into, 26
  traitor, as possible, 116
  trial of, 98, 100, 118, 120, 145,
    146, 148, 151, 155, 161,
    163, 173
Baynham, Sir Edmund, 165,
  177, 181
de Beaumont (French Ambassador), 5
Blount, Richard, 107
Bradley, Bob, 108, 109
Brewer, John Sherren, 49
Bright, Andrew 36, 73, 90, 123
Bright, Ellen, 90, 123
Brooke, Henry See Cobham,
  Baron Henry
Brunninge, Matthew, 120

Burghley, Lord see
  Cecil, William
Bye Plot, 5

Cambridge, Joan, 115
Carleton, Dudley, 63, 120, 122
Castlemaine, Lord Roger, 41
Catesby, Robert, 6, 9, 14, 24-6, 32,
  82-4, 86-9
  biography, 8-9
  death, 66, 93-6
  Essex rebellion, 74
  Garnet, duplicity towards, 18-19
    cited in trial of, 156, 159-63,
    165-69, 172-77, 181
  Holbeche, flight to and stay at,
    91-2
  Jesuits, connections with,
    17-18, 21
  Monteagle, relationship with, 50
  Plot, as instigator of, 59, 80, 86
  Plotters, relationships with, 10, 11,
    12, 13, 15, 16, 70-1, 100-102
  trial, 145-46, 149-53,
  traitor, as possible, 53-4, 65,
    95-6, 116-19, 124-25, 143-44
  Tresham, suspicions regarding,
    16, 58
Catesby, Sir William, 8

Catherine Wheel Inn, Oxford, 14
Catholics:
    measures against, 2-3
    Reformation, effects on, 1-2
    situation of before Plot, 2, 3, 5
Cecil, Robert, 38, 74, 81, 104
    Catholics, attitudes towards, 5
    Catesby, alleged meetings with,
        119
    Essex Rebellion, 7, 8
    Fawkes, arrest of, 63-4
    intelligence methods, 39, 40, 43,
        44, 53
    Jesuits, attitude towards, 4,
        17, 19
    'mine', 37-8, 109-110
    Monteagle and letter, 27, 48-50,
        54-5, 57, 113-15
    Percy, alleged meetings with,
        122, 123
    Plot, possible prior knowledge
        of, 5, 40, 74-5, 115, 116-17,
        121, 125
    Plotters, confessions of, 79, 125
        trial of, 98, 102
    spymaster, reputation as, 4,
        107, 108
    Tresham, alleged meetings
        with, 119
    possible escape of, 120, 1125
Cecil, William, 4
'Cellar':
    description and situation, 26, 32,
        36-7, 77, 109
    hiring of, 28, 36-7, 61, 66, 73,
        78, 85, 90, 122, 123-24, 138,
        146-47, 149
    search of and discovery of
        gunpowder, 28-9, 56-7, 60, 137,

    preparation of, 27, 34, 37, 73-4,
        75, 86-7, 90, 102, 147
Charles, Duke of Albany (later
    Charles I), 76, 106
Chartley Hall, 39
Church, Edmund, 53
Clink Prison, 20
Cobham, Baron Henry, 44-5, 104
Coke, Sir Edward, 5, 81, 89, 97,
    100, 102, 153, 157
Cornwallis, Sir Charles, 55
Coughton Court, 162
Creswel, Father Joseph, 149, 150,
    159, 172, 175
Cullen, Patrick, 158

Denny, Lord, 35
Destombes, Cyrille Jean, 41
Devereaux, Robert see Essex,
    Earl of
Digby, Sir Everard, 57, 77, 87, 142
    arrest, 58, 66
    biography, 15
    Catesby, betrayal by, 117, 118
    Gerard, cited in trial of, 162, 177
    Plot, enlisted in, 26
    trial, 99, 102-103, 148, 152-55
    traitor, suspected as, 53, 116
Douai (France), Catholic
    seminary, 19
Drury, Robert, 106
Duck and Drake, 25, 123

Edmondes, Sir Thomas, 49, 72
Elizabeth I:
    Catholics, situation of during
        reign, 2, 3, 7, 24, 41
    Essex Rebellion, 7
    Mary Queen of Scots, 39

Elizabeth Stuart, Lady, 76, 84, 85, 91, 99, 105, 142, 146, 163
Essex, Earl of, 7, 8
Essex Rebellion, 7-8, 9

Fawkes, Guy, 3, 15, 17, 20, 23, 25, 58, 81-4, 87
  arrest, 29, 55-6, 59-65, 113-14, 119-20, 121
  biography, 10-11
  'cellar', preparation of, 86, 87, 90, 112, 124
  confessions, 4, 66-78, 86
  Gerard, Father, cited in trial of, 156, 159, 161, 165, 168, 169, 177
  King's Book, cited in, 138, 145, 146, 147
  Lookout duties, 26, 34, 35, 36, 109
  'mine', 36, 37
  questioning and torture of, 30, 91, 111, 123
  traitor, as possible, 115, 118
  trial, 98-103, 148-55
Ferris, Mr, 71, 83
Fraser, Antonia, 49, 57
Frauncis, Jaques, 158
Fulman, William, 52-3

Gardiner, Samuel Rawson, 53, 89, 112-13, 124
Garnet, Father Henry, 20, 107, 145, 146, 147, 148, 149, 150
  arrest and interrogation, 19, 21, 22, 23
  biography, 18
  Catesby, betrayal by, 19, 118
  execution, 182

Owen, Nicholas, relationship with, 21
Plot, attempts to incriminate in, 17-18, 19, 97-8
  trial, 155-82
Vaux, Anne, relationship with, 22-3
Gerard, Father John (1564-1637), 13, 20, 99
  Catesby, betrayal by, 118
  execution, 21
  Plot, attempts to implicate in, 4
  plotters, relationships and meetings with, 4, 15, 25, 83
  torture of, 22, 68
Gerard, Father John (1840-1912), ix-x
Goodman, Bishop Godfrey, 42, 49, 96, 120, 121, 122
Grant, John, 13, 14, 26, 77
  arrest, 67
  biography, 14
  Holbeche,
    refuge and injury at, 88, 89, 92
    flight to, 91
  trial, 98, 100, 101, 142, 144, 146-47, 148, 149, 152, 155
  traitor, as possible, 116, 118
Gregory, Arthur, 42-4, 115
Greenway, Father see Tesimond, Father Oswald
Greenwel, Father see Tesimond, Father Oswald
Gunpowder:
  amount, 8, 34, 37, 38, 107, 111-113, 139, 146, 147, 149
  blast, possible effect of, 1, 26
  at Holbeche, 88-9, 92-4, 143, 152

cellar, storing in, 26, 27, 90, 102, 107, 109-11, 146, 147, 155

Lambeth, storing in, 12, 122

source, 84

Habington, Mary, 49

Habington, Thomas, 20, 163, 176, 177

Harington, Sir John, 99, 105

Haynes, Alan, 5, 6

Henry VIII, 24

Hindlip Hall, 19, 20, 21, 49

Hobart, Sir Edward, 49

Hoby, Sir Edward, 95

Holbeche House, 30, 57, 66-7, 80, 92-5, 101, 119, 124-25

Howard, Lord Charles, 5 (1st Earl of Nottingham, 2nd Baron Howard of Effingham), 5

Howard, Henry (Earl of Northampton), 102-3

Howard, Lord Thomas see Suffolk, 1st Earl of

Howes, Edmund, 104

Hoxton, London, 50-1

James I, 54, 79, 98, 105, 114

Catholic appointments, 3-4, 5, 123

Catholic hopes of toleration, 3, 11, 24

Catholics, attitudes towards, 5, 6, 24, 102

Fawkes, part in arrest and interrogation of, 55-6, 60, 62-3, 67-8, 69, 111

Monteagle, interpreting of letter to and relationship with, 27-8, 29, 47, 50, 55, 114, 115

Parliament, speech to after Plot, 48, 126-35

Jardine, David, 3, 14, 15, 25, 48, 49, 56, 58, 94, 99, 103, 110, 111

Jessopp, Augustus, 9

Jesuits, 2, 4, 5, 24, 122

Plot, attempts to link to, 5-6, 17, 97-8, 100

Jude, John, 120

Keyes, Robert, 15, 17, 58, 77

arrest, 67

biography, 12,

execution, 30, 155

Fawkes, suggested betrayal of, 64, 72

'mine', working in, 37, 72

Plot, enlisted in, 26, 72, 84, 161

traitor, as possible, 115, 118

trial, 98, 145, 146, 148

Knyvet, Sir Thomas, 56, 61, 63, 139

Lathbury, Thomas, 56, 93

Lenthal, William, 52

Lingard, Dr, 119

Little John see Nicholas Owen

Littleton, Humphrey, 21, 177

Littleton, Stephen, 88-9, 92, 95, 152

Longueville, Thomas, 100, 116

Lords' chamber, location and nature of, 26, 32, 33, 37, 78

Mary I, 2

Mary, Queen of Scots, 3

Mary Stuart, (daughter of James I), 76, 99, 146

'Mine' beneath Parliament, 18
  excavations, 36, 81, 83-4, 85,
    146, 149, 152, 161, 25, 26
  plausibility, 30-31, 33, 34, 35,
    37-8, 77, 107, 108-110
  situation, 26, 33, 36
Monteagle, 4th Baron, 50, 57
  Fawkes' arrest, 28, 55, 56, 60
  Cecil, possible collusion with,
    50-4, 116
  Essex Rebellion, 8
  letter, 27, 46-54, 87-8, 137, 151,
    155, 162
  preferential treatment, 48-9, 79, 102
Moore, Sir Francis, 122
Munck, Levinius, 79

Naunton, Sir Robert, 40, 107
Northumberland, Ninth Earl of, 4,
    49, 104, 123, 138,
  Percy, relationship with, 4, 11,
    87, 100, 122, 151

Oldcorne, Father Edward, 19, 20-1,
    56, 57
Oxford University, 19, 52, 13
Owen, Hugh, 74-5, 81, 86, 112,
    150, 158, 159, 161, 162
Owen, Nicholas, 20, 21-2 41

Palmer, Roger see Castlemaine,
    Lord Roger
Parker, William see Monteagle,
    4th Baron
Parliament, Houses of See
    Westminster, Palace of
Parry, Sir Thomas, 38
Percy, Henry see Northumberland,
    Ninth Earl of

Percy, Thomas, 33-4, 36, 61, 63, 71,
    78, 84, 85
  biography, 11
  'cellar', renting of, 26, 28-9, 36-
    8, 60-1, 73-5
  death, 66, 89, 94, 95-6
  Holbeche, 89, 91
  Garnet, Father, cited in trial of,
    160, 161, 168, 169, 176
  King's Book, cited in, 138, 141,
    143, 144, 145, 151,
  Monteagle letter, 56, 58
  Northumberland, relationship
    with, 4, 11, 87, 100, 122, 151
  plotters, meetings with, 24-5, 70,
    83, 84, 86-7, 88
  traitor, as possible, 93, 95-6, 119,
    122-25
  trial, 100, 104
Philip III of Spain, 2, 6, 10, 14
Philips, Sir Edward, 99, 103, 155
Puddle Wharf, 12

Raleigh, Sir Walter, 44, 45
Rookwood, Ambrose, 12, 26, 77,
    169, 173
  arrest, 66, 88-9, 92, 94, 95
  biography, 14-15
  execution, 152, 155
  traitor, as possible, 116, 118
  trial, 98, 100, 101, 143, 144,
    146-47, 149

St Michael-le-Belfrey
    (York), 11
St Winifrede's Well, 18, 162
Salisbury, Lord see Cecil, Robert
Shepherd, John, 66
Skinner, Mr, 36, 124

Spink, Henry Hawkes Jnr, 46-7, 56, 57, 65, 112
Stanley, Sir William, 82, 85, 86, 150, 158, 159, 161, 174
Stourton, 10th Baron, 58
Stourton, Edward see Stourton, 10th Baron
Stowe, John, 119
Streete, John, 96
Suffolk, 1st Earl of, 28, 54, 55-7, 60-1, 63, 89, 98, 155

Tesimond, Father Oswald, 3, 10, 5-6, 18, 58, 95, 97, 146, 148, 156, 159
  biography 21
  plotters, descriptions of, 9-11, 14-16
  regarding Holbeche, 95
  Garnet, cited in trial of, 156, 161-162, 163, 166, 167, 169, 170, 174, 175, 176-77, 179, 181, 182
  King's Book, cited in, 145, 149
  Monteagle & letter, 51, 67, 87
  Tresham, suspicions regarding, 119
Titchmarsh (Northamptonshire), 64
Topcliffe, Richard, 41-2, 45
Tresham, Francis, 17, 27, 50
  biography, 16
  death and mystery surrounding, 30, 67, 119-22, 125
  Essex Rebellion, 8
  Monteagle letter, suspected as author of 16, 49, 56-7, 58, 87-8, 115
Tunnel, beneath Parliament see 'Mine'
Tutbury (Castle), 19

Vaux, Anne, 18, 19, 22, 56, 164, 170, 178, 179, 181
Vaux, Eleanor, 22
Verney, Sir Richard, 92

Waad, Sir William, 44-5, 56, 65, 79-80, 89
Wade, Sir William see Waad, Sir William
Walsh, Sir Richard, 92, 94-5, 143
Walsingham, Sir Francis, 4, 39-40, 42, 108
Ward, Thomas, 14, 49, 57, 87
Weldon, Sir Anthony, 44
Westminster, Palace of, 25-6, 32, 62, 71, 84, 98, 107, 110, 121, 123, 139
Weston, Father William, 4, 18
White Webbs, 23, 58, 87, 124
Whynniard, Mrs (wife of John), 36, 66, 90, 124
Whynniard, John, 60-1, 66, 83, 120
Winter, Robert see Wintour, Robert
Winter, Thomas see Wintour, Thomas
Wintour, Robert, 13, 26, 67, 7, 116, 118, 145, 146, 147, 148, 155
Wintour, Thomas, 6, 10, 12, 13, 17, 25, 70, 74, 77, 145, 146, 148
  biography, 10
  confessions, 4, 37, 50, 66, 79-90
  Essex Rebellion, 8
  Garnet trial, citeded in, 156, 159, 160, 161, 167, 169, 172, 177
  Holbeche, capture at, 66, 94, 95, 101, 144
  flight to, 91, 93, 143
  'mine', 34, 37, 78, 110
  trial, 98, 100, 101, 148-55

traitor, as possible, 115, 118
Tresham, suspicions regarding, 58, 119
Wood, Anthony, 52
Wotton, Sir Henry, 53
Wright, Christopher, 14, 15, 17, 26, 71, 85, 86, 88, 89
  biography, 14
  death, 66, 89, 94, 95
  Holbeche, flight to, 91, 142

King's Book, cited in, 145, 148, 150, 159, 169, 172, 177
traitor, as possible, 57, 116
Wright, John, 11, 15, 17, 71, 83, 84, 89, 145, 148, 161
  biography, 9-10
  death, 66, 89, 94, 95
  Holbeche, flight to, 91, 142
  Plot, recruited to, 9, 24, 70, 80
  traitor, as possible, 115